Honorable Exiles

Honorable

Exiles

A Chilean Woman in

the Twentieth Century

Lillian Lorca de Tagle

Edited by Joy Billington and Chris Lucas

University of Texas Press 🔹 Austin

Requests for permission to reproduce
material from this work should be sent to
Permissions, University of Texas Press,
P.O. Box 7819, Austin, TX 78713-7819.

∞ The paper used in this book meets the
minimum requirements of ANSI/NISO
Z39.48-1992 (R1997)
(Permanence of Paper).

Library of Congress
Cataloging-in-Publication Data
Honorable Exiles : A Chilean Woman in the
Twentieth Century. An autobiography.
Library of Congress data pending.
LC 99-029839

ISBN 0-292-71606-0 (cl.: alk. paper)
ISBN 0-292-71609-5 (pbk.: alk. paper)

Frontispiece: Portrait of the author by Roberto Matta.

To my daughters,

XIMENA & ROSA,

who always stood by me.

They mean all in life to me.

CONTENTS

ACKNOWLEDGMENTS

My deepest gratitude to my niece Luz Lorca, who not only provided me with our family's documents and photographs but also established a bridge of understanding and love when circumstances had distanced us.

To Joy Billington, my editor and longtime friend, for her expert advice and guidance.

To Chris Lucas, for his patience and tactful suggestions during long reading sessions.

To María Isabel and Dave Oliphant for providing me with valuable information I would not have had access to without their help.

I am forever grateful to Ron Harris for his invaluable support in helping me solve all electronic glitches and getting me going to the finish line.

My granddaughter Tina Borja also applied for my benefit what she'd learned about computers during her stay in Washington, D.C.

To Suzan Cotellesse-Lowery, for making me face a painful incident in my life.

My gratitude to Theresa May at the University of Texas Press for trusting me.

INTRODUCTION

Usually the word *exiled* brings to mind suspicion of wrongdoing. Yet within the term there is a whole spectrum of categories, reflecting circumstances and personal motivations. The most common exile is the political dissident, rejected by his own country's government, accepted as a hero by another's. Manuel Seoane is in this category; so too Carlos Dávila, and also Miguel Labarca, although later he became a voluntary exile. In this latter category we find Roberto Matta, misunderstood in Chile and needing a more accepting atmosphere in which to develop. We have the economic exiles, the restless, the nonconformists, and the professional exiles whose work requires that they live away from their homeland.

During my life as a circumstantial exile I met them all, and I lingered in their ghettos to participate in the ritualistic banquets of their homesickness, momentarily soothed by food preparations, filling rooms with the nostalgic aromas of a faraway country, silently savoring the repast. Then letting down pretense to reminisce about the last authentic meal enjoyed with friends in the family's home. So, I introduce here the honorable exiles in my life, and my own experiences as someone cast out.

PROLOGUE

Has anyone ever seen a stranger moral fervor?
You who dirty the mirror, cry that it isn't clean.
— *Sor Juana Inés de la Cruz (1651–1695),*
Hombres Necios *(Foolish Men)*

A historian might question the specifics of my account of the Lorcas and the Bunsters in Chile. But who can deny the truth of word of mouth, carried through centuries with scarcely any change? In a land of earthquakes and tidal waves, not to mention political upheavals, official documents disappear. Family stories are more reliable sources.

The Lorcas and Bunsters are tribes in more ways than one. Like a maypole's entwined ribbons the two families came together, distanced themselves, drifted apart, and found each other again, either through commerce or in front of an altar reciting wedding vows. They gathered around a table, or over a fire in the woods, to lick wounds sustained during long absences and to celebrate the triumphs or overcome the tribulations that human creatures endure.

This is a story which, as a Lorca Bunster in name and blood, I feel compelled to recount. It is the sum of all that has happened to me, my relatives, my friends, and the world, from 1914 to 1996. Here begins our story.

Honorable Exiles

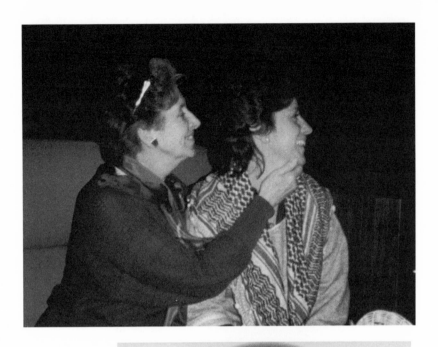

A distinctive feature in the Lorca family displayed by myself and my niece, Luz Lorca (top), and in the portrait of a Lorca ancestor found in the Governor's Museum in Valdiva, Chile (bottom).

The Lorcas from Spain

The first mention of the Lorcas' arrival in Chile comes from the seventeenth century. Most of them settled in the south, around Valdivia. This partially contradicts a theory among their descendants that their early presence was in Santiago and Valparaíso. But the Governor's Museum in Valdivia offers proof of high positions reached by the Lorca family. Oil paintings and daguerreotypes of family members show physical traits still detectable among descendants: high brows, long aristocratic noses, and large intelligent eyes. To this must be added courage, resourcefulness, and endurance. They had left Spain to live in a harsh climate and were threatened by periodic attacks of the most aggressive Indians in the area, the Araucanians.

The Spanish crown dictated the mission of the first Lorcas: they were to evangelize the natives. This meant a close cooperation between the church and the military. The latter was essential in view of the fierceness of the Araucanians. Little could be accomplished if the Indians were not subdued. So the first Lorcas were involved with the government, the church, and the military.

The story now jumps to the early nineteenth century and a man living in Valdivia. Lieutenant Mariano Fernández de Lorca y Albarrán of the 5th Company was singled out for his staunch defense of the colony when the forces of independence threatened it. Aware of the lieutenant's indomitable valor and loyalty to the monarchy, the king of Spain ordered him to restore the motherland's rule in Chile, but it was too late. The republic had already announced its victory in Santiago. Representatives, mayors, governors, and judges were being appointed by the new regime across the whole length and breadth of the territory. Similar processes were taking place all over Latin America. Spanish power was fast disappearing.

Lieutenant Mariano Fernández de Lorca decided not to follow his brother officers, who either returned to Spain or sided with the independence movement. He sent an emotional letter to the king of Spain, promising to remain on the desolate island of Chiloé to await reinforcements which would enable him to continue fighting until the colony was restored to Spain.

In Madrid the king merely shrugged his shoulders. Chile had never been really important to Spain. It lacked significant gold and silver. With one motion of his hand, the king abandoned this loyal subject. In making his decision to remain faithful, Lieutenant Lorca was obeying his ancestry: a Fernández de Lorca had defended the city of Lorca, in Murcia, against the Moors and had been victorious. A century later Lieutenant Lorca might have found a sympathetic chronicler in García Marquez, who would have exalted his useless loyalty to the monarchy as a noble gesture of total surrender to the king's will: Quixote still alive.

One can imagine an aging man wrapped in a heavy black poncho, typical of the chilly southern provinces, hiding under its folds the already frayed Spanish military uniform. He sits on the long open verandah of his house, his eyes scrutinizing the sea that refuses to bring the news from the faraway palace that can make him savior of the colony. He hardly reacts when his few remaining soldiers, one by one, kiss his hand in a sad gesture of farewell.

Later, his sons, grown into strong youngsters, discuss developments on the nearby Chilean mainland. They understand and accept the quixotic character of their father. Not a single one of the five dares speak of their desire to leave the island. Another restraining factor is their respect for their mother. Her blind acceptance of her husband's will is the foundation of her life. Many of the children she bore died in the polar weather of Chiloé. She unquestioningly believed that her husband would replace these lost children. She seldom resented it when, after the procreative ritual, Don Mariano dressed in his uniform and covered it with the Chiloéan poncho, without saying one word. Returning to his chair on the verandah, he continued grieving over the emptiness of the seas in front of him and the failed promise of a battlefield, as he slowly sank into the silent depths of madness.

Sometimes she sat next to him, her aristocratic beauty still holding up against the hardships of her life. She poured over him tenderness nurtured by compassion. Her dark eyes, less vivacious now and surrounded by deep shadows, look over Don Mariano's shriveled body, his head more bent each day, his hair sparse and white. She looks for the blue eyes that seduced her long ago, now murky and indifferent. Only when his breast exhales its last breath and his eyes close forever, do his sons depart for the mainland.

They chose Valdivia, where earlier Lorcas had settled and prospered long before. The stay on the island of Chiloé, so removed from civilized company and progressive ideas, made the brothers resolve to make up for lost time. They sought a project that not only might have a lasting effect on the family's fortune, but also would benefit the country. Chile's peculiar geography needed communication and transportation systems. A thin sliver of land, Chile is bordered on one side by the towering Andes and on the other by rocky shores barely holding back the wild force of the Pacific Ocean. The far north is barren desert, the far south windswept and icy. Within a few years they built a merchant marine fleet that served ports along thousands of miles of coastline, decreasing transportation time from one end of the country to the other.

Previously, passengers had traveled by horse, oxcart, or carriage, wading through streams and rivers, occasionally trusting their lives to fragile rafts, never knowing how long it would take to reach the capital. No matter how primitive, the ships of the Lorca brothers were a great improvement. Their long stay on the island had left the brothers with a dread of isolation. The Lorcas devoted themselves to overcoming the insularity of their country.

When their ships sank in winter storms, they sought other ways to reduce the distance to other countries. To reach Peru, where Lima, the former seat of the Spanish viceroy, was now a thriving independent capital, a safe route must be found through the Atacama Desert. One of the brothers, Rafael, tried to forge a trail but had to be rescued when his small group of explorers lost their bearings. They managed to save some of their horses by cutting their palates so the animals could survive by drinking their own blood. Eventually they all were rescued by experienced local scouts.

Apart from the Straits of Magellan, considered too dangerous, the only access to the Eastern world was by opening passes through the Andes toward Argentina. The existing governments were building a railroad between Santiago and Mendoza, but it was constantly threatened and damaged by avalanches. The brothers created a system by which they could transport passengers and cargo when avalanches disrupted the flow of traffic. Using hundreds of mules to negotiate an affected area, they safely delivered passengers and merchandise to the Argentinean side of the frontier.

When I was ten years old, I too had to trust the efficiency of the muleteers and the sure feet of the mules when they carried us through the narrowest of the cordillera's trails, flanked by cliffs and precipices. Few passengers complained. Most considered it a welcome adventure and a fine conversation piece. This resourceful service played an important role in Chile's efforts to end its isolation.

Of the five Lorca brothers, two became senators, one an admiral, and one, Arturo Lorca PellRoss, joined the Chilean Foreign Service. He was my father.

PRELUDE TWO

The Bunsters from England

About the same time as the fateful tale of Lieutenant Mariano Fernández de Lorca was taking place on remote Chiloé, a Royal Navy training ship, the "Catalina," sailed from England under the command of Captain Thomas Musgrave. From the rails, young cadets called goodbyes to the friends and relatives assembled to bid them farewell.

The first port of call was Rabat, the capital of Morocco, where they admired the horsemanship of the desert riders and the bazaars filled with art objects and exotic fruits. They stopped at Monrovia, Liberia's capital, where the stench of people dying of hunger or disease on the streets would stay with them for weeks. Not even the breezes from the sea were powerful enough to take away the smell of putrefaction. The next port of call was Luanda, in Angola, where the Portuguese ran things with implacable severity. Unaware of the effects of repression, the cadets thought they had found an ideal African country and expressed the wish to return later.

After a tempestuous sailing around the southern tip of Africa and a visit to Madagascar, where they were charmed by the hospitality of the islanders, they sailed through calm seas to Bangalore. There they saw fakirs climb up ropes suspended in midair by nothing except incredible trickery and make-believe, and they watched as the fakirs chopped up children bloodlessly. Later, as the young assistants were restored to their original forms, they ran among the spectators picking up coins. Was it collective hypnosis?, the cadets wondered.

In the Polynesian Islands they found the stuff that dreams are made of. Through transparent blue water they could see all the colors and shapes of fish and coral. Captain Musgrave overlooked the fact that some of his cadets slipped ashore at night to meet new friends with generous hips and slender waists. But if they failed to return by sailing time, Captain Musgrave departed as the schedule dictated. The sails were raised, and they soon left behind the Tuamotu Archipelago, loaded with a fragrant cargo of fruits, with their barrels sparkling and full of diamond-clear water.

After their next port, Valparaíso, Chile, they were scheduled to round the Horn, through the fearful Straits of Magellan, and thence to England. Yet something in the air warned of the unexpected. Hours before the storm came, a metallic taste to the wind cautioned danger. Gigantic waves, hurricanelike winds, and relentless rain beat down on the ship. Until then it had sailed majestically, but suddenly it was helpless in the fury of the storm. They lost their bearings, for days floating adrift in the wrong direction.

Finally they were able to make an estimate of loss and damage, realizing that their food and water had spoiled in spite of precautions. Their sails were seriously damaged. When they straggled into Valparaíso, Captain Musgrave requested a meeting with the local authorities. He explained the situation and asked for help.

Like many a young nation, Chile had been unable to avoid political infighting among those who sought to dominate the new republic. Valparaíso was under siege, and the governor told Musgrave that he couldn't spare food or water. Valparaíso's people would need it all before the siege was lifted. But moved by the English captain's situation, he suggested he sail south, find a cove, and send his men ashore to pick whatever they could find for their survival. Moreover, he'd ask landowners not to act against the English if they were caught. Captain Musgrave did just that. Sailing south he soon found a favorable cove with a small beach set among the huge boulders which characterize Chilean shores.

Captain Musgrave ordered several of his crew to man a boat under the command of Lieutenant Humphrey (later Onofre) Bunster Winckworth. They hid the boat among the rocks before setting out across the land in search of food and water. Wandering across a landscape of rough brush, they came to a spring, where they were beginning to slaughter some lambs when a sudden hammering of hooves stopped them. Bunster was determined to be the last to leave as the crew ran back toward the boat. He was "caught by a huge serpent and dragged to its lair," his

Grosvenor Bunster Winckworth, brother of Humphrey, the first Bunster to arrive in Chile. Photograph in the Revista de Estudios Historicos, Santiago, Chile. Their cousin, Margaret Bunster Knox, was often invited to Chile, but never complied. This miniature was a gift from my mother.

shipmates reported when the landing party returned to the "Catalina." These words were officially recorded in the Archives of the Royal Navy.

Back in England the Bunster family grieved over their son's death. The truth, of course, was far less drastic. In fact it was downright romantic. The "huge serpent" was a lasso, expertly handled by one of the "huasos" (cowboys) among a group of patrolling riders. Lieutenant Bunster was taken on horseback to the landowner's house for the "patrón" to decide his fate. The landowner found that he couldn't understand the prisoner's language. But judging by his manners and uniform, in spite of its being tattered in his capture, it was clear that the man was a gentleman. Lieutenant Bunster, in turn, made the best use of his imagination and talent for mimicry to explain what had happened. While enacting the scene of his capture he became aware of someone hiding behind a column on the porch. It was a young girl with long dark braids framing a lovely face, her eyes sparkling with curiosity. She followed every gesture and movement of the unexpected guest.

Finally the patrón gave orders to a servant, who guided Bunster to a room and in sign language told him to undress. A bath was provided, and the Lieutenant drank deep from a jar of water. Afterward he dressed in the clothes that had been put out for him. Looking in a mirror he saw that the British naval officer was no more. Instead there was an almost authentic huaso, except with blond hair and blue eyes. The tight black pants, the snow-white starched shirt, the red cummerbund with the long silk fringes, and the shiny black boots had changed his appearance almost totally. From that moment, a process of assimilation started that continued until his death. The new look did not displease him. The clothes he wore were not a costume but rather an attire that suggested a new personality and the start of an entirely different lifestyle.

When he walked out of the room, feeling somewhat self-conscious in his new clothes, the servant who had guided him earlier was waiting for him in the wide arched corridor with the broad clay flagstones. The man's ample smile, combined with the words foreign to him but whose meaning was clear, instantly put him at ease. Any doubts about his appearance were dispelled.

Signaling to him vigorously, the man made him follow once more. A steady murmur of voices, laughter, and the sound of dishes being moved around made him understand that they were approaching a dining room. A young maid in a neatly starched snow-white apron emerged from a door to look at him. She also smiled broadly, covering her mouth. She swiftly withdrew, and Bunster heard an explosion of words and exclamations preceding his entrance to the dining room.

Looking at him, the owner of the ranch — who had frustratingly interviewed him earlier — also broke into a big smile, pointed at a chair by his side, and stretched his hand to tap him on the shoulder in the universal sign of approval.

At the table, Bunster bowed to the landowner's wife. The girl with the dark braids and sparkling black eyes also sat ready to partake of the dinner. From the door to the pantry several small faces peered at him, giggling at the sight of the stranger.

Used to the Spartan customs of British home and navy, Lieutenant Bunster was in for a gastronomic surprise. On the table were stacks of different flavorful breads, cheeses, fruits, and nuts. The sequence of dishes being served left him aghast. A salad entree with shellfish and hard-boiled eggs would have been considered a meal in itself in his country. But then came the steaming soup, flavored with tasty herbs and spices. The main course of steak and sauteed potatoes preceded the fried river fish, with all of it washed down with delicious wines. A layered cake filled with milk jam was the quite unforgettable dessert.

Lieutenant Bunster's surprise at the variety and abundance of foods didn't ruin his appetite. He ate voraciously, enjoying all the new tastes and flavors that tickled his palate. His host appreciated his enthusiastic gluttony and again tapped his shoulder in an obvious gesture of satisfaction.

The ship must now be in some remote latitude. He had no way of telling his captain what had happened or where he was. There was nothing he could do but adjust and learn Spanish, perhaps with the help of the young girl with the dark braids. She was Rosario Ortiz de Montellan y Cuadra, the daughter of the patrón.

Time ran on imperceptibly, until one day he found himself easily conversing with his host, who asked him to perform certain duties. This made him feel like part of the family. Bunster soon learned to ride horses, to survey the property with the foreman. He got along well with the laborers, or peons, who approved of his progress in their language. He had chosen the Navy as a career and knew how to handle men with authority and restraint. Suddenly fate had given him a brilliant opportunity to improve his lot, make a fortune, and start a family, if the beautiful Rosario accepted his proposal.

In the meantime he had decided to set the record straight for the Navy and for his own family. He wrote to his parents, recounting his adventures and informing them of his decision to remain in Chile. To his brothers and sisters he extended an invitation to visit Chile, to see the opportunities the country offered. In time other Bunsters immigrated, settling in Valparaíso. Later this group became known as the British Colony. Their offspring hardly spoke Spanish, which was the case with my grandfather, Martin Bunster. Among the women, five o'clock tea was always a sacred daily ritual.

CHAPTER I

I was born in San Francisco, California, in 1914, my parents' third child after Eugene and Betty. At six months I made my first trip to Chile. It would not be my last journey on the Japanese Maru line.

During my father's twelve-year assignment as Chilean consul in San Francisco, my older sister Betty's frail health often required frantic trips home for consultation with physicians about her disturbing symptoms. California and New York physicians had given up on the child. They told Mother: "You are young. You can have other babies." In retrospect it is apparent that multiple allergies were the cause of Betty's problems, but back then the word *allergy* was unknown. The recurrence of the attacks seriously debilitated the child, and each ailment seemed a matter of life or death. The trips to Chile returned Mother not only to the familiarity of language and relatives, but also to native healing methods that Betty responded to.

Each emergency was met by precautions designed to protect others from supposed contamination. I recall vividly a vacation at one of Berkeley's most beautiful hotels when I was two; it was interrupted by a strict quarantine. Betty was sick again. All other guests promptly evacuated our floor while Mother, Eugene, and I remained isolated. Meals were left outside the room. We were forbidden access to the halls or even to open our doors. We'd become a threat to others. We waited forty days for the signs of measles to appear. They never did!

Once the incident was over, Mother insisted that she must travel to Chile to find out how to avoid a recurrence of such embarrassment.

Betty had been near death with the mumps, whooping cough, diphtheria, and sudden rashes that covered her body with blisters or swelled her up monstrously. Mother was resentful that the hotel's management had *dared* quarantine her and her family. Her pride as a Chilean aristocrat and wife of a diplomat was deeply hurt.

When we were on one of these trips to Chile in search of cures for Betty, our Japanese ship stopped in Panama. With the best Oriental courtesy, expressed with multiple bows and guttural noises, the captain requested that Mother and her children disembark. Betty was again showing alarming symptoms of distress. Captain Hakamuri sought to avoid the death of this small creature on his ship. It would reflect poorly on his impeccable record. Amid the turmoil of Carnival in Panama, we found a hotel.

For a short while that evening I had a respite from the worry of a sick sister and a frantic, distraught mother. With my brother, Eugene, at my side, my legs dangling between the rungs of the banister on the third floor of the hotel, I watched entranced as revelers danced below us on the patio of the hotel. Caribbean fragrances, colors of every hue, music, and laughter filled my ears and tickled my eyes. Finally the drinking and carousing became so uninhibited that my twelve-year-old brother felt he must shield me from the spectacle and sent me to bed.

For a woman with three children and no husband, to be stranded in Panama, a land reputed to be a haven for pirates and criminals, amid a variety of dubious characters, was an unpredictable situation. There was no easy or quick way to reach Father for help, but being a resourceful woman, Mother took matters in hand and soon had the Chilean consulate in Panama pulling strings on her behalf.

Mother was small in size, tall in authority. She had delicate fine-boned features made irrelevant by her two fiery, piercing eyes that commanded action. She knew how to exert that strong will on everyone, regardless of status.

When we finally returned to San Francisco, we came with assurances that my sister would grow sound and healthy. Several Chilean doctors concurred with this conclusion. Besides, the physicians were sure that Mother could handle any emergency, if it came to happen. One of them encouraged her to write a book about her observations and research undertaken for Betty. She did. It dealt with simple preventative and emergency measures in children's health care. The book had tremendous success and can still be found in many Chilean homes, particularly in rural areas. But the recurrent illnesses of my sister had affected four years of my life and seven of her own existence.

With her reputation as a healer, Mother became a sort of emergency physician during our vacations at relative's ranches. Once a peon had his arm pierced by a stake from his elbow to the shoulder. Nobody dared touch him. Mother gave him a glass of whiskey, braced herself and pulled on the stake with such force that she landed on the ground. She then poured iodine into the wound, bandaged it tightly, and sent the man to the nearest clinic. A week later he returned to thank her for helping him. Mother never took compliments gracefully. She once told me she found them redundant. She tapped the man on the shoulder, smiled thinly, and walked away.

At remote family ranches, Mother often helped out in deliveries, teaching the principles of hygiene to the mothers. As she taught the local midwives and healers, they also revealed to her their secrets. She watched as infected wounds, wrapped in moldy cornhusks and cobwebs, miraculously healed, treated by what we now know as antibiotics.

Betty was six years old when we returned to San Francisco. She seemed fine but soon a whole set of never before seen symptoms developed. Mother was off again to consult her Chilean physicians. Following the Panama incident, Father was concerned about our safety on Japanese ships. He had been approached by a Chilean who had been unsuccessfully searching for a relative lured north, some years earlier, by the California gold rush. This man had used up his money and lacked his fare home. Father agreed to repatriate him, and in exchange asked Don Francisco to look after his wife and children. As a farewell present, Father handed him a gold coin to cover his arrival expenses in Chile.

Father's anxiety was well founded. One morning Mother opened the door of her cabin to find Don Francisco lying in front of it. During the night a fight had started among the crew and several sailors were dead or wounded. He wanted to be sure that Mother and the children were safe.

This story had a touching ending. Some years later in Santiago, between assignments, Father was walking down the street when he heard someone call out. He turned around and saw a tall sturdy man running toward him. He said, "Don Arturo, don't you recognize me? I'm Francisco."

"Yes, of course I do. It's been quite a few years since last I saw you. What are you doing now?"

"I'm working on my farm. But periodically I come to Santiago looking for you. I have something to return." With that he dug his fingers into his waistcoat pocket and brought out a small, carefully wrapped object.

"Here, Don Arturo. I have kept this for so many years hoping I would see you again. I never spent it. If I had, I probably wouldn't have done as well as I have. I'm now a landowner. You must come and visit me and my family."

Don Francisco unwrapped the gold coin Father had given him so many years earlier. It dropped out, shining like new. Father told us this story later. His only comment was: "We do get our rewards in life."

Even in remote locations, Father had always found Chileans experiencing different degrees of distress and sometimes success. His anecdotes ran the gamut from the admirable to the hilarious. Among the latter are the tribulations of a Lothario who arrived in Hamburg, in midwinter, barefoot and wearing only pajamas. He had crossed half of Europe, leaving behind all his possessions, escaping from an irate Italian husband. He was repatriated.

In Australia a Chilean "artist" requested an appointment with Father. He told about his very special talent as an opera performer. Father asked about his voice register. The man replied that he didn't sing.

"How do you do it then?"

"By breaking wind, Don Arturo. I can give you a free demonstration," he answered eagerly.

The "opera star" was thrown out of Father's office, never to return.

During his stay in the United States, Father had observed a number of enterprises. Reporting to the Chilean president he repeatedly recommended that the Chilean government select outstanding young men to come to the United States to study new techniques applicable to Chilean products and raw materials. Two prominent Chilean families — the Matte and the Edwards — followed this advice, sending their sons to the United States to learn paper manufacturing. Both men considerably increased their wealth, creating the only "Factory of Paper and Cartons" in Chile. The Edwards added an entree to political power by founding what became the most influential newspaper in the country, *El Mercurio*.

Father also studied the production and export of fruit. The Bunsters followed his reports closely, planting huge apple orchards on their ranches in the south of Chile. Another area he researched in the United

States was the recently opened Transpacific Railroad. President Alessandri asked him to reorganize Chile's railroad — the country's sole means of land-based transportation — which was near bankruptcy.

So it came about that in the spring of 1920 we sadly left San Francisco and boarded a ship bound for Chile. How often since then I've missed the pungent smell of cabins, the salt in the air, the swinging motion of ships. The Pacific rocked us in its powerful swells as the ship cut through waves splashing us with fresh, cool foam, cresting the deep dark green of its waters. I remember stopping in Callao, Peru's main port and the entrance to Lima. Father told me a little about the city, seat of the Spanish viceroys for centuries. I heard much later about the colorful history of Lima, particularly the amazing life of La Perrícholi. I wasn't aware then that someone living in that city would have a great influence over my life.

There were no docks in Valparaíso at that time. A large, wide, and tall staircase came down to the sea, where we disembarked from tenders. The sailors who had rowed us through the high tide rolled up their pants, stepped into the water, and carried us in their arms to the top of the staircase, where our relatives waited for us and showered us with questions:

"Do you remember me?" (Of course not.)

"Aren't you glad to be here?" (I don't know yet.)

"Come and meet your cousins."

CHAPTER 2

Mother was never an easy person to understand. Perhaps unwittingly she subjected us to a series of shocks that today would be regarded as psychologically abusive. At that time there was just no explanation for her behavior. Some of my older relatives took it upon themselves to instruct me about her background, in an awkward although well-meaning attempt to explain, and perhaps justify, Mother's emotional turmoil.

She was one of seven surviving children. I say "surviving" because infant mortality was high in the nineteenth century in Chile. At every social and economic level, women were pregnant almost every year. Under the best conditions, less than two-thirds of infants lived past their fourth birthday. Lack of proper medical attention and mistakes by inexperienced or ill-advised nannies were in part responsible for the high mortality.

Mother was the youngest in her family. Her own mother was in her late forties when she was born. Lovely as a rosebud, she was christened Rosa. She was spoiled and pampered by parents and siblings, who all considered her no less than a miracle child. She was so tiny that her eighteen-year-old brother Martín carried her around on his shoulders so that she didn't have to strain her neck to look at taller people from down below. Perhaps it was on those strong shoulders that she got the idea she was six feet taller than other people? Who knows if being so far from the ground led her to believe that she was superior.

When Rosa was fourteen, she fell prey to typhoid fever while on vacation at the family's ranch. A physician was summoned from Los Angeles. After an examination he told the family that her chances of survival were doubtful, unless his recommendations were followed to the letter. The girl's fever must be fed, otherwise it would feed on her body. She must be kept on a strict diet of fresh oysters. She must be wrapped in ice whenever her temperature rose. Otherwise, he said, she would die.

The family set out immediately to follow orders. Ice could be gotten from high in the Andes. Oysters came from a bay by the sea. The men of the family decided what had to be done. With a large number of peons, horses, and mules, a daily caravan traveled to the highest peaks. The mules were equipped with straw-lined baskets for the ice. Delivering their icy cargo at the ranch for the wrappings, they then continued quickly toward the bay, where fishermen waited with baskets of oysters. All this was done at top speed, using relay animals along the way. For several weeks they traveled back and forth to the mountains and the bay.

One day the girl opened her eyes. She was saved. Emaciated, Rosa had lost much of her hair. What remained was cut short. Her convalescence began under the apple trees in the orchard. There, her brothers and the peons who had saved her life visited her. Her own mother, Rosario, talked about the rescue mission while offering the men goblets of "chicha," the local fermented cider. They told about the guides who led them to the thickest ice, less likely to melt on the trip back. They bragged about suffering from the "puna," the altitude sickness, and how they never stopped until the child was saved. Rosario would ask if her sons were good patrones who looked out for their peons' needs, or had they just pushed them like animals?

The men laughed at this loaded question. Swaying on spread legs, they answered, "They were good patrones. Your sons pushed us hard, but we knew what was at stake. Good to see you well, niña Rosita."

Mother related this story many times. She never forgot the sturdy peons who helped save her life, although she couldn't remember their names. Years later she would return the favor by tending to the medical needs of the laborers and their families on the ranches.

Mother was a superb storyteller. One tale was about her brother, Martín, who had gone on an expedition on the Renaico River. It was early spring, and melting snow had swollen the stream. The rustic raft he and his men traveled on was threatening to split. Their cargo of tools, foodstuff, and valuable seeds was thrown into the raging waters to lighten their load. But still they faced danger. One of the peons turned to Martín. "Good-bye, patrón," he said and jumped into the river, sacrificing his life in a gesture of loyalty for the safety of his patrón.

During her convalescence Mother realized the lingering effects of her illness. She couldn't walk. She tried to read but couldn't decipher a word. She tried to write but the hand holding the pencil wouldn't trace a single letter. Rosa felt she mustn't trust anyone with her secret. But finally she broke down and confided in one of her sisters, who hugged her tenderly and promised to teach her everything that the fever had wiped out. Many months of patient instruction followed.

I never met this sister, who later was forbidden to marry the man she loved. She married the bridegroom chosen by her parents. She died in childbirth. I did meet another sister, Aunt Rosario, reputed to be a miracle-performing nun. I was eighteen when I saw her through a wooden convent grille. She said to me, "You are quite a little lady. You must promise me that you will rather die than allow a man to kiss you. Otherwise I never want to see you again." I never saw her again. Her entreaty had come too late.

Mother's pictures from the years between her illness and her marriage show a perfect oval face and a slightly receding chin that belied the strength of her character. My favorite picture shows her with a white camellia in her hair. She is wearing a high-necked dress that covers her delicate throat with a lacy material kept in place by whalebone stays. She complained that her neck was too long and constantly wrapped ribbons or bead-chokers around it. She disliked her face to the point of refusing to be photographed and even cut out her face if a snapshot of her was taken by surprise.

She had several suitors, but was irrepressibly domineering and devastatingly sarcastic. She got a reputation for being unapproachable. But then she realized that she was being left behind. At the turn of the century in Latin America an unmarried woman of over twenty was considered on the edge of spinsterhood. The options for a spinster were limited: the nunnery or a diminished status within her family. The possibility of working for financial independence was not even considered. If not in a convent, an unmarried woman remained at her parents' home, grateful for any meager allowance that her parents or brothers might give her.

So when a young lieutenant asked permission to visit Rosa, it was in the reality of her situation that she accepted. It was a brief courtship.

Arturo Lorca PellRoss was not as tall as her brothers, but his bearing was ramrod straight from military training. He had blue eyes, wavy blond hair, and an engaging smile. Soon they were married.

This decision, like many in her life, was sensible, practical, and without the passion she could never feel for another human being. Fierce determination she had. She could stand firm for a moral cause. But the tender emotion of love seemed to her irrelevant and confusing. I don't doubt for a minute that it was Mother who planned for Father to leave the military and apply for an appointment at the Foreign Affairs Department. Moreover she was right. For he succeeded, and together they embarked on an exciting life.

Their first child, Eugene, was born in Chile in 1906, a year after the wedding. Not long before an earthquake had destroyed much of Valparaíso. Father was still in the military, awaiting his first overseas assignment. Dispatched to the stricken area, he proceeded to help the victims and to put order back into an area plagued by panic. Overnight the young husband became the family hero. As soon as the authorities could do without his services, he resigned from the military and started preparations to leave the country.

His first diplomatic assignment was London. Mother had hired a wet nurse for baby Eugene, the ugliest woman ever seen. She was unusually short with a hairy face and hands, but she came with impeccable references from her doctor. Mother would keep her, but she must improve her appearance. To be born ugly was regarded by my mother as a tragedy, negating any chance of respect or happiness.

Covering the nurse's rough hands with gloves, changing her sandals for patent leather shoes, wrapping her squat body in a wide cape, and planting on her head a frilly white bonnet, Mother took the woman from one house to the next seeking the reactions of friends and relatives. Their opinions varied from mild approval to outright ridicule. While they were making the rounds, Mother noticed a trickle of blood coming down the nurse's cheek.

"What's happening to you?" Mother screamed.

"You told me to hold the bonnet in place with the hat pin!" came the frightened reply. She had stuck the pin through her scalp!

Immediately calling upon the pediatrician who had recommended the nurse, Mother told him she refused to take this woman to Europe. Besides looking like a Neanderthal, she was stupid. He must give her a prescription to feed her son with a bottle, something unheard of in Chile at the time. Never did Mother consider breast-feeding her son. Victorian influences prevented women of social standing from caring directly for their children. The doctor stood his ground: "You'll be risking your son's life if you don't take that woman with you. Just think of her as a cow."

Mother accepted that she had no alternative. Her problems with the nurse were just beginning. Crossing the Andes and the pampas to Buenos Aires to board a ship, they journeyed with the nurse, Olga, carrying their son in her arms, and finally arrived in London. They proceeded to the Kensington Hotel, where the Embassy had made reservations for them.

A footman opened the door of their carriage, then promptly retreated. A second porter repeated this odd behavior. Father promptly stepped out and called the porter. He stopped momentarily, and said the manager was on his way. When the manager arrived he said, "I'm sorry. The reservations for you and your family are correct, but we can't assign a room to the . . . to the . . ."

"What do you mean? She is my son's wet nurse. She must stay with him."

"But . . . she's a negress," the man protested.

Having witnessed Olga's patient care for their infant, Mother's resolve and Father's compassion had been aroused.

"She may have some Indian blood," Father allowed. "Our physician says that our child needs her. My son's life depends on your decision, so be careful that I don't have to report this silly incident to the Ambassador, with whom I'm having lunch tomorrow."

The nurse was allowed to take the back stairs to a room close to them. When Eugene outgrew his need for breast-feeding, a position was found for Olga with a diplomatic family returning to Chile.

Mother liked London. The ambassador assigned an aide to show her around. She read as much as she could about the city's history. She visited the Tower and the British Museum. The pomp and splendor of ceremonies at Buckingham Palace enthralled her. She would have liked to stay in London forever, but after a couple of years Father was assigned to Rome.

In Italy she found a world greatly different from what she had expected. Having lived all of her life in a country predominantly Catholic, her puritanical convictions were shaken to the roots in Rome, the cradle of her religion. The Italians' moral looseness came as a surprise from which she never quite recovered. It was about this time that she started to create her own code of conduct in matters concerning religion. Mass and fasting were customs she respected and had lived by in Chile, but no longer. She acquired a great flexibility in her religious practices. She was less judgmental, although she would revert to old habits when she later returned to Chile permanently.

Mother hired a German nanny, who set the strictest rules for little Eugene. In London he had learned English as his first language. In Rome he absorbed Italian by osmosis. His parents spoke to him in Spanish. The German nanny spoke to him only in German. She determined what they would do every day. For a while Mother enjoyed the freedom this allowed her. She could roam the city, meet people, take art classes, and shop for antiques.

She was shocked to find it was the habit of Italian couples to split up on vacation to enjoy sexual freedom. Husbands would go to the beach, while their wives preferred the spas in the mountains. During a stay on Lake Como, hotel gossip soon revealed to her what really went on. Adultery was not for her, but she learned to tolerate it in others. In no mood for adventures, Mother quickly returned to Rome.

Father was pursuing a project of his own, encouraging the emigration of Italians to Chile. He spent long hours selecting candidates. Once he had a sizable group, they departed from Naples. They arrived in Santiago but eventually decamped to Buenos Aires, the most Italian city in South America. Humans are like plants, extremely selective about the ground where they grow roots. In Chile the German, British, and French thrive, but not the Italian.

Father's next assignment took the family to Australia. Mother had rid herself of the German nanny, after realizing that her jealous power over Eugene was unhealthy. In an outbreak of passion, Helga screamed hysterically and threatened Mother with a variety of curses. When Father arrived that evening, Helga was gone. The trip to Australia soon became their only concern.

Mother often described sailing through the Mediterranean: the mysterious beauty of the Aegean Islands, the stifling heat of the Red Sea, interminable days spent sailing on a leaden, waveless sea. How difficult it was to resist the urge to shed tight clothing in the tropical climate. She envied the light, colorful saris of the Indian women. Holding to a dress code that called for women to be completely covered from neck to ankle, with tight corsets and layers of undergarments, required extraordinary strength of will. How hard it was to remain dignified as sweat trickled down face and body.

She described amazing performances by fakirs in the ports of India and the temptations of the rug bazaars. She told of graceful dancers in Bali. And then came Sydney.

Perhaps it was too much to expect for her to like it after London and Rome. In 1909 Australian cities were promising but actually little more than overgrown villages. The people were rude, unpolished, and proud of their toughness, unmindful of their dubious ancestry. They took pride that despite having been dismissed as criminals by the English crown, they had created thriving communities. All this was true and admirable, but Mother felt deeply deprived and in the grips of such loneliness that she couldn't appreciate that she was stepping onto the threshold of an important fragment of world history. To witness the birth of a nation had no appeal for her.

It was then that she started mutilating all photographs taken of her. She turned against herself. She had always been able to have her way. Not anymore. She was helpless, in a deeper exile, she thought, than even the earliest settlers had endured. They were supposedly guilty of crime, but what had she done to deserve this fate? Her English was inadequate. She had trouble communicating. Photos taken at parties show Father alone. Mother refused to attend.

She had been warned about poisonous insects, so even a stroll on the beach became a fearful experience. Australia was for her a frightening turning point. I doubt she ever entirely recovered from the shock of feeling she had been dropped off the edge of the world. No airlines existed then to whisk her away to a more amiable atmosphere. Letters from home took months to arrive. The questions she asked found no answers.

Father's assignments usually lasted two years. This was too long for her not to carry forever the scars of her loneliness and the aggravation of the loss of control over her immediate surroundings. Father started a steady correspondence with his government contacts and influential friends begging them to work out a transfer for him. He succeeded and · was appointed consul in San Francisco, California.

In 1910 the city was still recovering from the devastation of the 1906 earthquake. Whatever had withstood the tremors had been turned into ashes by fire, but Mother relaxed at once. Although a far cry from the attractions of London and Rome, she did not feel cut off as she had in Australia.

My sister Betty was born a year after their arrival in the United States. Soon after her birth she developed a series of strange symptoms that baffled the physicians in San Francisco. Betty's ailments eventually became a blessing in disguise for Mother. They gave her a reason to travel frequently to Chile in search of friendly physicians and compassionate understanding from relatives.

In 1914 I was born in San Francisco after one of these many trips. My arrival hardly caused a ripple in the activities of my family. Mother was busy taking care of Betty when she was sick, which was her permanent condition. Every childhood sickness was considered a life or death struggle. Each time this happened Mother would demand a trip to Chile. The truth was that only in Chile could she be the pampered, spoiled woman she was accustomed to being. The fact that her husband's career had taken her around the world added to her prestige. Her experiences overseas qualified her to influence every decision within the extended family. Only in Chile could she feel fulfilled, and Betty's health provided the excuse for frequent trips home.

CHAPTER 3

After living twelve years in the United States, Father returned to Chile because the president recalled him with a specific purpose: he must reorganize the country's railroad system. He would later resume his diplomatic career, but his assignments never took him back to the United States, where he most wanted to be. Father's inventive mind and curiosity were matched by the progress and enterprise found in this country. From 1910 to the 1930's was a period that saw the birth of much of the technology that shapes our world today. It was a time for adventurous and bold thinking. Father was more than a diplomat. He was a visionary, often frustrated by the confines of political loyalties. Later, when he felt pangs of nostalgia for the United States and its exhilarating atmosphere, he would ask me — a young woman — to keep him company on long and silent walks. What was he thinking? Then, I did not ask. I was sure of the nature of his regrets.

San Francisco, the city of my first six years, left deep impressions. There we had lived on Washington Street, which was lined with houses exactly alike, with views of the bay and its shimmering blue waters, dotted by sailboats and large steamers. The scene had kept me mesmerized for hours. One neighbor had a face that I can still see in my intimate album of memories. I don't think I ever knew her name, so I shall call her Janet.

The gardens behind the houses were small but fine. Mother had little patience for gardening, but Janet followed the seasons, filling her small plot of land with a profusion of aromatic bushes and colorful patches of flowers that she cut to share with friends. I learned from her to care for plants, tend to their needs, and enjoy fragrances and forms. She was a rather lonely and reserved woman, probably a spinster. Few people ever visited her. Yet I felt good with her, and I think that she loved me too.

Later in life I found out that love is far more complex and not always a good feeling, but then it was simple and sweet. She never refused to care for me when Mother was absent, and while she was silent, puttering with her plants, or explaining how to best help them thrive, a glow emanated from her. After we moved to a larger house in a different neighborhood, I didn't see her again, but I never forgot her.

The new house was large enough for guests, so Mother decided that she would give her nieces the chance to visit the United States. The first niece to come was Mary, daughter of Mother's eldest brother. Mary was very tall, very beautiful, and very dull. It was like acquiring a new piece of furniture. She looked good, was comfortable, demanded nothing, and scarcely ever gave an opinion. She stayed for a few months and left without leaving a mark. The second niece was Blanquita. She was exactly the opposite of Mary, although just as beautiful. She had a soul. She was vibrant. From the instant she awoke, her laughter rang out all day. Blanquita coined a phrase at the height of surprise or admiration for something new: "It's like in the movies!" All the family's friends fell in love with her. Rumors of her charm got around, and a reporter requested an interview. He instantly fell under her spell. In his description of Blanquita he became lyrical in praise of her beauty. The language barrier came crashing down. The reporter found ways to make her express her amazement at everything she saw. Later he wrote: "Her smile uncovers strings of pearls between her lips."

Hollywood was beginning to stir the world's emotions. Father thought that a visit to the studios might be something that Blanquita would appreciate. They left for Los Angeles, Father driving a new Packard, at the time an object of incredible luxury. The visit to the studios was memorable, not only for Blanquita, but also for the whole family. Blanquita was offered a contract to play in the movies. Never mind that she didn't have any training. They wanted her beauty, her spontaneity, and her ready laughter. She would rival Mary Pickford, said one director.

Father was pleasantly intrigued by this development. Could this be a lifetime opportunity for Blanquita?, he wondered. Consultation with her parents was out of the question as communications were unreliable, even through the Chilean Foreign Affairs offices. The decision — a

Picture taken in San Francisco, California
(left to right): Betty, me, Mother, and Eugene.

negative one — was made by Mother, who believed that anything connected with the world of entertainment was evil and corrupt. She clung to this belief all her life.

To Mother's further aggravation, Blanquita had fallen in love with a young Chilean tenor who would later become an international celebrity once he moved to perform in Europe. He was also deeply in love with Blanquita and wanted to marry her. Then along came another young Chilean, visiting the United States before entering the seminary to be ordained a priest. He too became enchanted with Blanquita's charms. He announced he would forego his vocation to ask for her hand. So Mother was saved. She wouldn't have to fight Hollywood or the opera. She returned to Chile with Blanquita for the wedding. Blanquita never had children. Our cousins mischievously attributed this to a failed libido on the part of her strongly religious partner. But Blanquita's laughter continued to ring clearly and convincingly. She seldom mentioned her stay in San Francisco, her visit to Hollywood, or the opera star who — it was said — pined for her a long time in suitable operatic tones.

As World War I raged in Europe, anti-German propaganda spread in the United States. Descriptions of atrocities committed by the Kaiser's troops filled every newspaper and magazine. Mother and her friends read these stories aloud amid expressions of outrage. After listening to them, I looked at the pictures. One evening, probably having heard about a particularly gruesome description of the abuses of German troops, I woke up in the middle of the night feeling an acute need of comfort and reassurance. To get to my parent's bedroom I had to walk past the stairs. As I did, I felt compelled to check sideways at the dark void of the stairs. There I saw Kaiser Wilhelm in full battle regalia, followed by his soldiers, climbing the stairs with their arms outstretched to catch me. They were upon me as I uttered the most horrified scream of my four years. In a flash my parents were by my side, the lights came on, and the vision was dispelled. But still I shivered. No power on earth would make me return to my bedroom past those stairs where the Kaiser and his soldiers were waiting for me. This incident would later help me understand why Mother refused to live in Germany, where Father had been appointed.

Mother always hired Chinese cooks and domestics in San Francisco. I was allowed to sit with them as they talked to me about the food they were preparing. Often I was given gifts so fine that I developed a lifelong appreciation of Oriental art. Father too felt close to these men, who did their work fast and silently, who demanded so very little. Mother used to say that she only knew they had taken another job when she found a taller or shorter man than the one she had dealt with the day before. Father appreciated the attention they gave me, their presents, and their patience in teaching me how to handle small jobs around the kitchen.

On Sundays he took me to Chinatown, where we saw funeral processions, with relatives carrying large pictures of the deceased perched on the back seat of their cars. There were extravagant displays of dragons and monsters for special occasions. Father would buy me exotic toys or the sweets our cooks had taught me to enjoy. Slanted eyes, yellow skin, overcourteous manners, funny turns of phrase, none of it surprised me. It was there, in San Francisco, that I first came to appreciate human-kind's great variety of color and class.

I had little contact with my sister, Betty. She was permanently ill and demanded Mother's constant attention. When Mother wasn't preparing some potions for the child, she would be reading any medical book that might give her a clue as to what could best soothe Betty's symptoms. Unable to play with a brother eight years older — who had little patience for the games of a young child — I learned to play by myself. I created a world of funny creatures with whom I sustained endless dialogues.

While Father was consul in San Francisco, he didn't restrict his activities to his job description. The United States was a nation in the midst of an extraordinary transformation. World War I had ended its isolationism. The country was beginning to see itself as a world power. A monumental national pride seemed to take hold of Americans. The automobile and civil aviation industries were creating new services. Agricultural production was soaring to incredible levels.

Transcontinental transportation by land and air were a field that Father followed closely, as usual watching for the systems that would be best for his own country. His official reports were not treated as diplomatic communiques. Many were published in Chilean newspapers. Father believed in the power of reiteration. Time and again he would bring up the need for bright young men — regardless of their family's financial means — to be provided with scholarships to study in the United States the most suitable industries for the advancement of Chile. The youngsters who were challenged by such progressive ideas were later the founders of industries that still exist and have for more than six decades met vital Chilean needs.

Father's contacts with American leaders of industry had resulted in exciting offers of employment, should he choose to remain in the United States when his president recalled him. But Mother wouldn't hear of it. She must return to Chile, be close to family and friends. Father gave in, responding both to his wife's demands and his deep loyalty to the land of his birth. It was the same patriotic pull that kept his forebears in the island of Chiloé years earlier. It now dictated Father's abandonment of his own bounteous interests. It was thus that we returned to Chile and I was thrust into a flock of my cousins.

Among treasures from all over the world, Mother had a Chinese vase decorated with a multitude of tiny faces. What awaited us at the top of those steps in Valparaíso's quay was a replica of that vase. The faces on it were silent. Those that greeted us were distorted by a series of emotions. Open mouths emitted sounds that were incomprehensible to my ears. Women's shrieking voices grated on my senses. I wished only the men would speak in their stronger, deeper tones.

The cousins we were to meet either hid behind their mother's skirts or looked at us suspiciously. I asked Mother a question. "Wait," she answered peremptorily. A similar appeal from Betty brought a series of exclamations from the grown-ups and snickering among the cousins. We spoke only English, which they seldom heard.

"¿Qué dices? ¿Qué quieres?" What did you say? What do you want? Father translated and I insisted: "I want to go to the bathroom."

"I'm thirsty," Betty said, pleading with her eyes.

"Control yourselves. Wait," Mother ordered.

We started to walk, and I quickly forgot my urgent need. We were to ride in handsome, shiny black coaches drawn by beautiful horses. Their hooves clicked a lively rhythm on the cobblestones. It seemed a long but delightful ride by the sea, tall waves splashing the road with their foam. The hotel at Viña del Mar was a one-story building around a large court-yard full of blooming vines in bright yellow and red flowers. Big round clay pots disgorged multicolored geraniums. We might have enjoyed the whispering of a fountain in the middle of the terrace if it had not been drowned by the excited prattle of aunts, uncles, and cousins.

The next day we took the train to Santiago to stay at Uncle José María's home on Ejército Avenue, in the heart of a remarkable residential neighborhood. It was one of the widest avenues in the city, flanked by spectacular homes built in pure English Regency style. At the end of the avenue, turning left, it led to the Military Academy. On the right was the fashionable Club Hípico, where on Sundays horseracing provided women the opportunity to display the latest Paris fashions, while the men risked their fortunes on the speed of the horses.

Uncle José María, Father's eldest brother, was a small, silent man who walked through the house with his hands firmly clutched behind his back. He stooped badly and was totally oblivious to his surroundings. Founder of the Villalonga Express, the rail transportation to Argentina, he was also a senator. This uncle's family became my first haven, filled with laughter and outrageous activities from the mischievous cousins.

José María's marriage to Aunt Esther had produced several children, only five of whom survived infancy. One boy, Fernando, turned out to be an unmanageable eccentric, who was sometimes funny but more often obnoxious. He failed in his studies and had no way of holding a job. Being a senator, his father found him a niche in the diplomatic service, so he was shipped overseas. Somewhere along his career, his eccentricities mellowed and he performed brilliantly for his government. The high point was his intervention in negotiations to avoid a war with Argentina due to border conflicts.

The rest of Uncle José María's brood consisted of four daughters, who came under the care of two "mamas" who had nursed them since birth. These women watched over the girls in every aspect of their development: health, manners, and education. Each one supervised two girls. One of the mamas took me under her wing. She was tall, slender, and quite handsome. She had a son she scarcely ever saw. Nobody knew who the father was. There was an air of distinction about her that gave ground for speculation about her origins. Aunt Esther wondered if she was the illegitimate daughter of some distinguished person. The second mama was quite the opposite: heavy, dark skinned, and sloppy in her manner. Yet she showed a gushing tenderness to her charges, the two youngest girls in the family.

At six years of age my first weeks there were a lesson in patience and painful adjustment. My cousins delighted in making me speak English, laughing at a language unfamiliar to them. I didn't know a word of Spanish, and they had not a clue about English. No one could help me. My brother and Betty were in the same predicament. Father was deeply involved in his new assignment. Mother was working with architects on a second floor that was to be built onto our late grandparents' home at the other end of the city. It still intrigues me how it happened but one day I just started to communicate in Spanish. The same miracle happened to Betty. Only my brother was behind. Being years older than us, he found picking up a strange language more difficult. His classmates were extremely hard on him when he made mistakes. But we all learned.

After we moved into our grandparents' remodeled home I was sitting on top of a trunk stored in a living room, when Eugene walked in and asked what I was doing; "I'm reading," I said, matter-of-factly. He laughed.

I offered to read to him, lifting a yellow bound copy of the Espasa Calpe "History of the Rise and Fall of the Roman Empire." As I read a passage my brother showed a reaction that would characterize him to me for the rest of my life. He turned around without a word and walked out of the room. Whatever emotion he felt was immediately controlled so no inner workings would show. If he had asked me who had taught me to read, I could only have answered the truth: nobody. I could read just as I could speak Spanish.

We felt proud of our new home. It was cleverly designed with living room, salon, and dining room to the front of the building. Each room had a balcony on the street. The bedrooms, bathrooms, and large family room were at the back. The kitchen and maid's quarters were on the south side, next to the stairs leading to an attic. Memories of my friendly relations with the Chinese domestics in San Francisco made me seek company in the kitchen. But I got a quick rejection from the cook.

"Don't come in here when I'm working. You curdle the mayonnaise with your eyes."

I retreated. I just had to find something else to do. Mother was always out, and Father working. Eugene and an apparently fully recovered Betty were at school. The stairs to the attic seemed mysteriously attractive. What was up there? Among empty trunks and boxes, I found the sad figure of a carved wooden Saint Anthony that Mother had ordered banned to the attic. At Valparaíso's customs her trunks had been ransacked and her most precious possessions stolen. Saint Anthony had not protected them. Even a saint was not immune from Mother's wrath. I sat for a while, wiping off cobwebs from his enamel face and crystal eyes. Then I found a more dignified location for him among the discarded objects in the attic. I could now be satisfied that Saint Anthony was redeemed.

Noticing a trap door in the ceiling, I pushed it open and stepped out onto the roof. The sight took my breath away. It was late afternoon, and the sun was setting over the Andes. The mountains absorbed all the light, and the sky above was tinted red, orange, and pink in a spectacular display of colors. Then night took over with its dark velvets, star studded from one side of the horizon to the other. From that day on the rooftop became a daily pilgrimage. As I grew older I would take pencil and paper in an attempt to capture the beauty of those moments.

Mother's eldest brother, Martín, occupied the first floor of the house. We seldom saw him. Most of the year he stayed at his ranch in the south of Chile, waiting for summer when his wife, children, friends, and relatives arrived to spend vacations at San Martín. His wife, Aunt Celmira, their three daughters, and two sons spent most of the year in Santiago in order to be part of the city's social life and attend schools and universities. I had a crush on both of the sons. They were sensationally handsome.

Gonzálo was tall, blond, and blue eyed, reminding me of some of the young Americans I had seen in San Francisco. Ivan could have passed for an Oriental prince. His black hair, dark eyes, olive skin, and sinewy body were a sight to behold on a horse. It was difficult to tell where man ended and animal began. In the summer I rode his horses, rather than ponies, although my heart was pounding with fear. At seven I stuck to the saddle, always following him and making him proud to be my teacher.

One year at spring carnival, an incident involving Gonzálo confirmed that women had an irresistible attraction to him. In the middle of the night I heard voices raised in anger in the hall downstairs. Moments later Mother was summoned. Curiosity led me to follow her quietly. Looking into the hall I saw my aunt and cousins — Mary, Aida, and Perla — holding onto her. Apparently she was about to faint. Their horrified expressions and large frightened eyes spoke of tragedy. I moved cautiously lest I be spotted. Lying on a couch and deathly pale, Gonzálo held a towel to his chest. Its whiteness was stained with blood. Mother bent over him. She held his hand away from his body to look at the wound. A jealous husband had shot Gonzálo, I found out later.

"He must be taken to the emergency clinic immediately," said Mother, who I could see was alarmed. Aunt Celmira screamed in anger: "Never! We can't face such a scandal."

"Would you rather he die here without any help? What kind of a mother are you?"

"His father would find out through the newspapers. I can't stand the thought of it. The scandal might ruin the girls' betrothals. I will not damage my daughters' lives for the folly of their brother." Aunt Celmira sounded firm.

Ever resourceful in emergencies, Mother remembered that another nephew was a medical student about to graduate. Quickly she dispatched a couple of maids to bring him to the house. Soon Eduardo too was leaning over Gonzálo, examining his wound and asking questions.

"I can take care of this right here," he reassured Gonzálo. "I brought some instruments. I just need hot water and clean bandages."

Knowing Mother's reputation as a sensible, strong woman who had faced wounded workers at her brothers' ranches, Eduardo told her to hold Gonzálo tight.

"I must get the bullet out quickly. Fortunately it's not too deep," he said with great authority.

After cutting into Gonzálo he pulled out the bullet. Aunt Celmira fainted. Her three daughters wailed uncontrollably, and I began to shift my allegiances to Eduardo. I decided then to become a physician. Notwithstanding his princely beauty, poor Ivan was suddenly a notch lower in my affections. Granted he rode magnificently, but he had never stepped onto the stage of heroic performers, like Gonzálo and Eduardo did that night. Definitely, I would become a physician, but since this couldn't be attained overnight the thing for me to do was to nurse Gonzálo back to health, under the daily supervision of Eduardo.

One day I was taking a bath when Mother walked in and sat on the edge of the tub.

"You've grown so much. All of a sudden I realize that you exist! You know I've been busy with many things, but I wanted to tell you that even though your birthday is coming up you mustn't expect any presents, because Christmas is too close. You'll get presents then."

She left without looking for a reaction from me. The water in the tub seemed cold. I turned the faucet to achieve a more pleasant temperature but then decided instead to get out, dry myself, and go to bed. Sleep would help. I couldn't remember having had a birthday celebration, so I didn't much care for failing to have one now. It didn't hurt as much as the fact that Mother had not been aware of my existence for all the years of my life.

However I did get a gift after all, although not on my December birthday. Mother hired a nanny called Carmelita. She was very short, hardly taller than me, all pudgy and soft, but amazingly agile and fast on her feet. She kept me entranced listening to her stories of elves, dragons, fairies, and heroes.

At this time I started school at the Sacred Heart Academy. Carmelita was supposed to take Betty and me there every morning and pick us up in the afternoons. Home was quite a distance from the convent and we were expected to take the tram, but Carmelita made us walk, with promises of a surprise later in the day. Betty wasn't interested in the surprise but she walked anyhow, and Carmelita saved the tram money everyday both ways. Betty never knew what she missed by refusing to share in Carmelita's surprise: tickets to the movies. Carmelita was delighted because she paid only for her own ticket. Mine was free since I was under age. This was my introduction to the world of entertainment. I saw Rudolph Valentino in "The Sheik," "Riders of the Apocalypse," "Blood and Sand"; the sublime Bertini, the Italian rival of Sarah Bernhardt; Pola Negri, Mary Pickford, and all the stars of the twenties.

Our adventures continued until one evening when a particularly strong tremor forced the manager to evacuate the theater. Chile, just like California, suffers frequent tremors and unannounced earthquakes, followed at times by tidal waves. To remain undetected by family or friends, Carmelita would get us seats in the balcony. When the earth started to shake and the lights went on, I climbed onto the banister, my frightened body improvising an acrobatic act toward the exit. Spectators below paused in their flight, horrified that I might loose my balance and fall.

A group of neighbors visited my parents that evening. When Carmelita was called in to explain our presence at the theater, I panicked. I didn't grasp all the implications, but soon Carmelita's tears told me that something was terribly wrong. That same evening she left us forever. No more the softness of her body embracing me. No more storytelling to put me to sleep. No more walking to school in order to save money for movies. No more exciting pictures that taught me acting by osmosis. Little did the nuns know, when they assigned me a role in a play, that I *was* Bertini, not the studious little girl who won all the first prizes.

Years later, living in Chile as a young adult, I looked up Carmelita. It was difficult but I finally found her address, a dreary tenement, with a windowless room and a shared toilet. Her body seemed to have lost its softness. She kept her mouth pursed to hide decayed teeth. She didn't recognize me until I told her one of her own stories. I enthusiastically related tales of movies I had seen in Europe and bragged about French and German stars she had never heard of. Tears started running down her cheeks, and then I realized how selfish it was to look her up. I was disrupting her slow slide into oblivion to satisfy an obsession of mine. A voice inside me whispered: "Let her sleep. Let her sleep. You can't do anything for her." I had little money at the time, but I slipped a few pesos into her pocket saying, absurdly: "Movie money."

In California my brother, Eugene, had become interested in radio, then the craze among young people. Our father encouraged him to research and experiment. Our basement on Presidio Terrace had turned into a workshop full of books and tools. There he held meetings with the friends who shared his hobby. Eugene was extremely adept at building things, so he had no trouble putting together small galena radios that worked the miracle of broadcasting and receiving messages. Gradually he eliminated the scratchy sounds, a triumph that Father celebrated by providing him with new materials. This allowed Eugene to beam still farther — and clearer — to friends in the outskirts of San Francisco. So he was desolate when he was told that we must leave for Chile for an indefinite period of time. What would happen to the arsenal of materials accumulated in his workshop? Would he be able to keep up with fast developing techniques? Even at fourteen he understood perfectly that the radios he built were no toys, that this amazing scientific development must certainly influence generations to come.

Eugene asked Father if he could stay, at least temporarily, in San Francisco. But this was out of the question. His tools and materials would be shipped. To soften his disappointment, Father promised to introduce him to friends who shared a love of technology and would appreciate Eugene's pursuits. Eugene accepted grudgingly, fearing that Father's friends would be older people who wouldn't see the potential of the new science. He considered Father to be different because he had lived so long in the United States. Fortunately he was wrong. Father's recommendations had unexpected results.

Soon after arrival in Santiago, Eugene was contacted by a curious group of Father's friends. They discussed the possibility of setting up a workshop, with him as the instructor, to start the manufacture of radios. Eugene became responsible for a weekly class eagerly attended by a growing group of adult students.

Eugene returned from one class unusually subdued and depressed. He told Mother that he refused to go on teaching. He wouldn't go into details. He offered no valid reason. Mother asked one of Father's friends if anything had happened to discourage Eugene from teaching the radio class. The friend couldn't think of anything but came to speak with Eugene.

"I understand that you don't want to teach us anymore," he said.

"That's right," answered Eugene, showing no feelings.

"Why? Do you realize how much we appreciate your help?"

"I guess I do, but . . ."

"Let me tell you why this is so important to us. Think of Chile, this long, narrow island in the middle of nowhere, cut off from the world. Why do I call it an island when we know it is not? Bring me a map," the friend ordered.

Eugene left the room and returned promptly with an atlas.

"Look at this narrow strip of land. In the north the Atacama Desert acts like a barrier. In the east the Andes is like a forbidding wall. The Pacific isolates us and the near polar conditions in the south add to our insularity. Communications from one end to the other of the country are of vital importance. This is what you have brought to us with your classes — the possibility of creating a network that may allow us to overcome our isolation at little cost. Do you realize now why we must continue to learn from you?"

"I understand," Eugene replied, "but some of you make fun of me."

"What do you mean? I'm not aware of it."

"I heard somebody say 'Look at this kid in short pants teaching us.' And they laughed."

Father's friend burst out laughing. Then he explained.

"There's two sides to that remark. I don't think that whoever said it meant it disparagingly, only that at our age we know less than a boy in short pants. The joke is on us."

Father's friend then gave Mother the address of his tailor. The next day Eugene was properly fitted. At the next class he appeared handsomely clad in long trousers. This simple garment transformed the brother I knew into a young man now ready to take his place as a teacher. His new suit also enabled him to participate in the courtship rituals of the young. It was a custom for a suitor to walk up and down the street in front of the home of one's beloved. Because of his reserved nature, we never knew the real outcome of Eugene's mating dance, but it was clear he was no longer a boy in short pants.

More important, Eugene was now aware that he was doing something sorely needed to alleviate Chile's isolation. He was helping to place the country on the way to higher technology. He understood more fully

Father's preoccupation with adapting scientific discoveries to his country's needs. He felt proudly that he was following in Father's footsteps. Pride was a sweet sensation.

Vacations were the highlights of our year. We divided our time among relatives' properties in the south. At Uncle Alberto's ranch, Llallauquen, six cousins awaited us. Other cousins came and went, the numbers often rising toward twenty or thirty. In the mornings we would get a glass of milk at the dairy barn, each glass filled directly from the cow's teat. It was frothy and warm, and I was the only child who refused to drink this delicacy. I was disgusted with this exposure to nature. In the States milk came in a bottle. I was shaken by the knowledge of its true origin. But I loved the workers' freshly baked loaves of multigrain bread. Warm and fragrant, it stayed inside my shirt and I would munch on it all day.

Then we mounted our horses and left for unknown destinations. A postillion, assigned to our care, accompanied us armed with a first aid kit and tools to repair saddles or bridles. Exploring the ranch to its farthest limits, where the land stretched into the lower slopes of the Andes on one side and the beaches of the Pacific at the other end, we visited the families of men who worked in the fields. With the generosity of the poor, they never failed to offer us something, sharing with us fruit, eggs, or a drink.

Aunt Graciela was a beautiful woman, but she had an oddity. She proudly displayed several baby teeth still in her mouth even though she was over forty. Alberto, Graciela's husband, was nicknamed Rapalo by his closest friends. It came about in this way. Graciela's parents belonged to a family that in the last century held important positions in government but were not wealthy. When Graciela met a member of the Bunster family they rejoiced, for the Bunsters had a reputation for being the most powerful landowners in the country. Unfortunately, Alberto Bunster belonged to the least wealthy branch of the family. When Graciela's family discovered this, they forbade her to see Alberto again. The couple eloped and disappeared. A long and discreet investigation located them in Rapalo, Italy. One of Aunt Graciela's uncles was sent to bring them back to Chile. For years a few close friends used the name Rapalo with a smile of complicity.

Graciela's uncle, a beautiful old man in his late seventies, told me this story. I always suspected that he was the envoy responsible for returning the young couple to the fold. I liked older men. They usually had such lovely tales to tell, and this friend in particular wrote for me the most stirring poems of love, tragedy, and death. Having lost his fortune, he lived with his sister in a big old house with palm trees around a garden which led to stables where old carriages were kept, although the horses were no more. While we talked about many things, my favorite cousin, Eliana, visited his sister, her grandmother. Eliana usually asked to see her jewel box and quietly picked a few pieces of gold that we later sold to go to the movies!

While vacationing in Llallauquen we had to help out during the missions. These occurred once a year when the landowner hired a Catholic priest to perform religious ceremonies. All the eight-year-old girls were instructed for their first confession and communion, for which they received a new dress and veil. Aunt Graciela would bring out several bolts of white cotton percale, usually with small blue dots. She put all her nieces to work on these dresses, all cut in the same size with hems reaching to midcalf on some girls and as miniskirts on the taller ones.

Multiple weddings were held in the afternoon. Aunt Graciela donated the veils and a modest boutonniere for the grooms. After a luncheon where communicants and parents enjoyed a buffet of empanadas and watermelon, the couples to be wed lined up in front of the chapel, and the priest gave them his collective blessing.

On one occasion Graciela's eyes focused on a sobbing figure by a tree. She knew her. The girl had occasionally worked in the kitchen. She'd lost her slender figure. Her protruding belly proclaimed her condition. She was alone. The white veil covering her dark hair floated about her head like a bird trying to fly away. Aunt Graciela was compelled to do something to stop the woman's humiliation. She walked down the chapel steps, where a line of young men stood. Grabbing one by the hand, she pulled him toward the sobbing girl.

"Now, you marry her. She is a good, honest girl. I know her well. She'll take care of you. Cook, sew, mend, and clean. Besides she already brings you a child to help you later. Quick, take her hand and join the others."

Blushing to the roots of his hair, the youngster obeyed.

That day I celebrated my aunt's initiative but took exception to the priest's acceptance of her spontaneous gesture. It belittled the sacrament he was performing. I told him so later, but he only answered, "You don't know what you are talking about." He was probably right. Yet I felt there was more involved in a well-meaning gesture intended to soothe the humiliation of a girl. The young man's situation and future were entirely overlooked. His feelings were of no concern. He had obeyed the patrona's order, and the priest had sanctioned it without question. He had bowed his head but later would he react with anger? Most people present considered the incident humorous and didn't give it another thought.

By 1923, after three years, Father had corrected the problems of the Chilean railways. As promised, President Alessandri fulfilled his commitment, returning Father to his diplomatic career — with a considerably higher rank as Consular Inspector for Europe with residence in London. Mother was pleased, for she had always felt closer to her British blood than her Spanish heritage. We traveled across the Andes by train, mule, and train again, sped through the pampas to arrive in Buenos Aires, where we took a British ship to Southampton. Another train ride took us to London, where my parents had earlier spent some time. It was fall. The fog seemed to penetrate the hotel rooms, dimming lights and making it practically impossible to tell day from night.

While Mother boasted that Betty and I had been born in the United States and were fluent in English, I could not understand the first question asked of me. Mother translated, urging me to answer. I could sense her embarrassment and aggravation. I had tried so hard to overcome the language barrier in Chile that I had completely forgotten English. I realized I was facing immersion in a different culture and would be verbally isolated yet again.

We had only just begun to settle into life in London when word arrived that a coup in Chile had ousted President Alessandri. His decisions were rescinded, and hardest hit was the Chilean diplomatic corps. No salaries were sent. Not a hint came of what would happen next. For six months Father and other Chilean officials abroad waited anxiously. Finally, Father was notified that his position in London was canceled and that he must move to Germany, where he would be the next Consul General in Hamburg.

CHAPTER 4

While World War I was raging in Europe, Mother became immersed in anti-German propaganda, which had a lasting effect on our lives. When Father was appointed Consul General in Hamburg, she refused to follow him. It was for this reason that we four went to nearby Belgium, and Father proceeded alone to Germany. We all experienced the consequences of this. As far as we, the three children, were concerned, Eugene would study civil engineering at the University of Ghent, while Betty and I were enrolled as boarding students at the Sacred Heart Convent in Lindthout, Brussels.

Eugene was liberated from Mother's demanding tutelage. Notes among his papers, found after his death, speak of those years at the university in Ghent as full of personal development. He made friends with local students and other South Americans attending the university, without having to seek Mother's approval for his choices. He started to lead a man's life, going to bars, drinking beer, ogling girls, and laughing at the crude remarks of his companions. Mother would have frowned at such boorishness. Eugene only laughed.

Betty and I rarely communicated despite the fact that we were in the same school. She was in a higher grade. I had been assigned to a lower class until I was fluent in French. This soon happened, but the nuns forgot that I was supposed to be promoted. We were not seated near each other in the refectory nor were our beds close in the dormitory. The situation became critical the day I started to menstruate. I hadn't the foggiest idea what it meant and wanted to die of shame. Severe cramps gave me away. When taken to the dispensary I left a large spot of blood on the chair. Given a sanitary napkin and shown how to hold it in place, I was dismissed without any explanation. Gathering courage, I tremblingly asked the sister, "Will I bleed to death? Can you give me something to stop it?"

"You'll be all right," she answered. "Don't worry so much. Every woman goes through this."

"Why?" I asked, shocked that a cure had not been found for this excruciating experience.

"You'll find out later. Ask your mother."

"But I won't see her until next visitation day." I could feel the panic rising from unanswered questions.

"Be patient. I will send you more sanitary napkins. Don't bathe or shampoo your hair until it's over."

Every two weeks we were allowed a parental visit. In our case only Mother visited us. It was only then that I saw Betty; otherwise we lived in different worlds. After these reunions with parents, the nuns called us for tea, clicking the little wooden boxes they carried in the palm of their hands, never uttering a word, yet controlling our every move. Click to get in line. Click click, to start walking. Click click click, to stop. Hard click, somebody is talking! The nun flies down the line to catch the culprit. Click click, to resume walking. But when we reached the refectory, the rule of silence was lifted.

At our assigned tables sat big tin boxes with all the candy and cookies our parents had brought us. For the next twenty minutes we had a choice: speak or eat sweets. We usually did both simultaneously, and the spectacle of chocolate drooling down the corners of our mouths, while we talked and laughed, was gross. Then silence would prevail again. The tin boxes were closed, and the remaining candy and cookies we had been unable to gobble up were shut away. The clicking wood boxes snapped us back to order.

Mother requested that we be provided with milk but was told this was totally unavailable due to postwar circumstances. Shortly afterward we were to discover the alternative to the requested nutritious supplement: two pitchers on the dinner table. One contained water, the other beer!

Sister Ann was hardly taller than a midget. Her wrinkled little face, framed by the white starched material that didn't allow her to look sideways, always had a ready smile and twinkle for the girls, particularly the younger ones. We would often hear a "pst, pst" in unexpected places, such as from behind a bush at recess or in a corridor from behind a door. A small hand would emerge holding out a candy bar or a couple of cookies.

Sister Ann was never short of ideas to help us or lighten the deadly monotony of the system. We loved her but feared we might get caught conspiring with her. If this happened we would be punished. Every Saturday students assembled to receive their report cards. Three consecutive demerits called for a three- to seven-day suspension. I would find out that was no picnic.

Father could only visit us in school every other month, when he came to Brussels to see Mother. Meantime he'd started a courtship — perhaps the most high priced in the history of forlorn lovers. It was his attempt to persuade Mother to live with him in Germany. A floor-length sable coat announced his campaign. After briefly trying it on, Mother let it slide from her shoulders with a nonchalant shrug.

"It's too heavy," she remarked.

A stole, made with the skins of four silver foxes, was the next gift.

"You should know that I can't possibly handle these animals," she said, dropping the wrap on a chair. She accepted a three-strand pearl choker with mild enthusiasm.

Many years later I found the stole in a trunk. I shook off the hairs loosened by neglect and the voracity of moths. I wore it defiantly. It indeed proved hard to handle. Apparently my body's warmth instilled life in the foxes that slithered around my shoulders and waist as we walked together down the street, the foxes and me. I had the inner satisfaction of having done justice to Father's generosity.

One spring morning the manager of the hotel on the Avenue Louise knocked on Mother's door. Somebody was waiting for her downstairs, he said. I happened to be suspended from school at the time and realized something important must be happening for Monsieur Dubois to call on Mother personally. His obsequious demeanor, the bending at the waist, the ingratiating smile gave him away.

In the hotel's courtyard — where I imagined elegant carriages drawn up by fiery horses — was a shiny black Mercedes Benz. A smiling chauffeur opened the door for our inspection.

"With Monsieur Lorca's compliments," he said respectfully.

Mother didn't crack a smile. She looked at the car only for a second, then turned slowly toward the chauffeur.

"What is your name?"

"Pierre, Madame, Pierre LaSalle," he replied.

"Pierre, go now and have that gilt braid removed from your cap and sleeves. Return at three o'clock."

She turned her back on the stunned Pierre, took my hand, and dragged me to the dining room for breakfast. In one quick embarrassed look I took in the shocked faces of the hotel manager and the chauffeur. Their expectations of how this dazzling gift would be received were shattered. But the Mercedes Benz and Pierre soon became the centerpieces of an important period in my adolescence.

Mother had left the hospital not long after an almost-fatal car accident. When she arrived at the hotel, she found me in her suite. I didn't know she had left the hospital. She didn't know I was suspended from school for a week. It was a pleasant surprise for us both.

I had already been admonished by waiters and maids, who took it upon themselves to make me feel guilty about my lack of appreciation for the privilege of an education in the same school that Princess Marie Joseph of Belgium had attended. They refused to serve me in the dining room. I was confined to the pantry. My bed was not made. Now I hoped that Mother would protect me from their hostility. She did, and she allowed my company to distract her from her pain and, for a short time, soothe her loneliness.

After I explained to Mother the reason for my suspension — interrupting the teacher in class with an answer to a question not addressed to me — Mother never spoke of it again. So having each other for company and Pierre to drive us around, we had a splendid time. For the first time in three years in Brussels, I saw the magnificent Grande Place, the historical center of the city. Pierre told us that the architect of the city hall building committed suicide when he noticed that the tower was not properly centered.

We stopped at galleries of modern art, regarding the artists' creations without much understanding. It was a time of radical changes in art. Cubism, Dadaism, and other schools were intriguing experiments. These works seemed to stay with me, creating persistent visions. Figures, shapes, and colors couldn't easily be dismissed, no matter how unusual their structure or bold their shadings. I longed to return for a second look, but Mother preferred to go on, looking at other things.

When the time came for me to return to school, Pierre drove us to Lindthout, obviously sad to see me go. Mother wasn't happy either although she didn't show it clearly, except when she hugged me good-bye, she whispered: "Not for long." I treasured these words from a mother who I knew did not display tenderness easily.

Three days later Pierre came to pick me up on Mother's orders, for an indefinite absence. I looked into his eyes, and a beautiful friendship was instantly established. He looked very much like my absent Father; not too tall, a little stocky, blond, blue eyed with a big smile. I tried to sit next to him in the passenger's seat, but he stopped me: "Pas ici, ma petite. You sit in the back."

Feeling like a solitary pea on the deep velvet seat, I complied, primly crossing my legs. I turned to look back at the convent. Several faces were watching my departure. Sister Ann was one of them. My dearest friend, Nathalie Wrangel, was there too. She was the daughter of the White Russian leader Baron Petr Nikolaevich Wrangel, the gallant general who fought the Bolsheviks. Nathalie lives now in the United States, and we still correspond. The story of her family's escape from Russia sparked forever my interest in world politics.

I could also see Yvonne Kemp, whom I loved because of her spontaneity, her irrepressible joie de vivre in a place where all was gray and smothered. She was Dutch. Her handsome sculptured features, as though cut in stone, made her beautiful in an unconventional way. Another friend, Françoise Descamps, who wore with pride a patched handed-down coat because her parents were intent on building dowries for their five daughters, was also there. Would I ever see them again? Jumping up to my knees, I faced the back window, waving desperately.

One might ask, how were friendships made under a strict regime that practiced the rule of silence at all hours? How do prisoners communicate in solitary? It can be done. A slip of paper with tiny scrawled words, eyes speaking, gestures carrying a message. It works. Many years later I met Nathalie for lunch in New York. I was able to trace her thanks to Princess Obolenski, the doyenne of White Russians in the United States. But I have always wondered what became of Yvonne and Françoise during World War II.

CHAPTER 5

At the Hotel Wiltchers in Brussels, Mother had a large suite with a bathroom at the end of the hall. Adjoining bathrooms were not yet in practice, no matter how prestigious the hotel. There, Betty and I bathed before entering Mother's rooms. Mellifluous André, a hotel employee in charge of our floor, scrubbed our backs and supervised our soaping. I never inquired why he and not a proper maid did this chore. It was enough to be able to take a bath whenever I wanted, instead of waiting for the weekly convent immersion, which required a thick cotton tunic to cover us from neck to toes. We must have stunk to high heaven. No wonder that on periodic visits, Mother forbade us to enter her suite until we had been soaked and scrubbed by André.

Our school uniforms were sent to the cleaners, and we dressed in clean clothes before approaching her. Betty enjoyed the ritual, splashing wildly to André's aggravation. I had reservations about the whole cockeyed ceremony, but those were Mother's rules. Also I disliked the taffeta dresses she picked for us, and the patent leather shoes were sheer torture. But this was required for us to attend a mahjong evening, with a collection of hotel guests, like the Comtesse de Rochechouart and a general who had lost his right arm in World War I.

Betty usually excused herself. I wouldn't have missed mahjong for the world. I delighted in the design and feel of the exquisite ivory and bamboo chips. Sometimes I was allowed to play. I listened to the gossip about the royal family, past and present, anecdotes about opera stars, actresses (at times involved with the royal family), and other celebrities.

Mother often asked questions that led to fascinating revelations. The daughter of the Comtesse, Hermine, was about to become engaged. One evening the couple visited the mahjong players. The contrast between prospective groom and bride was striking. He must have been at least twenty years her senior. Hermine was in her early twenties and she physically mimicked her own name, with a snow-white complexion, deep blue eyes, and raven hair, which brought to mind the image of the white- and black-tipped ermine. After they left, Mother tactfully expressed her surprise about the age difference. Without seeming offended the Comtesse explained that Hermine did not have a dowry, therefore she was lucky to marry a man of solid means. Age and love were of no concern.

I suspected that Hermine might have seen in her fiancé more than her mother surmised. Older men are often extremely attractive to young women. After the age of forty this process seems to be reversed. Women find themselves besieged by and yielding to younger men. Certainly the Oedipus complex plays a role in both cases. A thorough explanation of the dowry as a safety measure for a woman, with everything stipulated in a marriage contract, with both sets of parents and their respective attorneys insuring a fair agreement, was offered by the Comtesse.

Brussels had become a haven for Russian emigrés. Many stopped at the Hotel Wiltchers until they found their own places. Each arrival was the focus of attention for several days, as they told about their escapes and what they had witnessed or heard rumored.

Two stories remain in my mind. A nobleman, owner of a large estate, planned his family's escape. While making the necessary arrangements, he left his wife and children alone. One evening, arriving cautiously at his home, he saw no lights except in the dining room. When he walked in, he found his wife, her mother, and the children murdered. Their severed heads were placed on their respective dinner plates.

The second story, not only told by the emigrés but also widely published, described the situation of abandoned children during the revolution. They formed gangs that robbed and looted stores to be able to feed themselves. Several hundred of these children developed typhus. Hospitals were overcrowded and lacked medicines. Authorities decided on a radical solution: troops were sent out, and the children were gunned down.

A world away, Mexico was under similar civil war conditions. In school the nuns told us about the burning of churches and the humiliations to which priests and nuns were subjected. Much later I realized that the term *humiliations* covered rape, torture, floggings, and murder.

Throughout the history of humankind we find a multitude of charismatic but pernicious personalities. In this century Lenin, Mussolini, and Hitler. They emerged and used their power to fuel the emotions of the masses. They all followed a similar technique. They found a reason to hate and whipped it into a frenzy. "Give me the power to change the ills in our society," each said, "and I will do it no matter the cost." I heard them. They never mentioned the real tools of redemption: discipline, education, and hard work. Their motto was: destroy and rebuild on our terms. I heard them. I also saw their victims, their violated bodies, their minds haunted by shattered dreams and torture.

During one mahjong session the general addressed Mother in his gravelly voice:

"Madame Lorca, you are a young and attractive woman. Do you have a lover?"

"How dare you ask such a question," Mother bristled. "Lillian, wait for me upstairs," she said to me. I didn't leave, and she didn't insist. She probably thought it would be better if I heard her answer.

"Madame, I have asked myself many times why you stay here when your husband has an important position in Germany, unless you have a powerful reason to stay apart. The Countess shares my curiosity."

"I shouldn't honor you with an answer," Mother replied, looking at him proudly. "I do have a powerful reason. I loathe the Germans for the atrocities they committed during the war."

The general burst out laughing. "Ah! Madame, how naive you are. If you only knew what we did to them!" His pride in having resisted brutality, not allowing it to victimize him, was clear.

When the long summer vacation arrived, Mother took us to a spa. Pierre drove us across Belgium to a large four-story hotel amidst fragrant gardens. There we met other vacationers and became friends with the son and three daughters of the Brazilian Ambassador to Denmark. We devised amusing tricks to play on the hotel guests. As we were the only teenagers around, we were forgiven for our antics.

Years later I found out that one of our Brazilian friends, Isabel Bueno, had become an ace pilot in her country, often competing in international meetings. On one of these occasions I was working at the *Voice of America* and had a chance to interview her. It was a great reunion full of happy memories.

Father visited us briefly, with unexpected results from Mother. We would come to Germany after all. To Father this concession of an indefinite stay in Wiesbaden was the first favorable sign in his battle to bring his wife and children to live near him.

On the way to Wiesbaden, we spent a night in Cologne. It was here that for the first time I experienced the delight of a down bed. Lumpy beds in Chile, solid bunkers aboard ships, and hard ascetic convent beds were all I had known before. At first encounter Germany showed me a sensual refinement I was to find in food, manners, and every walk of life.

CHAPTER 6

Wiesbaden was a land of enchantment, and Father wasn't pressing on any move to Hamburg. Although Pierre didn't speak German, and the occupation of Belgium during World War I was still painful, he managed to find something exciting for us to do every day. A cruise on the Rhine, castles open to visitors, Black Forest inns, where the food was superb. Sometimes Mother agreed that we could spend a night in one of these places. Pierre would wake us up early each morning for a stroll in the woods. Having lived all his life in a country as flat as Belgium, he delighted in the views from the top of hills and the outline of mountains at sunset. He never stopped smiling, as though he was catching up on bad times. There was a light in his eyes I hadn't noticed before. He read scrupulously about every place we visited; the flora and fauna in the forest, legends and superstitions, and he would eagerly tell me about his discoveries. If we visited a castle, he would research the lineage and history of the owners.

Pierre explained to me that the nobility did not work like ordinary people. They had to pay extremely high taxes to cover reparations agreed upon at Versailles after the war. Opening parts of their historical and art-filled homes to visitors was the only way they could raise the necessary money to pay taxes. Before every visit, Pierre reminded me not to touch anything and to pretend not to notice if we stumbled on the privacy of someone we suspected to be the owner. These visits were an education in art and history. Pierre failed in art but was strong in history, and I took advantage of his research.

Pierre finally allowed me to sit next to him in the car, while Mother dozed in the back seat. Pierre was really the first man with whom I communicated without feeling uncomfortable. Father was a distant presence to whom I longed to get closer. My brother, Eugene, fell in the same category. Our relationships would later develop happily, but meantime Pierre took their place. His maleness never threatened. While hiking in the Black Forest I would sometimes fall and scrape a knee or a hand. Pierre would investigate the extent of the damage, wash off the dirt in a clear brook, bind it with a clean handkerchief if it was bleeding, and comfort me with a hug if I cried. He even carried me piggyback when I had trouble walking or was too tired. I was twelve years old and very naive. In retrospect, I can see there were certain looks and gestures that could be seen as sexual. The word wasn't yet in my vocabulary, nor was the idea in my head. Pierre himself would have been shocked if accused of any sexual intentions.

Once when I was traveling on a train with Mother, a handsome man and a woman were in the same compartment. I must have stared at him, and he responded likewise. After a while I felt the intensity of his eyes conveying a message I couldn't understand. Instinctively my shoulders rose in a protective movement, but I never stopped staring at him. Mother started a conversation to break the spell. Later she warned me that I must never look at a man "that way." I didn't know what she meant, and she did not explain.

For a long time I had been waiting for an occasion to ask Mother how babies were born. I didn't ask about conception, about the relationship between a man and a woman. I missed the connection. I only wanted to know how babies were born. The answer felt like a slap on the face. Mother answered irritably, "You are intelligent enough to find out by yourself."

Find out for myself is what I did. During the quest I made many mistakes and put myself in risky situations.

Yet Pierre remains the sweet memory of a man who became a reliable friend. One day he disappeared. I was unable to find out what had happened. Was he fired? Why? Had he found a better job? My questions got no answers. He was a friend, and he hadn't said good-bye. I felt rejected but mostly confused and terribly sad at the loss. Later I came to suspect that Mother did not understand the innocence of our closeness and possibly made untrue accusations.

Father and Eugene took the car to Hamburg. Mother and I left for

Nice, where she hoped the warm weather would relieve the pains in her legs, which had been broken in the car accident in Belgium. From our hotel's location on the hill next to the Roman ruins at Cimiez, the view of the Mediterranean was dazzling. The blue waters sparkled like sequins dropped on the sea. Yachts and powerboats cut through the waves, leaving long trains of white foam. Each color seemed to respond to the sun with an intensity that I later found in Matisse.

I decided to learn tennis and met a couple of young men willing to teach me. I had a daily session with them and thoroughly enjoyed the exercise. It made my body come to life. For too long I had been quietly sitting with adults, listening to their chatter. I loved to run, hit the ball, and move every muscle with an energy that tinted my face with the color of good health.

There was weekly dancing at the hotel. I distinctly remember a young girl with a marvelous smile that went straight to her eyes. Her hair was jet black, her nose aquiline, her eyes black and slightly slanted, her wide mouth cut across her face, displaying a row of perfect teeth. She danced, and her feet didn't touch the floor. She used a delicious perfume that I have never been able to identify. Mother noticed my admiration. "She is Jewish," she warned. So what? What difference did it make? She was a joy to look at, and her Jewishness didn't change that. Besides the issue of Jewishness had always been a matter of contention to me. In the convent the nuns warned us about the wickedness of Jews. I found their accusations preposterous. I puzzled over the fact that Jesus was Jewish yet we worshipped him.

Sometimes Mother would take me down to the Promenade des Anglais. We would have tea at the Negresco, and she'd point out to me the celebrities who were spending the winter in Nice. Coco Chanel was a regular guest at the Negresco, and when she walked through the halls of the hotel one could feel a flutter of excitement among the visitors.

We were invited to the casino at Monte Carlo. The drive along the Corniche was magnificent, with the sea on one side and a cascade of flowers on the other. The casino was grandiose, and the gamblers impressed me with their almost religious silence. We saw the place where heavy losers committed suicide. Then I understood the silence around the tables. Perhaps I felt cautious because of a premonition of the bitter hours I would spend in another casino, thousands of miles away, watching my husband win and lose fortunes.

Back in Nice I told my special friends, John and Bette, my impressions of Monte Carlo. John was a talent scout for a London theater. He often said he wished I lived in London so he could teach me to act, dance, and sing. I was sure that I could dance, I also knew I could act, and for them I improvised plays with Pola Negri, Bertini, and even Valentino in the main roles. They loved it, and we laughed together at the stories I concocted and the tricks I invented to switch from one role to another. I had never felt so uninhibited.

John insisted that I must go to London with them. With the proper training and encouragement I would follow in Gertrude Lawrence's footsteps. I had never heard of her. He showed me her pictures and told me anecdotes about her. He said my body called for beautiful clothes because the fabrics seemed to come alive with the rhythm of my hips and shoulders. John had a theory about women and nakedness: "Women with the ability to turn garments into second skins should have every chance to show their skill," he said with authority. John talked to me as a grown-up woman. It made me feel older, sophisticated beyond my years.

Then John made a serious mistake. To show how earnest he was about "Project Lillian," he talked about it with Mother. The next morning we were on the train back to Paris. To Mother the world of entertainment was for prostitutes, not her daughter. I remembered Blanquita and her visit to Hollywood. John had inadvertently stumbled on a cultural concept that Mother and many others believed.

This time Father joined us in Paris and we had much to talk about. Mother remained in considerable pain. After a series of nurses she thought to be incompetent, she kept me out of school as her companion and helpmate. Father worried about her decision to take me out of school so young. So wherever we went, he sent bundles of books, with commentaries about them. At the time my chief language was French, so he introduced me to the old and new masters in literature. This came as quite a shock because my earlier reading had been limited to the lives of saints, with emphasis on martyrdom as a goal in life, and the Comtesse de Segur stories about infantile mischief. Switching from this to Hugo, Balzac, Flaubert, Maupassant, Duhamel, Eça de Queiroz, and Blasco Ibáñez (the latter two translated into French) contributed to the creation of a rather unusual teenager. Also, my "university of hotel life" was teaching me things, as long as I kept eyes and ears open. When I saw a girl I had known in school wrapped in a stunning white fox cape, at the side of a much older escort, my mind jumped to the correct conclusion.

In Paris, when Father visited, he attended the Banco Sudamericano de Londres (London South American Bank), where former Chilean president Arturo Alessandri held court each day. Clerks' desks surrounded a main hall, with offices on the second and third floors reaching up to a glass dome. Power and money there affected decisions of international import. It seemed strange that they would allow an exiled South American president to hold court in their main hall, but there he sat in a leather armchair conducting appointments as if he were in a private office. Chile still belonged to the powerful ABC trilogy of Argentina, Brazil, and Chile. Chile's nitrate was the foundation of its economy. Its potential was awesome. Nitrate supplied material not only for ammunitions, but for fertilizers and iodine as a byproduct, the latter under the aegis of a consortium in London.

Father had a special relationship with Alessandri. In the early twenties, the first time the president was ousted by the conservatives, he found refuge in the American Embassy in Santiago. After several weeks and almost daily demonstrations organized by Alessandri's enemies, the U.S. ambassador tired of the situation and called on Father for help, knowing Father well and trusting him. He asked for a prompt solution, which had unavoidable risks.

The dangerous part for Father was to get Alessandri out of the embassy without alerting the demonstrators. He succeeded and drove Alessandri to the railroad station, where a special rail car awaited. Father stayed with Alessandri until they reached the Argentinean frontier. By spiriting Alessandri out of the country, Father had risked his life and his career. He continued to put his career in jeopardy by those visits to Alessandri in Paris.

I recall visits to the bank as one remembers visits to a cathedral. However low the voices, they were carried by an echo all around the building. Alessandri usually beckoned me to approach him. He mumbled some inane questions. "So you are Arturo's little girl? What's your name? How old are you? Come and sit here. I miss my children." He pulled me down to his lap. This I found embarrassing. I disliked the smell he exuded, like an acid odor from someone who has been sweating out a sickness. His clothes were impregnated with this odor. His breath was foul. Later I would identify this as the smell of treason. Despite what Father had done for him, when Alessandri returned to power in the early thirties, he denounced Father for having worked for the man who kept him in exile. Father answered this accusation by saying that he had worked for Chile as a diplomatic officer, not for any particular government. Others in the Foreign Service had similar experiences with Alessandri.

We survived, yet never forgot. The sons and daughters of Alessandri's victims grew very close. We had known each other in the good times of our fathers' careers. Later we supported each other in adversity. We seldom reminisced; it would have been too painful. Rather, we worked together at adjusting to different circumstances.

Sickness was one of Mother's obsessions. Having received a clean bill of health from her doctors in Paris, she focused on my slender body and decided that there must be something wrong with my lungs. Tuberculosis was in fashion. The daughter of a well-known artist had just died of it. Mother took me to her doctors, who subjected me to a battery of tests and X-rays. When they finally said that I was perfectly healthy, Mother decided that we must go to Switzerland anyhow, where the most fashionable sanitariums were located. The doctors begged her not to put me in such an institution, where I would surely be infected. Father sent Eugene with us to ensure that the doctors' recommendations were carried out.

When we arrived in Lausanne it was late, and we were dead tired. The next morning Eugene and I opened the French doors onto a balcony. We were entranced by the view of Lake Geneva, surrounded by snow-capped mountains. The shimmering waters of the lake, the trails climbing up majestic mountains, the beautiful villas, the small towns that were built to resist snowstorms, it all seemed like an illustration for a romantic novel.

Mother was looking for the right school for me. What was needed was to fill the academic gap that had grown considerably wider since I left the Sacred Heart. The school she found wasn't strong in education, but it offered an intense program of sports: tennis, swimming, sailing, horseback riding. I found sailing new and exciting. Granted, there were no academic challenges, but we all enjoyed sports.

In the evenings the students got together to tell stories, the scarier the better. We would go to bed fearing that the monsters we had invoked would jump on us and carry us through damp, cob-webbed tunnels to the depths of the earth. Movies and television today fill the human need for the abominable, making us face the horrible unspeakable creatures they create with special effects. Such appetite for horror responds to a deep human need to glimpse the menace, certain that a familiar voice or the turning on of a light will restore safety.

After Eugene left Lausanne, Mother and I went to visit a Chilean family in Geneva: Moisés and Graciela Poblete. Moisés was Chile's representative at the League of Nations' Labor Organization. He explained that in the search for peace the League believed that through labor legislation, the unrest that led to wars might come to an end. Moisés was an extraordinarily eloquent man. We listened to him entranced. I noticed that his wife also listened to him in awe, although she must have heard him speak about his work many times. Many years later they found themselves in a quandary concerning a problem that affected me directly. They failed in their romantic mission through no fault of their own.

The ski season was about to start. All the sports practiced at the school seemed but a preparation for when I would clasp my boots onto the skis and slalom off a slope. But it was not to be. We were about to move yet again.

CHAPTER 7

We were to return to Paris, where Father would meet us. Eugene would be there, and Betty was supposed to join us from her finishing school in London. We all showed up at the Hotel Regina, across the street from Joan of Arc's equestrian statue, almost at the same time. Mother's sense of drama had set a scenario in her hotel suite that resembled a stage. On an alcove raised a few steps higher than the rest of the room, she and Father sat. We were asked to enter. Three chairs had been placed in front of the alcove. Something serious awaited us.

Mother began. "I want you to prepare yourselves to leave for Chile as soon as possible. Your father will not be with us."

She paused for us to take in the import of that terse statement, then continued: "We are going to start a new life. I don't know yet what it will be like, but I'm sure my family will support us when they find out what you are about to hear. Your father has been having an affair with a German woman for a long time. I can't tolerate this situation any longer. I must separate from your father, who has become a man without principles and honor."

She went on, describing her feelings of revulsion, stressing the fact that the mistress was a German woman. I stopped listening and looked at my brother and sister. Eugene was very pale and obviously distressed. Betty was sobbing, the tears ravaging her face. Neither was in any condition to take the initiative and stop the accusations against Father, who looked as though his heart was breaking. I never loved my Father more intensely than I did at that moment. I had to stop the humiliation to which he was being subjected.

He couldn't deny what Mother was saying. It was true. He did have a mistress. During a pause in Mother's tirade, he managed to say that he was ready to give up the woman if we all moved to Germany. Mother became even more enraged. She said that that would be blackmail, to force her to live in a country she detested. Then I heard myself speak. My voice wasn't strong enough, so I stood up, an instinctive motion intended to demand attention. I began by using a term that always infuriated Mother.

"Madame," I said, "you chose to leave Father alone for years. You should have realized that he might take a mistress. You share his guilt. He was unfaithful, but you were unreasonably selfish. You brought this upon yourself. I don't think that we, your children, should be deprived of the love and company of a father we cherish because of your mistake."

I still remember the leaden silence that fell when I stopped speaking. Slowly I realized that Betty's sobbing and Eugene's throat clearing had stopped. They each stood up to say they agreed with me. I blew my nose to avoid breaking down in a flood of tears. I never before had had the courage to stand up to Mother. I felt completely drained. I wondered if she would strike me.

From the corner of my eye I saw Father stretch out his hands to grab Mother's in a powerful and tender grip that she didn't reject. Then he turned to us.

"Eugene, take the girls to the Bois and don't return until after lunch. Go now. Quick. Don't think about all this anymore. We'll be all right. I love you all. Go."

Father was again in command. Mother sat frozen, but her pursed lips and fixed stare told me she had in no way been defeated. At the end of the day we had a second meeting. The earlier tenseness was gone, and we were told what our parents had resolved. Eugene would return to Hamburg with Father, while Mother, Betty, and I would spend two months in Chile before joining them in Germany.

We arrived in Chile in the spring, when the sweet aroma of flowers and fruits in stalls in the streets fills the air. Our vacation was a pilgrimage from one family ranch to the next, from San Martín to Llallauquen, from Pichilemu to San Carlos. All our cousins were now grown up. With few exceptions, the girls were all beautiful, consummate coquettes.

The boys we'd known as obnoxious kids were now handsome young men, some of them in military uniforms, others flaunting their intellect as university students, using a vocabulary so highbrow that we girls hardly understood their meaning. Whoever insisted a few years earlier that I must meet my cousins was right. Back then they were merely a promise of things to come. It was now fulfilled.

Many of them had turned into hunters, each with a different seduction technique that was interesting to observe. The "uniforms," either military or navy, usually brought flowers or candy to start a conversation leading to a date. They were extremely sensitive to flattery and delighted in having their picture taken with the European cousins. I didn't mind acting the adoring fan in exchange for flowers or candy. Soon I switched my attention to the intellectuals, the medical students being my favorites.

The brighter among them didn't limit their aspirations to relieving pain and mending bones. They observed the deterioration of the human body and asked themselves why and what to do. The first answer was usually poverty and ignorance. The second question concerned their professional responsibility, and to face it they read and exchanged information. I was proud to sit with them during discussions, although I was advised to keep my opinions to myself. Listening to them was heady wine.

When my affections found a focus, it was my cousin Hernán. He was the least handsome yet he embodied a serenity not found in others. His sincere interest in me sustained my spirit in a way that gave me strength and confidence. This was the beginning of a friendship that would last a lifetime. He died a few years ago of a heart attack, but I still talk to him in times of stress because it was he who taught me to live fully, with the courage of my convictions. There is a simple piece of advice Hernán gave me. It has served me well on many occasions. "Ask yourself what is the worst that can happen if you do or not do something? If you can face the worst, you have no problem."

When we later moved to Chile permanently, Hernán continued my education. He was surprised that having lived so long in Europe I hadn't read Proust. No matter how hard I tried, I didn't like Proust. I found him obsessed with small, banal details. However, when Hernán insisted that I read Freud, I was fascinated. A whole new world opened up to me. I was able to understand people's reactions in a far clearer way. Later when I was confronted with surrealism, I could more confidently interpret its motivations and expressions.

On this vacation I was sent to San Martín in the far south. The ranch there bore the name of Mother's eldest brother, Martín, but Aunt Celmira was the strongest personality around. She was stunning, a cameo beauty but a little too "rondelée" at a time when flappers were in fashion. Having no qualms about her weight, she concentrated on the care of her complexion. To avoid wrinkles she used to stick stamps on her forehead, the corners of her eyes and mouth. Once the stamps were secured, she rubbed cream on the rest of her face and throat. She would then join us, and we purposely told her stories that made her laugh. The stamps would become loose and drop off. She screamed that we were destroying her beauty treatment.

One day I found her youngest daughter, Perla, crying. Her cheeks were flushed, her hair a mess. I asked what was the matter. She made me swear that I wouldn't tell anybody. I didn't, for a long time.

"Mother makes me stand in front of a mirror and orders me to cry. I have no reason to, so she slaps me, pulls my hair and stamps her feet saying: Cry, cry pretty! Learn to cry pretty so you can handle any man in the world!"

I was an adult before I realized that Aunt Celmira was training her daughter in the art of manipulation in a world where men owned everything and women gained power largely through their ability to manipulate, seduce, or cajole.

Aunt Celmira was socially ambitious. Families at neighboring ranches all had pianos, so she must have one. A Steinway was imported from Europe. It landed at the nearest port, Talcahuano, and was shipped by train to Mulchén, the closest station to the ranch. A team of peons traveled several weeks to bring it by ox cart to the ranch. When it arrived, no door was wide enough to get it into the house. A wall was knocked down and the piano found a home. Nobody ever played it, but it looked elegant.

Our male cousins had grown up and now occupied their own quarters, which were open all hours to friends of both sexes. The Puelmas, friends from a neighboring ranch, were the most assiduous female visitors. The girls were very attractive. They broke all the rules: short hair, riding pants, vibrant, loud, independent. Traveling often to Europe and the United States, they were considered too avant garde and finally decided to stay abroad. They were an interesting lot, and I often wished there were more chances to talk with them. They were in their mid twenties, so the gulf was too great between us. I could look at them from afar, enjoy their antics, and wait for my own turn to come.

A painful incident put an end to our stays at San Martín, and our relations with that branch of the family were never the same. We were sitting one day by the tree next to the dining room. We had just finished lunch and were trying to figure out what to do in the afternoon. Aunt Celmira didn't want the youngsters to go swimming in the river because it was swollen by the Cordillera's thaw. Mother insisted that the younger cousins in the group must stay to learn the multiplication tables. She already had in her hand a slender twig that she used to illustrate the Spanish saying "Letra con sangre entra," or "lessons are learned with blood."

My cousin Lola was sitting next to me embroidering her new initials on a pillowcase for her trousseau. Her wedding would be held as soon as we all returned to Santiago. My older cousins were set on going hunting. Ivan held a gun on his shoulder. My brother, Eugene, stood next to him. The loud conversation, the laughter, and the teasing around the tree was such that later nobody remembered hearing a shot. The realization of what had happened came only when Lola collapsed on top of me, then slowly slid to the ground.

I was unable to hold her and wordlessly stared at myself covered with Lola's blood. My hair was dripping blood. My hands were sticky with Lola's blood. Lola was unconscious, while blood gushed out of one ear. After a minute of shocked silence, pandemonium broke out.

Ivan and Eugene stood frozen, looking unbelieving at the scene in front of them. Aunt Celmira wailed uncontrollably. Her daughters repeated incessantly without much conviction, "It's nothing. It's nothing. Everything will be all right."

Mother jumped to my side and gave me a quick examination to see if I was hurt. Then she kneeled next to Lola and confirmed that she was seriously wounded but still alive. With the lucidity that she always displayed in a crisis, Mother immediately took action to reach Father by telegraph. A rider was dispatched with a written message, and he was ordered not to stop for any reason until he arrived in Mulchén, normally a four-hour drive by coach. If his horse failed to cover the distance, he carried enough money to buy a replacement. Whatever happened, he mustn't stop. Once the telegram was sent, he must wait for the answer.

Mother's plan was to have Lola carried by oxcart to the railway station in Mulchén, where hopefully Father would be waiting with a physician. In her message Mother had explained the nature of the wound, as far as she could tell: the bullet had penetrated Lola's ear, she had lost much blood, she was alive but unconscious.

Once the rider was on his way, Lola was placed on a mattress on top of the oxcart. As Mother readied herself to accompany her, Aunt Celmira detonated a second explosion.

"Whose gun was it?" she screamed.

"It was Eugene's gun," Mother answered.

"He didn't have the safety latch on. Eugene is responsible for her death!" Lola's hysterical Aunt Celmira accused.

"Lola is not dead!" Mother answered emphatically.

"She will die. Nobody can survive such a wound. It's useless to take her to Santiago. It would be better to let her die here in peace. Leave her alone!" screamed the hysterical woman.

Aunt Celmira was desperately trying to deflect any blame from her own son, Ivan.

"As long as she is alive something must be done to save her." Mother's voice was calm and persuasive.

"No. I know what's going on. It was Eugene's gun that Ivan was using and Eugene failed to put the safety latch on. Now you, Rosa, decide to take Lola away to cover up your son's fatal mistake."

"Ivan had the gun on his shoulder. He could have checked the safety latch."

"He trusted Eugene."

Mother would never forgive Aunt Celmira for blaming Eugene. Neither could she forget that her decision to take Lola to Santiago in search of medical care was questioned. Lola survived but was permanently disfigured. One side of her face was paralyzed. Her fiancé behaved nobly. He married her. They had three children, but after about ten years he abandoned the family.

Lola lived to be eighty, enjoying her children and grandchildren. She had a full, although at times painful, life.

Eugene could not shake off the feeling of guilt that Aunt Celmira thrust at him. Although he never talked about it, nearly sixty years later, shortly before his death, he confided to his daughter Luz that "Ivan shouldn't have been pointing the gun toward the people around the tree. He should have had it pointing backwards. He knew enough about guns to check the safety latch himself." The incident had continued to haunt him despite the years.

We never returned to San Martín for a vacation. I never saw Uncle Martín or Aunt Celmira again. When I met my cousins after many years everything was different. The magic of our closeness was gone, and we looked at each other like strangers.

CHAPTER 8

It was time for our return to Europe, at last to join Father in Hamburg. The thought of becoming a family again was appealing and yet frightening. We were not sure how things would work out between our parents. What would happen if they didn't get along? We should have trusted Father, who had on many occasions given proof of his infinite patience, resourcefulness, and love. He would do anything to keep us together. But still we worried.

Father rented a beautiful apartment and invited his German friends to meet his family. He neglected to advise Mother about German punctuality. The first dinner party was almost ruined when all the guests arrived on the dot of eight. Mother was still in the tub after a day of shopping. Father, Eugene, and I excused her the best we could. Twenty minutes later she showed up and without qualms inquired of her guests how they managed to be so punctual. Her question seemed to amuse them. One of them said: "We come ten minutes early and sit outside, until the time we can ring your bell on the dot, all together."

Father explained that after spending two months in Chile Mother had reverted to the custom of lateness, as a sign of nonchalant elegance among Latin Americans. Everyone laughed.

Mother invited another of her nieces for a stay abroad to expose her to European society. Rebeca was not pretty like Mary and Blanquita, but she made up for it with personality. She was handsome, her features almost too strong. She had big myopic eyes, a solid jaw, dark straight hair cut short, a wide mouth always in motion, because she talked incessantly, and she laughed uproariously and ate with the healthiest of appetites.

Mother objected to her table manners and noisiness. She was tall and slim, with the legs of a tennis player. Although totally different from Blanquita, Rebeca had the same effect on everyone who met her. Her liveliness, her straightforward approach, and her flair with clothes made her extremely attractive. Although she didn't speak a word of German, she managed to make herself understood. She made friends everywhere, and nobody ever made an unkind remark about her name, for this was pre-Nazi Germany.

Rebeca was several years older than I, but we got along famously. She told me when she fell in and out of love. She taught me what to expect from a kiss, how to recognize danger signals with men, and the best techniques for a dignified retreat. She sang with such enthusiasm that all her off-key notes were forgiven. Even in the most conservative clothes, picked by Mother to ensure that she wouldn't shock her new friends, she nonetheless looked provocative and daring. Was it the beads that Rebeca added or the jaunty angle of her hat?

In the role of confidante she had assigned to me, I often turned the tables, and she listened to me. I once explained that when we lived in Belgium we spent our vacations at Ostende in a rented apartment on the esplanade. Mother heard one day that Anna Pavlova would be performing soon at the Kursaal. I knew who Pavlova was, but I was unprepared for the impression she would make on me. The night of the show she danced "The Swan." Her image became for me an unforgettable vision of beauty and gracefulness. I must become a ballerina, I told Rebeca with all the passion of my heart. She promised to help me. I warned her that she would have to confront Mother. She didn't seem intimidated.

CHAPTER 9

There were few signs in Germany in 1928 of the storm that was gathering strength, nurtured by enormous pressures that made life extremely difficult for the majority of the population. The Germans were eager to accept any leader who'd restore their self-respect and the comfortable lifestyle they'd enjoyed before the First World War. It was impossible to see that ten years later Germany would be ready to strike at its neighbors and start a world conflagration.

A period of runaway inflation had set a pattern of instability in the early twenties, but it had passed, leaving no apparent scars. The people never ceased to work, rebuilding the country's economy, notwithstanding the restraints imposed by the Treaty of Versailles.

Father observed that Germany was creating a police force disproportionate to its needs. He noted that the Treaty of Versailles forbade Germany to have an army but didn't limit the size of its police force. It was easy to see the implications of his remark. In the parks of Hamburg we saw young men and women marching and drilling in a military manner. Was this simply for exercise, or did it have a purpose beyond health? Was it a preparation for action? In retrospect it is certain that the German youth were looking to the future without any doubt that they must be ready to fight.

Hitler was an emerging figure. He didn't yet have the power that he sought, but his *Mein Kampf* was widely read, discussed, and admired. Anti-Semitism and anti-Communism were vigorously stressed,

*The family is finally reunited in Germany in 1928
(left to right): Betty, Father, Mother, Eugene, and me.*

both blamed for Germany's economic woes. Hitler also advised that the Treaty of Versailles must be abolished. Germans saw in him the leader who would restore their world status.

Our first year in Germany caused mixed feelings in the family. We were surrounded by Father's friends, many of them linked to Chile by important businesses such as Siemens Shuckert, H. Folsch & Company, and others who sold Chile heavy machinery and bought nitrate, copper, wines, and fruit.

Hans Folsch, founder of the company that carried his name, lived in a magnificent mansion by Lake Alster. A pier onto the lake was equipped with boats and canoes that he encouraged us to use. He was a most gracious host. He acted like a year-round Santa Claus, dispensing gifts, throwing parties, and calling just to say hello and ask if we wanted anything, from theater tickets to something new in the stores. A little on the heavy side, not too tall, with stark white hair and blue eyes happily squeezed by a constant smile: that was Hans Folsch. It was difficult to estimate his age, he was so agile and lively. I absolutely adored him.

It was at this time I dreamed of becoming a ballerina. Pavlova's performance at the Kursaal Theater in Ostende was still fresh in my mind. I was resolved to emulate her. As a token of my infatuation I decided to show my friend what I could do in the terpsichorean art. I had learned to dance en pointe by myself, without expert instructions. I also learned to sew and create costumes and tutus for my rehearsals in the basement of the house we had moved into on Harvestehuderweg.

Father had invited Folsch and other friends to dinner. After savoring our excellent cook's cuisine, the guests moved into the adjoining living room for coffee and liqueurs. I dressed in my tutu and ballet slippers. Rebeca started the music for the "Swan" on the record player and pushed open the sliding doors. I danced in.

My performance was so obviously addressed to my friend Hans that when I lay dying on the floor, after a tremulous fluttering of arms and hands, he stood up clapping loudly, walking forward to lift my breathless body from the parquet. The rest of the guests followed his example with another ovation. Hans put his arm around my shoulders and whispered: "Wunderbar, wunderbar, wo hast du gelernt?" (Wonderful, wonderful, where did you learn?)

Turning to Mother he asked, "Which academy does she attend?"

Peeved, Mother replied, "None. This is just a foolish idea of hers."

Every year on Chile's Independence Day, September 18, Father organized a party at a fashionable restaurant on Lake Alster. All Chilean residents in Hamburg were invited, plus German friends and businessmen associated with Chile. Hans Folsch was, of course, one of the honored guests. His son sat next to Mother and his American wife, Lillian, next to Father. She was a beautiful woman, although frail compared with the sturdy frauen around her.

Midway in the dinner a commotion at the door of the dining hall called everyone's attention. Father's assistant was dispatched to find out the reason and quickly returned.

"Chancellor Hitler wishes to present his respects to Consul General Lorca, his family, and friends."

Surprised, Father stood up and walked to the door. Hitler, followed by his retinue, walked in with hand outstretched. Father signaled Mother and his children to join him. Hitler turned to the guests and barked a few words, which I didn't understand except the name Chile was repeated several times. Everybody applauded while he again shook hands with Father and Mother, touched my shoulder and Betty's, and grabbed Eugene by one elbow, forcing him to follow as he retreated to much applause.

How often I have remembered this scene, and my impression of him. He didn't smile once. He appeared nervous, highly strung. He moved and walked like an automaton. I have tried not to let subsequent events color my impression of him during those few minutes, when he came to perform a courtesy to the representative of a remote country. But there was no warmth in him, no lightness. He was fulfilling an obligation and wanted to be done with it as fast as possible.

Afterward I asked Father why he'd come. "Because there are many Germans in Chile," he replied.

"But they are so far away and they aren't German anymore. They are Chilean citizens," I observed thoughtfully.

"Origins are hard to lose. There's always something to remind you of where you came from, even generations later. Also Hitler is aware that I'm gathering immigrants to settle in Chile."

Years later, when the Nazis invaded Eastern Europe, the existence of a Fifth Column in the South of Chile was a subject assigned to me for research by *Ercilla* magazine. Suspicions were confirmed when a group of students took over the University of Chile, demanding that President Alessandri step down. Their leader, originally German, called Von Marees, escaped before the police subdued the rebellious students. They were marched by the presidential palace, unarmed, hands raised in surrender. They had already passed the Social Security Building, ironically named and ever since mentioned in shame, when an order from the highest authority made them turn around and enter the basement of the building. Inside over one hundred young men were mowed down with machine guns. Later a congressman entered in the hope of finding survivors. He commented, horrified, "The blood reached to my ankles."

This event increased my disgust for Alessandri tenfold. Additionally, the massacre had a deep impact on me because a young friend of ours, the only son of a widowed mother, happened to work in this building of death. Notwithstanding his protestations, the police grabbed him and executed him with the students. On the day of the funeral, my friends and I were speechless as his mother confronted her tragic loss.

The Fifth Column was never mentioned again in Chile. But the dreadful incident at the Social Security Building raises the question: did Hitler know about its existence as early as 1930 when he crashed our Independence Day party?

As we rejoined the guests that day, I sat by my friend Hans Folsch. He seemed strangely subdued. Since he spoke fluent Spanish I tried to start a conversation. No matter what I said it fell on deaf ears. So I just sat by him, while he dwelt on whatever thoughts tormented him.

I was back in Chile when Nazism began to sink its claws into Europe. I heard subsequently what happened to him. His fortune was confiscated, and the beautiful mansion by the lake was occupied by the S.S. In one last grand seigneurial gesture, he requested permission to invite his friends to a farewell party before retiring to a "home." For a long time people talked about Folsch's retirement party. The lights were tripled all around the house and the pier. Boats and gondolas took the guests to the pier. Every room was covered with flowers from floor to ceiling. Chilean lobsters from Juan Fernández Island and Valdivieso champagne were flown in from the land that had made him wealthy. Three inside and outside orchestras took turns playing tangos, his favorite dance, fox trots, and waltzes. Scott Fitzgerald and Truman Capote should have been there to see and record this last grand gesture of hospitality. He was taking leave from the loyal friends who cherished him. At 4 A.M. he called for his chauffeur and slid into anonymity.

In 1930 Mother and Father were often traveling about Germany. They both seemed more relaxed, if not deliriously happy. During their frequent absences I was entrusted to Eugene's care. Betty had returned to her finishing school in London, and Rebeca was back in Chile. Eugene liked to take me for long walks. He preferred the old town, where he could see ancient buildings and teach me to appreciate different architectural styles. He instructed me: "Don't just look in front of you.

Move your eyes to the top of the building and bring them down slowly. Observe the different shapes of the roofs, the decorations around the windows or on the ledges between floors. Find out the relation to neighboring structures."

These walks through Hamburg had a specific purpose: to teach me his own love for classic styles, to identify them for me, and to communicate his dislike of the Bauhaus, which was then influencing construction everywhere.

Music was another field where he never failed to instruct me. Through him I discovered Bach and Stravinsky, and later returning home from concerts I made him laugh by performing the "Fire Bird."

"What are you doing? You want to be a ballerina but what you are doing is not ballet! Be careful you don't ruin your back with all that twisting. What are you doing?"

"I don't know. The music makes me do it."

"Do you feel the same about Bach?"

"Do you have a record? Play it. Let's see what happens."

Bach was a different experience altogether. Just as wonderful and powerful, but totally contrasting. Stravinsky made me want to jump and never come down, turning and twisting, free of gravity. Not floating inertly but dancing and sliding freely like today's astronauts about which we knew nothing at the time, although I had read Jules Verne.

Bach called for restraint, a tempered formality, a symmetrical expression of movements, a solemnity in each thrust of leg or arm, an elevation of the chin, and rigidity of the neck as though the head supported a royal crown. With Bach the body danced with majestic discipline while the head remained aloof of its motions. Matter and spirit used the music to stress their limitations and differences. I didn't know it then, but I had already moved from classical ballet to the free interpretations of Isidora Duncan.

I never succeeded in making a career out of dancing, but two of my favorite nieces have done it for me: María Eugenia Lorca with her own academy, and Luz Lorca as a ballerina and assistant to director Ivan Nagy of the Ballet de Santiago.

After a trip to Saint Moritz, Mother decided that I must learn to ski. Friends of Father in Munich offered to take me to Garmisch Partenkirchen, then uncontaminated by politics, and before Hitler built his Eagle's Nest on top of the mountain. I would travel alone and stay with strangers. Incredibly excited at this first unexpected opportunity to fend for myself, I wondered what I would do if I found on the train a man like the one who had earlier mesmerized me with his stare. What if this time he talked to me? Once more I would confront the unsolved mystery: "You mustn't look at men that way!" All right, Mother, not ever again.

When I stepped into the compartment I saw that I needn't have worried. My travel companion was a mother with three children. The oldest boy, about seven, was a handful. I felt his mother slapped him too often and hard, but how could I stop her?

At Munich's railway station a tall, attractive woman of about thirty was waiting for me.

"Hola, ¿qué tal el viaje?" (Hello, how was the trip?), she asked in Spanish.

I must have looked so relieved that she laughed. "I lived several years in Chile. My parents also speak Spanish, so you'll feel comfortable. Would you like to see the city before we go home?"

Munich's wide, beautiful avenues, flanked by impressive buildings, vaguely reminded me of Paris. Remembering Eugene's lessons in architecture, I looked upward for details I could describe to him later. We drove by the Pinachotec, the art museum, and Helen told me we would visit it in a couple of days. The next morning we took the train to Garmisch Partenkirchen, where I had my first ski lesson. Following instructions carefully I remained upright, turned and managed to slow down and stop. Helen was delighted. We retired early. The excitement had taken a toll on my energy. The second day I took a few steps and landed on the snow. A passerby helped me to my feet. I slid down a small hill, mostly on my rear. Somebody else helped me again. What happened to what I had learned the day before? Helen comforted me saying that it was a classic occurrence with beginners. I had become overconfident and made mistakes. "Don't worry. It will all come back. Let's have lunch."

If Helen hadn't insisted, I would have gladly remained on the terrace sipping a drink. But I followed her, and this time did considerably better and was proficient by the end of the day. As a reward for my courage, Helen took me after dinner to a bier halle, where a band of Bavarian musicians played. One of them performed the typical dance of the mountaineers, hopping around and slapping his leather shorts to the rhythm of the music. I felt very grown-up and sophisticated. I must have had on my face that beatific smile that absolute happiness brings out. Helen looked at me and teased me about my ecstatic expression. As we walked back to the hotel I enjoyed the constant greeting of passersby saying "Gruss Gott!" (God's blessings.)

I returned to Hamburg after warmly hugging Helen for providing the most exciting experience of my young life. Helen was a photographer. Several years later she visited Chile when we had settled in Santiago after Father's retirement. Helen took then a photograph of me that I still cherish. But by then I no longer wore the smile that had struck her back in Germany. Disturbing experiences had changed me, and this shows in the picture she took.

Helen was proud to know that a large group of friends and I had started a ski club in Farellones. Accommodations were primitive, but we didn't mind and went on practicing and promoting the sport. Today a village has been built where sixty years ago this enthusiastic group of youngsters started a trend that still develops.

When I returned home, Betty was back from London. Mother looked different. She was no longer relaxed. An expression of bewilderment dominated her face. Father seemed calm, self-assured. There was a spring in his step that I hadn't noticed for a while.

At dinner that evening he announced: "Tomorrow we leave for Berlin. I must visit the ambassador and consult with him about some decisions I must make. I have been promoted to the rank of Minister at the Legation in Quito, Ecuador. We will be leaving in about a month. We'll have plenty of time for farewells. It will be a long trip. First New York, then through Panama to Guayaquil and Quito. But first things first. Tomorrow, Berlin."

After dinner I looked for Eugene and asked him about Ecuador. "Fascinating country. Pray that the mosquitoes don't bite you in Guayaquil and kill you with malaria or yellow fever. Two days by train to Quito. No air flights. The train goes through jívaro country. If they catch you they will turn your head into a zanza."

"What's that?"

"You don't want to know."

"You are teasing me."

"Have I ever? You know I'm humorless."

"You'll protect me from the jívaros."

"I won't be there. I'm going straight to Chile."

"Why?"

"Because I'll represent there an important German firm. Sort of an industrial diplomatic job."

"You are lying."

"Watch your tongue."

"Come on, Eugene, tell me the truth."

"You just heard it."

I was trying to fall asleep when Betty walked into the room. "Are you asleep?" she asked.

"Who can sleep in this crazy family?"

"What's bothering you? We are going on a fabulous trip to New York, then to a country where everything will be new to us, unexpected, waiting to be explored. We'll be so close to Chile. We can go there whenever we wish," she said.

"But we are already in a country that we scarcely know. There's a lot more to it than we have seen. I'm sure that we have barely scratched the surface."

"It means no more problems with languages, different cultures, and customs. It will be like being in Chile, with the same language, same habits, and interests." But Betty didn't know how wrong she was.

In Berlin we were introduced to the ambassador, a tall, distinguished man with a surprisingly thin voice. After the usual courtesies, Mother said we had to leave, and Father remained with the ambassador. That evening we went to the opera, courtesy of the ambassadress. I had already seen the Nibelungen before in Brussels and felt undeservedly punished for having to sit through it once more. A late dinner at an elegant restaurant made me feel a little better. I must speak with Father and find out if Eugene had been pulling my leg, and if Betty was overoptimistic.

Returning from Berlin I noticed that bewilderment was still written all over Mother's face. For the time being she was only interested in shopping in the manner befitting her husband's new rank. The Baccarat crystal, the Rosenthal china for eighteen, the solid silver flatware with the family initials in relief, LB: these were her first acquisitions. Then she must order the dresses from Paris. She never bought clothes in Germany. She wrote to a friend in Paris who had dressed her for Hamburg and told her that this time she must be outfitted for Quito, Ecuador. For days the correspondence by letter and telegram ran steadily between Hamburg and Paris:

PARIS: "Rosita, I have no idea what you may need for Ecuador. I'll try to find some Ecuadorian diplomats in Paris. I've been so careful, even asking for the color scheme of the hostesses' homes in Hamburg to avoid your dresses clashing with their decor. But what am I to do now?"

HAMBURG: "Yes, Anita, you have been wonderful. I'm sure that you will do just as well in this crisis. I will also try to find out more about Ecuador here or in Berlin's embassies."

PARIS: "Finally I've found some information. There's only two seasons in Quito: rainy and dry. The temperature is rather mild all year round. Women are extremely conservative. They wear mostly black and navy. Two good, safe colors."

Thus they reached an agreement, and Mother filled trunks with beautiful clothes. Also there was the delicate matter of interviewing for the butler's position. It was no easy matter to find a presentable, well-trained human being, willing to travel across the world into the unknown. A young Dane was finally chosen. Tall, blond, the longest neck ever, slumped shoulders, flat feet, and large hips, but with the kindest and most unflappable disposition that anybody ever possessed. Even his name seemed strangely appropriate — Gottlieb, or "God-loved."

The farewell parties were a succession of events that pleased Father immensely. His stay in Germany had been considerably longer than ours, so the parties were his exclusively. The one given by the city's mayor was particularly lavish. Mother was seated next to him, and at one point he turned to her and said: "You may remember that when we first met I said that everybody in Hamburg knew why you didn't come earlier to Germany. I also warned you that we would take revenge and make you love us. Have we succeeded?"

Mother smiled coyly and replied: "Mr. Mayor, you can be sure that my feelings have changed."

In Germany, Father had picked up his lifelong project of the immigration to Chile of suitable candidates for citizenship. He had interviewed many people eager to leave Germany and try their luck on American soil. At the same time Father had stressed to the Chilean government the need to provide immigrants with new homes and plots of land where they could grow vegetables for their immediate needs. Fruit trees must be already planted and close to producing pears, apples, and oranges. The colony should be near the capital to facilitate the adjustment of people used to urban life who were starting an experiment in agriculture.

Father was pleased with the people he had selected. He told us one anecdote that we enjoyed, although it clearly proved the difficulties of life in Germany in the late twenties. When one candidate showed up for the preliminary interview, the title on his calling card claimed he was a baron.

"Why do you want to live in Chile?" Father asked.

"I've read a lot about the country, its political system . . ."

"You know then that after decades of democracy, Chile has a dictatorship."

"I know, but General Ibáñez carries on a progressive plan, building roads to improve transportation and communication, public pools and stadiums to promote sports among the country's youth. His dictatorship is a mild 'de facto' government. No repressive measures against his opponents. I can live with that."

"You seem well informed. What are your reasons for leaving Germany?"

"I can't pay the taxes on the family's estate."

"Why isn't your wife with you?"

"I'm single."

"But we must select married couples, preferably with children. I'm sorry."

Father and the baron wound up their conversation, and the latter departed. Three days later the baron returned, followed by a typical German frau and three children. Father's expression of surprise clearly asked for an explanation. The baron graciously complied.

"Mr. Consul General, may I introduce widow Karlsen, now the Baroness, my wife, and her children, Johan, Ilse, and Sebastian. Do we qualify now?"

Father smiled widely, stepped forth from behind his desk and shook hands with the baron, the baroness, and their children.

Eons passed and I was living in Washington, D.C., working at the *Voice of America*, when I hired as my secretary a young Chilean woman who spoke fluent English, Spanish, and German. I asked her if she knew anybody at the "Florida" German colony that Father had sponsored. "We are all related there," she said. "I have many uncles and aunts in the colony." She proceeded to bring me up-to-date on their many accomplishments in business, industry, and politics. But she knew nothing about the baron. Her name is Karla Parodi, and she has been highly successful in Washington, where she holds an important position at the Library of Congress.

We went to Paris to take leave of our friends there. As usual we stayed at the Hotel Regina, across the street from Joan of Arc's equestrian statue. Management graciously provided a large salon for my parent's flow of visitors every evening. A smaller room was reserved for Betty and myself and our younger friends. The night before departure I noticed that our cousin, Pepe Bunster, was obviously delaying his departure. Once everybody was gone, he approached Betty and I saying:

"It's a shame that you'll be leaving without knowing the real Paris. You have spent all your years in Europe in schools and nunneries. Let's go. I want to give you an experience you won't forget."

We didn't think twice about his offer but ran out of the hotel with him. Pepe stopped a carriage that swiftly drove us to Montmartre. As we passed the Moulin Rouge, he told us that Maurice Chevalier and Mistinguette were playing there. Pepe seemed to know everybody and kept calling from the coach, waving at friends who approached and we were introduced to a number of them as "ces jeunes filles du Sacré Coeur." Later he said that there was an amusement park nearby. Would we . . . ? Of course! Let's go! We went twice on the roller coaster, and from the top of the Ferris wheel we felt awed by the view of Paris' lights stretching into the night. Then we realized how late it was and rushed to the hotel in a cab. Father was waiting for us in the lobby.

"Go upstairs immediately and talk with your mother. You, young man, you stay with me and explain what happened," he told Pepe.

Mother was pacing the floor, and as soon as she saw us walk into her room, she addressed her fury to us. We had been lost for hours. Where did we go? What had we done? Nobody slept that night. Early in the morning we headed to the railway station to take the train that would carry us to Le Havre to board the ship to New York.

We were about to climb the steps of the train when we heard a voice calling us. Pepe came running down the platform carrying flowers and boxes of candy. Betty and I were stunned. Mother waited for Pepe to get closer, then with a sweeping motion of her arm she sent the candy flying, grabbed the flowers, and hit Pepe with them. He lost his hat and lifted both arms to protect his face from the rose's thorns. His eyes bulged. His usually happy expression gave way to another of horrified surprise. He turned and fled. Father only mumbled: "There goes the Bunster Carmonas."

Pepe was a nephew of José Bunster Bunster, the "King of the Wheat," the most successful of the Bunsters in Chile. He had founded mills and banks throughout the south. His annual yields of wheat were recorded as extraordinary in financial and trade publications in England, where he died at the turn of the century. Persistent rumors indicated that in his life he had tumbled as many women as he had trees when clearing the land for his crops.

But Mother's volcanic temper wasn't always spent on trivia. I distinctly remember an occasion when, still in Germany, Father invited to lunch at home a Chilean government official who had attended an academy near Berlin. He was the chief of the Bureau of Investigations in Chile. During lunch he expounded on the goals of his training. He must learn the latest in systems of torture. He described what repeated doses of castor oil would do to a prisoner. He was about to launch into a variation on the subject when Mother stood up, threw her napkin on the table, and shouted:

"Get out of my house this instant."

"You don't understand. Sometimes it's necessary . . ."

"Not another word. Leave this instant."

We departed from Europe and on we went to yet another country, to meet new people and face different experiences. Neither Eugene nor Betty had been right in their appraisal of Ecuador. It wasn't as dangerous as my brother had made it sound.

Although it was a South American country like Chile, the differences in culture and customs were stark. It wouldn't be easy to travel to Chile. But once immersed in a society so different from any other we had experienced before, we wanted to know more about it and our understanding of it became a challenge.

CHAPTER 10

Eugene left for Chile before we departed Germany. His absence was for me particularly painful, as I had finally established a warm relationship with him. Chile seemed close geographically, yet in reality we'd be many rivers and mountains apart.

The stopover in New York was my first taste of adulthood. Although I was only fourteen years old, I was tall and slender, and apparently my eyes conveyed messages of curiosity or awareness that made my father's friends grant me special privileges that were denied others.

I was a good listener, quite decorative, and my innocence made me harmless or enticing, depending on the circumstances. The wives didn't feel threatened by this child-woman attending lunches and dinners at the Plaza or the Waldorf Astoria.

My favorite escort was the exiled political leader Carlos Dávila, short in stature and tall in ambitions. At lunches and dinners he always asked me to sit next to him. Once the eating rituals were finished, he invariably found something for us to do together. Having heard about my weakness for the performing arts, he took me to Broadway and let me choose any movie or show I fancied. Then he took me out for ice cream or shopping on Fifth Avenue. I was unaware that during those three days before our departure, he totally neglected his office. Meantime Mother and Father were too busy with their own things to pay any attention to me.

Only a couple of years later Dávila returned to Chile after the dictator who had exiled him was himself ousted. Carlos succeeded him, presiding over the 1932 Socialist Republic, which lasted only one hundred days.

It was a time of turmoil, and although I was also in Chile I didn't see him before he left the country after his failed government. He returned to New York, where he married, bought a house in Connecticut, and picked up where he had left his career in journalism. Our friendship resumed in 1954 when he was elected Secretary General of the Organization of American States and I was assistant editor of the OAS Spanish *Americas* magazine in Washington, D.C.

But that time in New York, when at fourteen I was beginning to make a social impact, came to an end when we departed for Ecuador.

We bypassed the Caribbean islands. They had not yet become the tourist attractions of today. Before going through the Panama Canal's locks, we visited Colón's shops run by Hindu and Chinese merchants. Mother was reminded of the Far East bazaars she had seen on her way to Australia. She thought that the quality of the merchandise in Colón left much to be desired. Nevertheless she acquired intricately embroidered tablecloths and colorful gifts for Christmas presents.

We crossed through the Panama Canal, and I must confess that its importance as an engineering feat escaped me. If Eugene had been at my side he would have opened my eyes.

For Helmuth Gottlieb, our Danish butler, Colón was his first encounter with a crossbreed Latin American country where every existing race seemed to have mixed. For me also Colón was a revelation. Chile is almost one hundred percent European. Like Argentina and Uruguay it has an exceptionally homogeneous population.

After our ship crossed the canal into the Pacific, we touched land at the Colombian port of Buenaventura. The captain set a curfew for anyone interested in going ashore. Because we'd listened to some dismaying reports, there were no takers, and we left soon after the captain had completed loading mounds of delicious tropical fruit, intended to last until our arrival in Guayaquil.

At the captain's table, as we gorged on pineapple, fresh coconut pieces, and other fruit whose names we didn't know, Father inquired about the country we were coming to. He would be heading the Chilean mission in Ecuador, and he wanted to know if there were frontier problems between Colombia and his host country. He could have an official report if he wanted, but he had always felt that inquiries at the grassroots were extremely valuable. At the time everything seemed very quiet. Besides Bogotá, the capital, there were two growing towns, Cali and Medellín. Neither one had the reputation it later acquired as a center of drug traffic.

Emeralds were then the main Colombian source of revenue, and violence in the countryside was a thorn in the flesh of the authorities.

When we reached our destination of Guayaquil, Ecuador's main port, we were surprised to find that a fire had deprived the town of its much touted grandeur. In a pathetic effort to recreate what it had lost, empty "Potemkin" facades had been erected along the piers. Most of the town's visitors were crocodile hunters, who quickly got in their boats with their guides to reach the best hunting grounds on the river Guayas. Passengers who stopped in Guayaquil only waited long enough to catch the train to Quito.

We stayed a week at the consul's residence before boarding the train. Father took a look at it and turned to the consul, asking:

"Is this supposed to carry us to Quito?"

"It's far more reliable than you might think. It takes two days to climb the Andes to reach Quito, but it hasn't failed yet. You will overnight at a hotel in Riobamba."

Father was right to be surprised by the looks of the train. It was a vintage model, worthy of a museum. It had no essential facilities and, of course, no dining car. But it stopped often, and vendors would besiege us offering their wares, mostly food like cookies, breads, tamales, and a colorful array of fruits which Mother forbade us to eat except for the pineapple slices that we devoured. She didn't have to stop us from buying the roasted guinea pigs displayed on a double cross of twigs that the vendors stuck insistently through the windows. The poor creatures were really too repulsive.

By the time we got to Riobamba we were too tired to judge our accommodation. But before collapsing on our beds we had to go to the outhouse. We were all given a candle and a stick.

"What's the stick for?" Father asked.

"To shoo away the dogs."

The next morning we started early. We faced the longest trek to Quito, and the train would prove its worth by climbing the high peak called "The Devil's Nose." It was an unforgettable experience. If by now the little train has been retired, I suggest that it be brought back as a tourist attraction, for lovers of roller coasters. The zigzagging route bordered precipices and turned out to be fascinating to Father, who reminisced about his years in the Chilean railway system. We had all crossed the Andes by train, mule, and car, but it couldn't compare to the steep climb of this train over the Devil's Nose.

At one point Father couldn't control his curiosity and stepped down from the train to inspect the system of track that held the cars in place and pulled them up the mountain. In about two hours we reached the summit. The descent didn't take that long, but it was just as frightening to think that the system might not hold and we would be precipitated toward the foot of the mountain. Anyhow, by then we were a little more confident about the reliability of the locomotive and the expertise of the engineer.

We reached Quito late that day, and a large retinue of Ecuadorian officials and the first secretary of the legation were waiting for us at the railway station. After a few days at the Hotel Metropolitano we were to move into the legation in the residential sector of the city. Mother insisted on inspecting the premises before the local contractor finished the preparations for our stay. She returned from this visit determined to introduce a series of changes. She objected to the colors selected, to a pretentious mural in the living room that tried to pass for a Corot. It must be covered! Father accepted her ideas for inside the house, but put a stop to her plans when she wanted to knock down balustrades, turrets, and gargoyles from the castlelike exterior.

When we finally moved in, our social life began at a frantic pace. Father presented his credentials to President Isidro Ayora in the heavily embroidered diplomatic garb and plumed hat customary at that time. We were awed. Once accredited, he and Mother had to visit every diplomatic mission and cabinet member's home, which called for some discreet ceremonials. Then such visits were reciprocated, and the round of social events went on and on. Betty and I were sometimes called to participate in these events.

Mother suddenly became worried about my helter-skelter education. She tried to get me back in school, but after a thorough examination, the Sacred Heart's head mistress suggested that a tutor be hired to help me fill in the gaps resulting from my very odd upbringing. Mother accepted a highly recommended man called Señor Aníbal Unzueta, who would help me improve my Spanish and erase all traces of other languages. He would come three times a week, go over the essentials of Spanish grammar, and assign my homework, usually readings of classic Spanish authors such as Cervantes, Góngora, and many poets. One day I told him that I had read Blasco Ibáñez, in the hope of getting into contemporary literature. He looked at me horrified.

"At your age?" he exclaimed.

Señor Unzueta reminded me of a cricket. Rather small, very pale with thinning hair, a receding chin, bad teeth, and narrow shoulders, he walked as though his hips lacked a joint. Every step was half the length of a normal man's stride. He moved his hands without ever stretching his arms, which seemingly were glued to his rib cage. I often wondered how he could dress in his tight black outfit without unfolding his arms.

Señor Unzueta must have worried about my manners. He thought them far from ladylike. He brought me a book that I should have kept as a curiosity. Some highlights of it were:

• For sports a woman must choose those that never expose arms or legs to onlookers.
• Horseback riding is allowed sidesaddle but a lady does not gallop.
• To swing is definitely out as it is too violent an exercise. Hammocks are recommended instead.
• A lady must never blow her nose and then look into her handkerchief.

Señor Unzueta eventually gave up on me. As he said in a letter to my parents, in his most florid style, he felt that I was too advanced in some subjects while in others it was too late to even try to put me up to date. Never again did Señor Unzueta's cricketlike countenance set its slender shadow on the legation's door.

But Father decided that I must do something. He suggested that I learn to decode messages arriving from Santiago. My instructor would be the first secretary, Julio Prado. So each morning I ran down to his office on the first floor to see if he had any work for me. Telegrams were scarce, but Julio always found something to keep me busy. We enjoyed each other's company. He was a splendid raconteur and made me laugh with his stories. He asked me questions that showed he wanted to know more about me. Sometimes his wife joined us, and we would walk to their small house in the compound for a cup of tea. Julio was collecting antiques in Quito. Despite all my years in Europe, I had not been taught much about art collecting. Museums, cathedrals, galleries, I thought, were the logical repositories for such treasures. Julio taught me differently.

Pilar was the opposite of Julio. While he was tall and handsome, with black wavy hair, sparkling blue eyes, and a carefully trimmed little goatee, she was also tall but gangly, colorless, and as listless as though suffering from acute anemia. But Pilar Carvajal y Colón was the niece of the duke of Alva, the Spanish grandee famous for raising on his estate the best fighting bulls to display their fierceness in the arenas of the peninsula. Pilar never talked about her uncle. Julio did and plenty. I didn't judge him then to be a social climber.

Christmas was close. Betty and I were invited to a party at the home of the Secretary of State, Gonzálo Zaldumbide. Mother felt flattered and so did Father, although he expressed some concern that we would be the only young persons attending a party for grown-ups. Julio assured him that it didn't make any difference. Besides, he and Pilar would be there, and if we felt out of place they would take us home.

Dinner was very lively. Betty and I seemed to be the big attraction. We were showered with questions, and our answers seemed to amuse the guests. Their favorite story was one about our brief stay in a school in Brussels recommended to Mother by a friend. Once we had left it, she was told it was known as the "École des Cocottes."   prostuk

Later things got still more animated. We were invited to dance, and they asked if we knew the Charleston, which we did. We gave a clumsy demonstration of it, and I started to feel embarrassed. Gifts were distributed, and loud laughter celebrated each unwrapping. I was given a book that Pilar promptly took out of my hands and never returned. I looked for Betty and found her in a small salon. She was deeply flushed and looked strange.

"Are you all right?" I asked her.

"Of course. Why do you ask?"

"You just look kind of funny."

"What do you mean?"

"You look flushed and unsteady, and have a stupid smirk on your face."

"Why don't you mind your own business."

"You are my sister. You are my business."

I went looking for Pilar or Julio. Somebody intercepted me showing a matchbox with a miniature man and woman in an awkward position. I pushed him aside. A door opened and amid applause and guffaws the wife of the Argentinean ambassador, followed by a male friend, stepped out laughing. She was dressed in his clothes and he was wearing her evening gown. Julio and Pilar came up to me.

"Where is Betty?"

"She was in that room a minute ago," I pointed at the salon.

"Fetch her and let's go."

Early next morning the town's gossip was knocking on our door, asking to speak with Mother. She knew everything that had happened at the party and more. Betty and I were summoned and subjected to the third degree.

Finally Mother ended the interrogation with these words: "They couldn't possibly understand the implications. Let us change the subject and have breakfast."

Some Chilean exiles were living in Quito. Father found out about their backgrounds and decided to invite them all to lunch, on condition that they accept this as a friendly gesture and not discuss politics and the present dictatorship in Chile. Two guests made an impression on me: Gonzálo Rivas, a student who fell in love with Betty, and Miguel Labarca, who fell in love with me. Rivas requested permission to visit Betty. Labarca did not ask to see me, but he later surfaced in my life for decades.

My relationship with Julio was changing from a platonic friendship to a far more exciting phase. Decoding telegrams had become a pretext for arousing me with kisses and caresses. In spite of my extensive and indiscriminate reading of modern and classic authors, in whose pages I found explicit descriptions of lovemaking, I never imagined that a kiss or even a slight touch could leave such a longing. Anxiously I waited for the next opportunity to feel his lips searching for mine and his hands touching my body, although never intimately. One day he asked how old I was.

"I'm fifteen."

"My God! Go away. Never come back!"

"Why?"

"Don't you know?"

"No, I don't know. What do you mean?"

"Just my luck. I had to fall for a girl who is either stupid or totally innocent. Don't come near me again."

But I did go back. I couldn't help myself. We never did have intercourse, but the lovemaking was so delicious that I was hooked for life.

The Christmas dinner at the foreign secretary's home had unexpected repercussions. Betty and I were suddenly *in*. We were invited everywhere, to parties, excursions, horseback rides, and lunches at country estates. One of these gatherings was sociologically revealing to me.

A large group of friends got together with us for a picnic in the mountains. I'm sure that most of them knew where we were going, but Betty and I thought that a picnic in the mountains would be just that. After about a three-hour drive over rough dirt roads, we arrived at the gates of a manicured lawn, surrounded by rose bushes, in which was set a perfect replica of the Petit Trianon. As we entered the house, we saw that the furniture, chandeliers, silver, crystal vases, porcelain figurines, and original paintings were obviously priceless. The administrator who was acting as our guide explained: "The family is still in Paris. They show up any time they please. That's why everything is kept ready for them. Their horses are in the stables, ready to be saddled in case they want to ride around."

Several months later we heard that the source of the owners' wealth, cocoa, had been destroyed by the plague called "Escoba de la Bruja," the Witch's Broom. They returned to their estate, which they found as though they had never left it, but this time their stay would be long, until the cocoa bushes overcame the plague or another profitable crop was raised. This was a typical example of owner's absenteeism, the scourge of many Latin American economies.

As that first year progressed, the diplomatic corps and Ecuadorian aristocracy prepared for the festivities on Mother's Day. The children were invited to participate in a show to be held in the city's main theater. Betty was asked to dance as a chocolate soldier, to the tune of Tchaikovsky's "Nutcracker." She rehearsed for hours under the supervision of a young man from the American Embassy. After numerous exhausting and frustrating sessions, Betty confessed to me:

"I can't do this. You must take my place."

"You're crazy! I can't take your place. Mother has been so looking forward to seeing you dance."

"If you don't do it there will be an empty stage. I'm staying home. I refuse to make a fool of myself as a little chocolate soldier. No way," she said, adamant.

Picking one of my records, Grieg's "In the Hall of the Mountain King" (from his Peer Gynt Suite), I stitched up a costume to which, not knowing any better, I gave an Oriental flair. Then I ordered a fake fire set up midstage and improvised a dance.

Next to our box sat the Secretary of State, Gonzálo Zaldumbide, and his family, including a sister-in-law who had been a pupil of Isadora Duncan in France. During the applause she turned to Mother and asked:

"Where did she learn to dance?"

"Nowhere."

"You mean she has never attended an academy?"

"Never."

Encouraged by the applause and the young American instructor, I danced again. Mother told me later that Zaldumbide's sister-in-law had said:

"You're right. She has no training. This dance was as beautiful as the first but entirely different. Let me teach her."

After the show there was a ball for the performers and their families. Julio asked me to dance with him. An artist in the audience made a sketch of us, with Julio leaning toward me as I lifted my face to him in utter adoration. I kept this sketch for many years until the paper crumbled with age.

I continued to decode telegrams in Julio's office, until one day I decoded a message recalling Father to Chile for consultations. Once again we would have to move, leaving behind a world that I was beginning to like.

I was learning things about the indigenous Indians. I had come to know that in construction work, women worked alongside their men. They carried their babies with them, leaving them beside the ladders they climbed with loads of bricks on their backs. I watched them at lunchtime breastfeeding their babies and delousing their husbands.

I learned what tribal distinctions their colorful clothes indicated. There was a striking solemnity and dignity to their every movement. The labors they performed did not change this demeanor. The men clad in white pajamas with a colorful sash around the waist sported long braids down their backs. Cutting the braid was severely punished by the elders, and sometimes the penalty was death. Our gardener had committed this offense, and the visit of an Indian calling at our door to sell a zanza so frightened him that he ran away. When he returned three days later, he explained that the man was the chief of his tribe and he must never see that he had cut off his braid. ·

Father explained to me that the Ecuadorian Indians were in great measure self-sufficient. They raised their animals for food, grew their corn and vegetables, and wove their clothes. They contributed little to the country's economy but were in no way a burden. In a subtle manner they practiced passive resistance to the white man. This was the high Andean Indian. If there was an undertow of discontent that would change things, we had no time to detect it. We had to leave with an impression too shallow of a people that intrigued us. Ecuador is a country of sharp contrasts. During excursions through the mountains, we came sometimes to deep, abrupt valleys peopled by African Blacks who had come centuries earlier. Their personalities contrasted with the sober, dignified demeanor of the Indian. Their loud laughter and expansive gestures clearly told of the differences. But whether Indian or Black, the Ecuadorian people were outstanding in their artistic manifestations, and some years later they took their place in international exhibitions.

But leaving all this mattered little compared to the wrenching pain I felt at the thought of leaving Julio, the blue-eyed, dark-haired, goateed man who had awakened my senses to forbidden pleasures.

Years later I saw him in Santiago. The magic was gone. He told me that he was moving to Spain, where the Duke of Alva had offered him a position in Franco's government. My sympathies were always with the Republicans. Years later again, I saw him at Malaga's airport. I approached him.

"By any chance, are you Julio Prado?" I asked.

"Yes, yes." In his eyes I saw the fast rewinding of memories' images. Finally he exclaimed: "Lillian, how strange to see you here. What's happened? Tell me."

"It would be too long a tale," I told him, "and my husband is now coming with my suitcases."

CHAPTER II

In July 1931 we arrived in Valparaíso in a steady drizzle. The family and many friends awaited us, their clothes soaked and faces flushed by a cold wind blowing in from the sea. All had come dutifully to meet us, but this time there were no happy faces, no easy laughter. Something had to be very wrong, but we weren't able to guess the cause of the melancholy we read on everyone's faces. Father's friends seemed intent on drawing him aside to talk confidentially. This made us extremely nervous. I heard a snatch of their whispered conversations with Father.

"It can't last, Arturo. This is really the end."

"We know about offers they will make to you. Don't accept anything."

"The appointment as envoy to Egypt is already in the papers."

"Delay any decisions. Don't accept anything."

Once again we took advantage of Uncle José María's hospitality. The day after our arrival in Santiago, Father was summoned to the Presidential Palace. One of General Ibáñez' aides de camp came for him in a limousine. Curious neighbors and passersby stopped to look at the official seal on its door. Mother walked with him, repeating in a whisper the warnings of their friends received since our arrival.

After Father left, Mother announced that she wanted to see things for herself and she refused all admonitions against it. So she and I set out together, because I couldn't let her go alone. The streets were empty of traffic with very few people about in the downtown area. As we drew near the center of the city, we heard voices raised in anger, shouts, and the sound of horse's hooves clashing against the pavement. As we turned into a main avenue we met crowds of demonstrators running away from the mounted police, who were charging them with lances lowered. Mother grabbed my hand and pulled me into a shop doorway, but she was too late. A policeman came up to us and placed the tip of his lance against Mother's chest. She didn't panic. She brushed the lance away and shouted.

"You fool! Don't you know who I am?"

The policeman lifted his lance and slowly retreated, pulling at the reins to get his horse away from us. Then he turned and yelled:

"Lady, whoever you are, you'd better get out of here."

Soon the street was cleared. A handful of demonstrators were lying about, obviously hurt. We stepped out of our inadequate shelter and hurried home.

Father wasn't back, but Uncle José María's house was teeming with people waiting for him, all wondering about the reason for his tardiness. I told what had happened to us, and Mother was severely scolded.

"How could you do that, Rosa? It was sheer foolhardiness. Besides risking your life to satisfy your curiosity, you also put Lillian in danger. In his desperation the president has ordered a crackdown. You were lucky. You and Lillian could be now lying on a slab in the morgue."

Father finally came home about midnight. The same questions were voiced by everybody assembled in the living room. "What happened? Why were you so long?"

"I have accepted the position of Secretary of the Treasury. We discussed this all day. At first I refused, but the president insisted with such powerful arguments that I finally yielded. All my conditions were accepted. I really think I can help straighten out the country's economy and . . ."

"Arturo, you are naive. Your acceptance just buys the president some extra time. But he is doomed. No doubt about it. Come with us. There's something you must see."

Two of his friends took him on a tour of the hospitals. In the emergency rooms downtown and in the suburbs he was shown the wounded and counted the dead. This was an experience he wasn't prepared for. There had been coups in Chile before, but always bloodless ones. For the first time he was faced with a brutal reaction from a regime that would stop at nothing to remain in power.

Several hours later, when he returned, his face was drained of color.

This was due not to fatigue, but to disgust and disappointment about the man he had mistakenly judged as a benign strong man, who on that very day had seduced him into joining his government, supposedly for the good of the country. It was now clear that the man had pursued only his own selfish goals.

Physicians and interns at the hospitals he visited that night told him that for days they had been patching up wounded people, some seriously battered, many beyond recovery, and there seemed to be no end to the repression.

Close to dawn, he shook hands with the friends that had waited for him all night. He sat next to Mother with his arm around her shoulders and kissed her forehead. Mother didn't say what had happened to us. Probably she had a sense of guilt. He had seen enough blood and gore. He didn't need to know that we also had been in danger. Announcing that he would resign the position he had just accepted, Father said he couldn't identify himself with such a brutally repressive regime. Following a couple of hour's sleep, he went into Uncle José María's office and wrote out his resignation. José María drove him to the Presidential Palace and waited for him.

The next morning President Carlos Ibáñez left the country.

Carlos Dávila, whom we had met in New York, arrived in Chile and set up a Socialist Republic that lasted only one hundred days. Dávila was replaced by another former exile who took over briefly. Then a merry-go-round of hopefuls passed through the Presidential Palace. One of them stayed long enough to allow the democratic process of elections to take place. Arturo Alessandri was the winner. His campaign brought back memories of fiery speeches of the early twenties, when his populist eloquence had earned him the nickname "The Lion of Tarapaca." In exile, however, he had radically changed his allegiances. No more wooing of the people with words about how "only love can bring prosperity." He catered now to the wealthy aristocracy and their vested interests. No sooner was power securely in his hands than he displayed the vengeful side of his Italian ancestry. He forced into retirement many Foreign Service officers who had served under the man who exiled him. My father was one of them.

Father bitterly witnessed how the plan for economic reform he had submitted to Alessandri's predecessor was implemented by millionaire Gustavo Ross Santa María, one of Alessandri's political mentors.

After Father was forced by Alessandri into retirement, he had to face one of the hardest tests of his life. He had to start from scratch. His pension was minimal. He needed to find an honorable job or business and earn enough to maintain the family's social status. He became hypersensitive and testy.

One day he walked into the house and asked me irritably, "What do you know about this book in which you are mentioned?"

"I know nothing about any such book. Why are you so angry?" I laughed.

"I haven't read the book but a chapter was shown to me. The author says that he fell in love with you when he saw you emerge from the sea like Botticelli's Venus. How dare he compare you with Venus? In the painting she is naked!"

"Aren't you blowing this story out of proportion? Who is the author?" I laughed again.

"Enrique Araya. He even lives in this neighborhood."

At this point the conversation was interrupted by the telephone. It was Rebeca.

"You are famous! Everybody is talking about Araya's book. Don't tell me that you haven't read it!"

"I haven't read it. But Father is here and very upset. He says that Araya has portrayed me emerging naked from the sea. Father is determined to confront Enrique and demand an explanation."

"You're kidding! A duel in the family?"

"According to Father the book is offensive!"

When I read the book I enjoyed its humor. Only one paragraph irked me, because what was meant as light mockery made me look foolish. Knowing that I was to leave soon for Europe, the author asks me for a souvenir: "May I have your handkerchief?"

"Do you have a cold?" I answered.

Many years later, Araya and I met again. I offered to translate his book into English. It was already in its thirteenth edition, and Enrique Araya had been acknowledged by the University of Florida as outstanding among Latin American authors. But I've been unsuccessful in finding an American publisher. Perhaps editors expect Latin American writers to be tragic, somber, or indignant at social conditions in their Third World countries. Araya's book is just good fun, at times touching on piquant mischief and foolish incidents. I feel I owe it to him to have him published. He gave me a taste of celebrity. The telephone kept ringing as people called to find out how I felt about Enrique's mentioning his crush on me. Was it true? Did he really write to me after I left for Europe? How could I remember. I was only eleven years old.

Winter in Santiago was not a pleasant experience. There was damp, bone-chilling cold, and the family broke. We could see no way out of our predicament. Mother was devastated. Although she had always hated leaving Chile to follow Father on his assignments, she wished now he were back in the diplomatic service. She couldn't tolerate the atmosphere emanating from friends and relatives. Father had committed a supreme blunder by rejecting the good advice they had offered on our arrival. Most of his friends considered his early retirement as a demotion, a punishment for having served one day in the dictator's last cabinet. Seeing us stranded seemed to satisfy the secret jealousies of relatives who for years had been forced to bow to Mother's assertive character and unsolicited advice.

We moved to the old home of our late grandparents. This time we settled on the first floor, which had two living rooms, a large foyer, a cloakroom, large hall, two skylights on each side, a dining room, master bedroom, bathroom, and three bedrooms, stretched out around one side of a central courtyard. Eugene had married a year earlier, and now occupied the opposite side of the courtyard with his wife, Luz. They had a separate suite of two bedrooms and bath. It was there that their first child was born. I loved her dearly, and when it was discovered that she would need surgery for a birth defect, I devoted myself entirely to her care.

Meantime, Mother decided that to relieve the family's economic situation, the best solution would be to marry Betty off to the wealthy son of a good family. The chase was on.

Betty would have to be properly dressed for the seduction project. Mother took her to the most exclusive private boutique and bought her an expensive trousseau, cost to be worried about later. I can still remember a dark green wool coat with ermine collar and cuffs in which Betty looked stunning. But she unwittingly sabotaged Mother's plans through her risqué style of conversation. She tried to impress her suitors by appearing more sophisticated and experienced than she really was. For example, when Pepe Bunster took us to see Paris' nightlife we had driven past the Moulin Rouge. Betty's description had us walking in, looking at the half-naked chorus girls, listening to the crude remarks of the men, and even making dates with them. Or, reminiscing about the suspect

Christmas party we had attended in Quito, she made herself sound like a participant rather than an innocent observer.

Suspecting something was amiss, Mother was uneasy. Beautifully outfitted and groomed to perfection, Betty wasn't getting the response she had hoped for. She decreed that I must attend parties with Betty and act as her mini-chaperone. Then I found out what was going on. Our new acquaintances identified me with my sister as having learned more in Europe than the nuns at the Sacred Heart could possibly teach us. I had to do something about this quickly, before Mother found out.

"Betty, the story you told today is not true," I protested.

"But it's far more interesting than the truth."

"You are playing a dangerous game."

"Leave me alone. I won't listen to you."

"If Mother hears about your lies, she'll die."

"Only you can tell her. Be careful what you do. I can crush you. I know more about you and Julio than you think."

I realized then that Betty was a pathological liar, but she also had an ugly streak of vengefulness that I had never suspected. If I had had any knowledge of psychology I might have been able to help her. But psychotherapy was then unknown in Chile, and my ignorance permitted her to continue making serious mistakes. In the society in which we lived, conservative, religious, and retrograde, her behavior was definitely self-destructive. Moreover, it seemed to reflect on me, suggesting I was Betty's accomplice. I didn't know how to extricate myself from her web of lies. Instead I gradually exited my role as a chaperone.

My sister-in-law, Luz, helped me in this predicament. She argued successfully to Mother that soon I'd be a débutante, and it certainly might seem odd that I'd attended so many parties previously with Betty.

When the time came for my debut, Mother declared that there was no money to buy me a new dress. I must wear a discard from Betty. Luz intervened again, and as a result I made my official bow into society in an exquisite peau d'ange ivory dress, a Paris import smartly cut on the bias. It clung to my body, stressing pure lines of waist, flat stomach, and long legs. That night I met many young men who wanted to dance with me, and I kept in contact with them for years afterward.

CHAPTER 12

But when they danced down the street dingledodies,
and I shambled after as I've been doing all my life
after people who interest me,
because the only people for me are the mad ones,
the ones that are mad to live,
mad to talk, mad to be saved,
desirous of everything at the same time,
the ones who never yawn or say a commonplace thing,
but burn, burn, burn like fabulous yellow roman candles
exploding like spiders across the stars
and in the middle you see the blue centerlight pop
and everybody goes, Awwww.
— Jack Kerouac, 1957, On The Road

In the spring we were invited to a picnic in the mountains. A narrow
gauge train would carry our party of about forty youngsters through a
gorge to a peak where lunch awaited us at a rural restaurant. Empanadas,
salad, and red wine were the menu. Some of the young men I'd met at
the debutantes' ball were on the train. That made me feel good. The
descent from the mountain was exhilarating. Laughter was loud and rau-
cous, and as we looked out of the window at a steep incline that de-
scended to the rushing white waters of a river, everybody exploded in
shrieks of simulated terror. A small group started rocking the train,

prompting an inspector to order them to stop. Another group got hold of someone in the party, lifting him over the heads of the others, depositing him on my lap. It was then I heard for the first time a distinctive laughter, a mixture of a donkey's braying and a goose's hooting. Roberto Matta had landed in my life.

A few days later he called me on the telephone. Could he pick me up and take me to a movie, or to a restaurant, or to visit friends?

"Which friends?"

"The Correa Gac. I understand that you went to school with Inéz."

The image of a beautiful little blonde girl sprung into memory.

"I would love to see Inéz."

"All right, that's what we'll do. I love the whole family."

My friendship with Inéz started all over again, and in time I came to love her whole family. Her mother adopted me when my relationship with Roberto became difficult because of Mother's fierce opposition. She forbade me to go out with Roberto. She intercepted telephone calls and messages. When she found out that friends were covering up our meetings in their homes, she specified that I could not leave the house except with assurances that invitations did not include Roberto Matta.

Her next move was to cut off my clothing allowance. When I started to raid her trunks of Parisian dresses, learning to fit her skirts and blouses to my size, she eventually began to recognize her cast-off clothes and put an end to my recycling operation. Cornered, I created my own uniform. I recut a pair of Eugene's old trousers, making a costume which, together with a black Castilla poncho, my German boots, a sweater, and a Stetson hat, looked remarkable and unique. Since I had no money for the beauty parlor, my hair grew long and hung down my back dressed in a braid. Roberto drew a sketch of me in the Stetson hat that I still have in my collection of his drawings.

Mother's opposition was based on Roberto's family background, which was rather colorful. She only met him once and the meeting was unsuccessful, although hilarious to me, much to her indignation. Roberto came for tea at the small ranch we owned on the outskirts of Santiago. A round table hugging an old tree trunk had been set with Mother's best china and silver, probably to impress him. The conversation, strictly between Mother and Roberto, dwelt on our years in Europe. Mother took the lead and I was grateful to Roberto for limiting himself to only a few questions. I suspected that he knew more about

Myself in 1936 as seen by Jorge Opazo (deceased).

Roberto Matta and I at the Parque Cousino in 1935.

the European society she was talking about. His grandfather, Victor Echaurren, Roberto's mentor and greatest influence in his formative years, lived permanently in Europe, visiting Chile only occasionally.

I was surprised in reading *Conversations with Matta* (1985) by Eduardo Carrasco to see that he mentioned a maid as the unforgettable personality of his life. He entirely overlooked the grandfather he adored and often quoted.

Anyway, at this amazing meeting with Mother, Roberto abruptly

Roberto Matta's study for my portrait
(photo from original by George Holmes).

changed the subject to describe an idea of his: why are normal men employed in slaughterhouses? he asked. Would it not be more logical to employ murderers to do this work, thus satisfying their lust for blood?

Mother was aghast. Knowing her every reaction as well as I did, when I saw her back stiffen, her chin raise, her eyelids cover her eyes in a gesture of definite condemnation, at that moment I knew that Roberto and I were doomed. But there was more to come. Roberto jumped on the table and climbed the tree to its highest branches. From this position he started a loud recital of Neruda's poems. Then he laughed! The sound of his joy shook Mother to the innermost core of her sensitivity. She didn't speak a word, but when she looked at me, I read disaster in her expression. Yet, how could I refrain from laughing?

The next day one of our maids called me aside. "Please come and see what we found in the trash can."

Broken but still raising its body in silent protest at the outrage, a cactus with a beautiful pink flower lay among the garbage. The maid handed me a card with the words "The beauty and the beast." I recognized Roberto's handwriting and realized that Mother had thrown away his gift. The inscription could be interpreted in several ways. Had she taken it personally? I cut the flower and kept it with the card between the pages of a book.

Roberto and I kept meeting at every opportunity. We attended the School of Fine Arts together. There we met Fernand Leger's student Hernán Gazmuri, who eagerly adopted Roberto as his own student. They became inseparable.

By this time we had become sort of a legend. Accomplices in our romance seemed to multiply. Even Roberto's mother cooperated. I sensed that his snobbish brother, Mario, didn't care for me, but the youngest brother, charming, restless Sergio Matta, looked up to me, and once Roberto had gone to Europe, he even proposed. I liked him very much, but marriage to him would have smacked of incest.

My relationship with Roberto went further than that with Julio in Quito. I was terrified of pregnancy, not knowing anything about birth control. But I couldn't resist Roberto's desire, which I fully shared.

Roberto's art was fast evolving toward surrealism. His hands were constantly moving, impelled by a creative force. In restaurants he covered napkins and tablecloths with vigorous and amazing sketches. In parks he grabbed twigs to draw in the sand a constant flow of ideas that

Roberto Matta's doodles on the envelopes of his letters
(photo from original by George Holmes).

he quickly turned into images or symbols. I was in awe of everything he did.

He founded a furniture manufacturing plant that turned out "nice copies" of French provincial pieces. Also he created tables, chairs, clocks, and beds in shapes and with materials never before seen or used in Chilean furniture. His brothers, Mario and Sergio, ran the business after he left for Europe.

It was obvious that Roberto needed space to grow. He had exhausted all possibilities of artistic development in Chile. He had become outrageously eccentric, and most people laughed at his creations. When he started his furniture business he had occasion to sample different upholstery fabrics. One he liked so much he had a suit made of it. I didn't find anything wrong with it, but people mocked him and because the fabric had small dots he got the nickname "Puntitos," or little dots.

Love blinded me. I could see no wrong in anything he did. The pressure of Mother's opposition was a small price to pay for our escapades. Mother held long sessions with me, attempting to convince me that I must give him up. She wasn't sure but suspected that I still met him, since no other suitor came near me. She offered to lift all restrictions if I stopped seeing Roberto.

Attempting to shock me, she told me of his grandfather's reputation as a philanderer. He had a castle by the sea in Valparaíso, and every time he deflowered a virgin, he sent a special signal to a friendly admiral who promptly ordered a ten-gun salute to his prowess. He'd squandered a fortune on women and art in Europe. One of his daughters was Roberto's mother. She had certainly tainted Roberto with insanity, to judge by his behavior that day at the ranch. Moreover, the grandfather's second daughter was married to the man who caused the accident in Brussels that sent Mother to the hospital for three months. She felt that they were not sufficiently courteous to her during her convalescence. Nothing good could come from such a family.

After three years of relentless harassment, I started to push Roberto into leaving for Europe.

"It's an experience you need," I said.

"Lillian is right. You have nothing to learn here anymore. You must go," affirmed Gazmuri, his mentor. Roberto agreed but then reconsidered.

"Let's get married," he said, presenting me with the blueprints of the house he would build for us in Las Condes. This would have been his first project as an architect.

"Roberto, before we get into this you must go to Europe. If you decide to return, I'll be happy to marry you."

"I won't return unless I'm successful," he vowed.

A year after his departure, Roberto sent a letter to Father asking permission to marry me. He couldn't return to Chile for the wedding, he said, but suggested that we marry by proxy. When Mother read the letter she had one of her grand opera tantrums. Her voice could be heard all day and into the night, a raging torrent of sound coming from her bedroom. Father played the part of a single chorus, a voice trying patiently to placate her.

"At least this young man respects our traditions and asks for Lillian's hand. Rosa, don't get so upset. We'll just refuse and that's the end of the story."

"He's been gone for a year but still writes Lillian, keeping her hopeful," she wailed. "When will he understand that we will never allow him to marry her . . . much less by proxy! Who does he think we are?"

The two voices went on incessantly, Mother's amazingly strong, fed by passion. Father's fading, getting gradually weaker through the night.

I argued that I didn't see anything wrong in marrying by proxy. Mother had two reasons to disagree: nobody in our family had ever married by proxy, and if he couldn't afford to travel, he certainly wasn't financially successful and lacked the means to support a wife. We would starve in France.

Eugene and Betty, who'd heard Mother's reaction to Roberto's letter, showed me little sympathy and blamed me for not stopping Roberto from writing such a preposterous proposal. Finally Father wrote Roberto a polite refusal, putting an end to the matter.

A few months later Father received a call from Moisés Poblete, our Geneva friend. He was in town and asked if he might visit. He insisted that I join Father and Mother for tea, as his wife, Graciela, remembered me well and wanted to see me again.

Just before 5 o'clock the front door bell rang, and Helmuth Gottlieb let them in. He then announced that Mr. and Mrs. Moisés Poblete were waiting for us in the salon, handing Mother their calling card. I was pleased to see them again. Moisés had made an impression on me as an idealist, and I wanted to hear more about his work as the Chilean delegate to the League of Nations' Labor Organization. Graciela was a kind and joyful woman, and I remembered how, in Geneva, she had made a point of including me in the conversation although I was only thirteen at the time.

After an exchange of news between Father and Moisés, Graciela, Mother, and I talked about our experiences since we last saw them. Graciela was interested in how we'd adapted to life in Chile. She said she looked forward to returning to Santiago. Suddenly Moisés turned to Mother and said that he had a special mission.

"During a stay in Paris before sailing to Buenos Aires, we had occasion to spend some time with Roberto Matta," he said.

I looked at Mother. An instant transformation had taken place. Her back had stiffened. The gracious hostess disappeared. The welcoming smile was gone. The lines that reached from her nose to her mouth deepened.

"He is an amazing artist," Moisés continued. "He is having the greatest success in Paris. André Breton, Max Ernst, Chagall, Léger, all call him a genius. We agree. He is an extraordinary artist."

Mother's lips were tightly pursed, her head lifted in a challenging attitude. Her black eyes blazed. I knew that if she managed to open her lips there would be an explosion. Father saw it also and tried to avoid an incident.

"Rosa, please, everybody is entitled to his opinion. We think differently, that's all."

But Mother couldn't restrain herself: "He's insane. He's a fool. He doesn't know what he wants."

"It seems to me that he is very clear about what he wants. He wants to marry Lillian by proxy, and we would be glad to take her with us to Paris, where he is waiting for the three of us," said Moisés. He turned to me: "Lillian, you are a woman, not a child anymore. Do you want to marry Roberto and leave with us?"

"Yes, I want to marry him and I appreciate your offer to take me to Paris."

"You can't make a decision without our approval," Mother interjected. "You are a minor and legally you can't accept this proposal without our consent."

Too ashamed to say that as well as being legally incapacitated I had no money for the trip, I felt hurt and helpless. I excused myself and left the room. I never saw Moisés and Graciela again, nor did my parents.

As for Roberto, he was an overnight success after he joined the Paris group of surrealists. In the circle of his admirers and critics he was called the "Formidable Matta." During World War II he was among the group of European artists who emigrated to the United States. Stephen Naifeh's biography of Jackson Pollock mentions Roberto extensively and acknowledges his efforts in launching Pollock.

Twelve years later Roberto returned to Chile. By then we were both married to others. He asked to see me. It was a lifeless meeting, and I regretted agreeing to the reunion. I should have known better. We both lived in different worlds. His interests and mine didn't coincide. In his characteristically abrupt manner, he asked me:

"Are you happy? Please tell me that you are happy."

His emphasis on the word *please* shocked me. Did he feel guilty for having left me? What arrogance to think that in twelve years I wouldn't have organized my life around other lovers and activities. He never asked me what I was doing, or what my children meant to me.

He suddenly turned toward the painting he had been commissioned to do for Sergio Larrain, his main financial supporter for many years. He grabbed a sharp knife from his painting table, swiftly cut off a slice of the canvas and handed it to me, asking me to keep it as a souvenir of his young love. I still have it, but I'm unsure why I keep it. I also have many letters he wrote during his first years in Europe. These describe his friendship with Gabriela Mistral in Portugal, his experiences with dip-lomatic relatives in Madrid, and a visit to Russia, where he decided he was a Communist at a time when others were already disillusioned with the harsh regime that had failed in its promises.

But what is the truth about my romance with Matta? The truth is that when I encouraged him to leave Chile, I was exhausted by Mother's intolerable persecution. Also, Roberto's overwhelming personality was losing its magic, and I owed it to myself to find an ambiance for inde-pendent growth and the development of my identity. I felt smothered and victimized.

Yet I did grieve when he left and thought I would never love again. For months I had a sense of mutilation, deprivation, loss of direction and purpose. It went on until a friend forced me to face a mirror and set me on a path. I discovered I could love again with the same willing sur-render and joy. And one day I found the man who would shape my life for years to come.

When I emerged from the near catatonic state I'd been in, I became aware of Father's desperate struggle to stay afloat financially. He couldn't look for a job. He was overqualified to the point that nobody dared offer him anything. What could fit a former diplomat and Secretary of the Treasury, even if the latter was only for a day? Besides, most of his friends and colleagues in the diplomatic service were in the same situation. Alessandri didn't need them around, as his policies had been so radically reversed.

Feeling that I must do something to help the family, I puzzled about what it could be. Eugene was quite successful as the representative of a German firm, but he was married and Father would have never accepted help that rightfully belonged to his wife and small child.

Deciding that the quickest and easiest method of earning money was to make hats, I improvised a shop in the linens room and bought a few felt cloches that I soaked, shaped, and decorated the next day with ribbons, feathers, or silk flowers. I called several friends, letting them try on my creations and model them around town. Soon the telephone was ringing from potential customers. Then after a good start, I noticed that my clientele was dwindling. A friend told me that Mother was preventing them from coming for fittings, telling them that I didn't know what I was doing and the hats would soon fall apart. When confronted, Mother told me why she was sabotaging me:

"It's too embarrassing. I don't want word to spread around that you are a milliner."

My next attempt was at a radio station, where I offered to teach French. The director turned me down, but he had attended Eugene's classes on the manufacture of radios and stopped me from leaving to ask questions about the family and the reason for my quest for work. He offered to recommend me as a translator in the publishing business, and soon afterward I was called by one of these entrepreneurs, thus beginning a lifelong career.

From that moment on Father's typewriter took a beating. My work went well, and I was soon to see my maiden name on title pages. The first publisher had a rather small business and eventually went broke. Next Editorial ZigZag, the most influential publishing concern in the country, got in touch with me. My editor there was José María Souviron, the Spanish poet who had left his country during the civil war. He became my mentor, and under his supervision my style improved and my vocabulary became richer and highly accurate. One day he told me that the Buenos Aires chapter of the PEN Club had called my translation of Somerset Maugham's *Of Human Bondage* the best of the year. Would

I get a diploma for it? I asked. No, he said, Editorial ZigZag wanted to keep this memento.

The only serious disagreement I had with José María involved a translation of Robert Briffault's *Europa,* a fascinating account of pre–First World War Europe.

Europa in Limbo was the second volume, published soon after I had finished translating the first. José María refused to publish *Europa in Limbo* on the grounds that he considered it shocking and amoral. Passionately I argued that we had no right to suppress half of Briffault's work. I lost. José María wouldn't give an inch, and neither did he commission any more translations. I was "Lillian in Limbo!"

Betty was dating a young Peruvian who had had a crush on her when we lived in Ecuador. Betty claimed that she wasn't interested in dining alone with him, so would I join them? I had no objection. I remembered Carlos Vidal and liked him. When he picked us up he said that another friend was joining us: Manuel Seoane, a political exile from Peru, leader of the APRA party (American Peoples Revolutionary Alliance). He was waiting for us at the restaurant.

Since his arrival in Chile, in 1938, Seoane had attracted attention as a powerful orator and a sensational journalist at the helm of the magazine *Ercilla,* the first in Chile to tackle investigative reporting.

"I know a lot about you both," he said. "Carlos has been coaching me about your life in Europe and what you are doing now in Santiago. I'm particularly interested, Lillian, in your work as a translator. Would you care to work with us at *Ercilla* magazine? Come and see me tomorrow if you are interested."

Since the fallout with Souviron I wasn't sure he would ever commission a translation from me again. So I decided to talk with Manuel about a job at the magazine. I had no experience in journalism, he said, so I'd have to scan European and American magazines and point out to him features I felt worth translating. I was delighted. I'd found a job I would enjoy, and I'd be paid regularly. Book translations were tied to contracts, and there was often a gap between assignments.

There remained one big problem: how to tell Mother that I would be working daily from nine to five? I didn't know if I would be up to the job. Manuel might fire me as quickly as he hired me. I decided to wait.

Two months later I was still waiting for the right time to disclose the situation to her. Then a friend at the magazine called me, sounding excited. "Your mother is here. She is asking the porter where she can find you. Do something, quick."

I stopped to warn Manuel about Mother's presence. He sent me to the pressroom, telling me to wait for him there. The assistant editor later gave me an instant replay of the conversation between Mother and Manuel.

Jumping out of his seat, Manuel walked to meet Mother. Before she opened her mouth, he shook hands with her, held her by the elbow, led her to an armchair in his office, asked if she was comfortable, and offered her a cushion for her back. Then he returned to sit at his desk, smiling brightly.

"It's a pleasure to meet the mother of such a talented girl as Lillian."

"Thank you, but will you please tell me exactly what she does here?"

"She is here as a translator in English, French, and German. Furthermore she is our adviser on European news. Having lived in Europe she has enough special knowledge to analyze the political scenario for us. You are certainly aware of how important that is for our publication. We really don't know what we would do without her. You should be very proud of her!"

Mother visibly melted, according to witnesses, totally seduced. Then Manuel stood up and led her to the building's front door. That evening, Mother remarked: "Why didn't you tell me that you are working for such a fine young man?"

The secret was finally out, and I was glad to contribute my salary to the household expenses.

Manuel had to travel on a brief trip to Argentina. The assistant editor said I might start doing interviews and reporting like a professional. I was terrified as I grabbed a small notebook, purse, and coat and went ahead to see my first subject. He turned out to be an old friend of Father's, amazed to see me working as a reporter. His reaction was:

"There must be a mistake. Let me call my wife, and you can talk with her about fashions."

"No, absolutely not," I told him. "I'm here to interview *you*. I want to know what you think about Chamberlain and the Munich Pact. Do you think it will work? Can Hitler be stopped? What will happen if he carries out his threats? Will there be war? Will the Maginot Line hold?"

"You've done your homework," he laughed. "I like that! Let me answer each question . . ."

After an hour, his wife walked in to remind the senator that they had an engagement. She was a beautiful woman, and I could quite understand the senator's falling in love with her. Her husband had shot him, and, though wounded, he'd shot back from the ground. Neither was fatally hurt. Her marriage was annulled, and even though the Church refused to bless their union, a civil ceremony legalized their marriage.

When Manuel returned, the assistant editor told him that I was holding two jobs: translator and reporter. He grumbled for a while but soon settled down. Together with Lenka Franulic, one of the first Chilean women to perform as a full-fledged journalist, I was now in that category, reporting on events, political and otherwise, breaking the barrier which had previously confined women to describing debutante's dresses, weddings, and birthday parties.

I told Manuel that I wanted to write features and investigative reports like the rest of the staff. After reading some of their material I realized that much of it was shallow and the data inaccurate. I felt I could do better.

At the same time my friendship with my cousin Hernán grew stronger. We comforted each other in similar painful experiences: Roberto was gone, and Hernán's first love had deserted him. So we found solace in each other's company. Hernán and his colleagues in medicine, all of them interns in Santiago's hospitals, found in me a sympathetic ear. I often sat with them and listened to their experiences and observations. Hernán planned to specialize in obstetrics, as did several of his friends. They were horrified at the often fatal damage that women inflicted on themselves in order to abort unwanted or unaffordable pregnancies, and at the carnage wrought by inexperienced or unscrupulous midwives.

One day, after Hernán lost a patient under dreadful circumstances, he and his colleagues said I must write about it. I discussed the idea with Manuel, and I wrote my first investigative report about the ravages of abortion, stressing the need for its legalization. It was 1939. I was a single woman in a predominantly Catholic society. Manuel approved the article but warned that it wouldn't carry my byline.

"I must protect you. The reaction could make your life quite unpleasant," he said. I agreed. The purpose of the article was to save lives, rather than to make me sound like a crusading journalist.

My first serious mistake as a journalist came when I interviewed a freshman in Congress, son of a senator who was an old friend of Father and Uncle José María. Chile was close to elections. As usual, everybody had an opinion about the candidates. When I submitted my interview to Manuel, he bristled; "I've never read anything so bland. I know this young man. He must have said something else. Try to remember."

Blushing deeply, I wanted to disappear. I knew that what I had left out was in consideration to Father's feelings. The young congressman had expressed an opinion that would be shocking to many, considering that the Spanish Civil War had only just ended, leaving on people's minds the horrors of the conflict. Finally I blurted out: "I'm sorry. He said that what Chile needs is a Franco."

"My God! How could you forget that? That's the title of the interview. I'll never trust you again."

But he did, after a while. There was a failed military coup, and Manuel sent me to cover it. I went to the garrison where the leaders were under arrest. The general who headed the conspiracy agreed to be interviewed. He was smiling when I walked into the room.

"My dear young lady! I'm sure that you bring messages from my friends. Sit down. Let me hear you."

"General, I'm a reporter from *Ercilla* magazine. I'm supposed to interview you. Didn't they tell you?"

"Perhaps I misunderstood. What is your name?"

"Lillian Lorca."

"Are you by any chance a relative of Arturo Lorca?"

"I'm his daughter."

"That's impossible. No daughter of Arturo would be a reporter for *Ercilla*."

"General, I'm a reporter for *Ercilla* and proud of it. I'm here to offer you an opportunity to tell your side of the uprising. Everything I write will be exactly what you tell me. I can show it to you for approval before publication."

He gave me the interview. I typed it before leaving and let him read it. He approved.

Because of my skill in languages, I was always assigned to interview foreign celebrities. Henry Fonda was one of them, on a promotional trip for *The Grapes of Wrath*. Then I was to meet the monosyllabic, overweight daughter of labor leader John Lewis. She was in Chile as an observer of the first Popular Front administration of President Pedro Aguirre Cerda. During his electoral campaign he had visited Father. Nordic Gottlieb had left him waiting outside our front door. When Father realized what he had done, he rushed to greet him and apologize. Later Father inquired why our butler had left him standing outside. Helmuth answered: "He is so ugly I couldn't think he was important. I suspected he wanted something."

"Just a bunch of votes, with my help," Father answered.

It was about this time that Miguel Labarca, the exiled student I had met in Ecuador, surfaced again. He worked as an assistant to the mayor Graciela Schnake, the first Chilean woman to hold that office. When he found out that I was a journalist, he offered to open doors for me. President Aguirre Cerda's government had made radical changes, and Miguel had strings to all the new personalities at La Moneda, the President's palace. Senator Santiago Labarca was his brother. His sister, Amanda Labarca, was Secretary of Education.

I realized that he was not just an assistant to the mayor; he was a sort of Richelieu without the trappings. He knew everybody and was informed of everything, almost before it happened. I suspected that if what he had in mind didn't happen according to his schedule, somehow he would make it happen. When I wrote a short story about this mysterious character who exercised power without anybody knowing about it, Manuel only laughed, saying that it was probably true. He published it, although the magazine had never before bothered with short stories.

However, there was a price to pay for Miguel's tutelage. He called me incessantly. He showed up on any pretext wherever I was and, on the eve of my wedding, picked me up at home, drove around aimlessly all day and only returned me home in the evening. I was angry. He had no right to kidnap me in an effort to convince me that I must not marry "this man called Enrique Tagle."

On the day of my wedding, among the guests, I spotted the entire staff of *Ercilla,* headed by Manuel. When I walked past him, he whispered, "Courage!" I would need it and he knew it. For I was leaving behind the work I loved, with the people I liked beyond simple friendship. I was stepping into a void where my love for Enrique and his for me might not fill my needs. I would have to work hard at adjusting.

When I first met Enrique Tagle years earlier, he was dating a cousin of mine. They broke up, and he faded away. I fell in and out of love with Roberto Matta. There were some tumultuous times and several lonesome gaps in my life, and during one of them, just before New Year's Eve 1939, my cousin Nana had come to see me.

"We are having a New Year's Eve party, and we want you to join us."

"I can't, Nana. I don't feel well, and I have nothing to wear."

"Let me see your closet."

"You'll be disappointed."

After skimming quickly through my closet she returned and said, "You're right, you really don't have anything to wear. Don't leave before I return. I won't be long."

Nana, twice my size in height and weight, returned with an armful of clothes. I started to try on dresses, skirts, and tops, but all seemed too large. Then we came upon a lovely lace-trimmed slip and a shawl, and I was ready for the party. I looked good, and nobody would notice that under the shawl I was wearing lingerie.

When we arrived at the Club de la Unión I found out that my escort was Enrique Tagle. He briefly brought me up to date about what he was doing. I knew that his father's untimely death had interrupted his education and that he didn't attend the university like many of his friends. He held a part-time job, yet lived like a prince because his name was his credit card. No bank in the land would refuse a loan to a Tagle Zañartu, member of honorably bankrupt aristocracy. It took some time before Enrique explained to me how his father had managed to lose a fortune in land.

After the club we went to the market, where modest restaurants served the traditional onion soup, which was said to help people avoid the effects of hangovers. The sun was coming up when we left. Notwithstanding the late hour, I didn't expect what happened next. Enrique took me home, but we didn't have time to ring the bell. The door opened, and Mother launched into a shrill tirade of accusations and insults. She was in her robe, her hair disheveled, her face contorted by rage. I was stunned with shame. Turning to Enrique I asked him to leave. He told me later that it was at that moment he decided to marry me to take me away from my mother's insane rages. Once Mother realized who was my escort that night, she kept a discreet attitude toward Enrique. Again his name acted like a shield, protecting him from any animosity. The fact that he was not wealthy didn't seem to bother her excessively, although she frequently suggested that he might look into finding a more rewarding occupation than the part-time job he held in a very reputable office.

I settled down to married life and motherhood. My daughter Ximena's birth came soon enough to make my life unexpectedly happy. I hadn't much cared for babies before, but her presence and her needs were suddenly almost everything I wanted from life. When her birth was reported in the newspapers, her name was misspelled. This prompted a sly call from José María Souviron.

"Lillian, you know better than to spell your daughter's name with a J. It's spelled with an X. I'm surprised at you. Send in a correction. And by the way, would you like to start working for ZigZag again?"

If the offer had come from *Ercilla* I wouldn't have hesitated. Journalism had always fascinated me, but it was impossible under the circumstances. My child needed full attention. As a second choice, translating again at home would be fine. Just before my wedding when friends asked me what kind of present I'd like — a crystal chandelier was first on their list — I told them that what I really wanted was a typewriter. They were shocked.

"What will you do with it?"

"Write, translate, a million things."

So with my first typewriter, a faithful Royal that followed me for years, I began work at home. José María Souviron could expect neat, clear manuscripts from my brand-new typewriter. He never failed me, and I translated more than thirty books in nine years. There were best-sellers by Axel Munthe, Yeats Brown, Thomas Mann, Franz Werfel. Once when I was reminiscing about these names and titles with an Argentinean friend, she recalled reading several of my translations in a remote city in Patagonia. It thrilled me to think that my literary work had reached so far. Most of those authors are now forgotten. The Second World War brought new talents, like Wolfe, Salinger, and Mailer. Most of them are American writers, but in the forties South American readers still reached culturally toward Europe.

In 1946 I had my second child, Rosa. Ximena started school to overcome a bout of jealousy that worried everybody in Mother's household, where I was staying temporarily during a difficult pregnancy. Rosa was a premature baby. A nurse's blunder forced me to leave the hospital before the doctors had released me. Wrapping the child in a blanket, I hailed a cab in the street and returned home. I wouldn't allow anybody into my room until the pediatrician arrived. He approved my decision when I described the situation. After examining the baby, he ordered a blood transfusion that was provided by Betty. The doctor also ordered that until further notice no one would be allowed in the room without a sterile mask. Ximena was no exception. No wonder she resented being ostracized! For the first six years of her life she had been the absolute center of attention. School was a wise decision. It took her mind off her sister and made her feel important.

Enrique also felt that his life was being shaken out of an easy routine. Daily contacts with friends gave him information about businesses and commissions to be earned. Following World War II, Chile was getting back to normal. Cars were running without fear of gas and tire shortages. The country seemed ready to bloom again into prosperity. Enrique resigned the security of his part-time job and started a business partnership with a friend. Expectations seemed brilliant, but results fell short of our hopes.

On the other hand, as the representative of a German firm, my brother, Eugene, had been blacklisted during the war, and his problems grew with his increasing family. But there was no end to his resourcefulness, and he survived financially with more than average success.

Meantime, Betty had at last found a husband worthy of Mother's approval. He belonged to a well-known family of British origin, with even a heroic Naval ancestor to add to his own military record as an adviser in the preposterous Chaco War between Bolivia and Paraguay. He sported the first name of Washington, suggestive of American heroes, with aristocratic Lynch as a last name, which linked him to Chilean history. He had the fine features of a blond Don Juan and the long arms and dancing legs of a swordsman, matched by a spirit so light and frivolous that nobody could resist his charm. All this and empty pockets!

Betty dragged him into the most unseemly of adventures, considering his qualifications. They were to till the soil, plant seeds, and care for animals in a plot of land next to a blank on the map marked "Unexplored," in the southernmost tip of Chile. Betty dreamed of the Bunster's exploits in similar regions a century earlier. They had subdued the Indians not with weapons but with reason. Betty had to fight her husband's love for the easy life. And in this conflict, he won. Betty had to be rescued. She was still protesting her right to fame, glory, and riches when Eugene packed her up, shivering and close to childbirth, on the train to Santiago. Her husband pursued other dreams in Southern urban centers, far from the unexplored areas that Betty wanted to challenge. He later moved to Peru, where, according to gossip, he married a rich widow.

In 1948 Mother was asked to lead a campaign for women's suffrage. She recruited me, and we targeted schools where the children's mothers attended sewing and nutrition classes. We spoke about the importance of being able to vote. It was a right they must claim. It would give them a voice to state their needs and be heard. I never told Mother that I had written the article on the legalization of abortion. She had read it and

strongly disapproved. Aiming at the women's vote I felt that I was strug-
gling for much-needed rights for Chilean women. Whereas abortion legalization was a farfetched dream, this campaign had real potential. We
didn't just speak with the women at their school meetings. We talked to
congressmen, bankers, university board members, in fact anybody and
everybody of influence whom we could approach. We recruited many
women to share our efforts, and we won. The law was passed. In the
next election the women would vote en masse.

Mother was a stoic, reserved kind of person who scarcely ever showed
emotions except anger. I know that when the women's suffrage bill was
signed into law, she was proud and happy, but she wouldn't show it. I
was elated and wanted to celebrate. Suddenly I realized that most of my
closest friends were men. They might have reservations about celebrat-
ing this yielding of power to women. Their wives might be reluctant to
touch sensitive areas in their husband's egos. I had to acknowledge that
our victory wasn't so cut-and-dried as I'd expected — that in fact the real
struggle was just beginning.

On election day I noticed, much to my surprise, that Mother was
close to tears. I asked her what was going on. She confessed that she had
forgotten to register, therefore she couldn't vote. I had to resort to old-
style feudalism to solve Mother's distress. I asked a group of men who
worked for Enrique in his new venture how they planned to vote.

"We don't know. You tell us!"

"I can't do that. But I can tell you who I'm voting for."

I was then able to assure Mother that she could count on fourteen
votes for her candidate and mine.

My husband was a dreamer. His father had lost every one of the seven
ranches his wife had brought to their marriage. Enrique told me how
it happened. His father had decided to improve his laborers' lot by raising their salaries. Neighboring landowners retaliated by boycotting his
crops. Within a few years he was bankrupt. He sold all the ranches,
barely managing to keep sufficient money to buy a single property near
Santiago. His wife and the children stayed there while he accepted a job
as an engineer in the construction of a tunnel. He was so successful that
his calculations are mentioned in engineering textbooks. Having failed
as an agronomist because of his political beliefs, Enrique Tagle Rodri-
guez could have started a second career in engineering had not cancer
targeted him for a premature death.

His oldest son, Arturo, had just graduated from law school. He could help the family by taking a job in the most remote city of the land. But the younger brothers had to drop out of school and go to work.

Enrique often talked about recovering at least the last ranch that his Father owned, the one they had to sell after his death. How would he get it back? He didn't know except that one day he'd win big at roulette at the Viña del Mar Casino.

After gambling sessions we used to meet at my cousin Lila's, or at the house of Salvador Allende's sister, Laura, where I met the future president for the first time. Chicho to his friends, Salvador had also spent the evening at the casino. He was impeccably dressed in a dark suit. After a while he disappeared, and when he returned we noticed that his clothes were different. His trousers bagged at the back. The jacket was too tight, and the shirt he wore under it was of the gray-white cotton that needed a good soak in bleach.

"Very nice for a costume party," someone observed.

Salvador laughed.

"I have a meeting with the comrades in Valparaíso."

"Come on, Chicho. What kind of comrades?"

"The kind that work the night shift on the docks. Stop kidding. I'm already late. Good night."

This charade seemed distasteful to me, but later when I came to know him better, I understood his motivation. Salvador Allende had to reach those people and if it took a change of clothes to make the approach, he didn't mind.

During my years at *Ercilla* magazine, I had developed a warm friendship with Hernán's mother, Mary Lorca. She was a stunning woman of no great stature, with pure classical features, a straight nose, blue eyes, perfect oval face, and a nest of Venetian red curls crowning her head. This set her apart from the clan of tall, dark straight-haired Lorca women.

Mary had married at seventeen and bore Hernán shortly afterward. She was abandoned by her philandering husband and thereafter earned a living by creating and selling cosmetics based on natural products and herbs, a novelty at the time. Mary's failed marriage placed her in a sort of social limbo. She was not a widow, but she had no husband. Her beauty was felt as a threat to prospective hostesses. She devoted her life to Hernán's upbringing, and the business she carried on at home. She lived with old aunts who doted on her and the child. She read voraciously to supplement Hernán's education by discussing with him European literary giants. I soon became a natural addition to their household.

During my years of rebellion and frustration, Mary was the balancing element I needed so badly. There was nothing in my life that I couldn't discuss with her. She was to me the chosen mother, sister, and friend on whose lap I could rest my head to cry without shame. At her side I could speak about what shocked me in the conservative, hypocritical society that I resisted fiercely, refusing to let it swallow me. Mary unfailingly supported my ideas, no matter how outrageous. With her I laughed and cried, and a stroke of her hand on my head could soothe any imagined or real pain. We loved each other. Perhaps she saw in me the potential she had had herself, without being able to develop it. I needed her tenderness, her intellectual stimulation, and her support for my individual growth and my painful emotional experiences.

Mary's father had been married in succession to two Argentinean Ortiz sisters from Mendoza. When Mary's mother died, her father had courted and married the younger sister, who also passed away without leaving issue. The Ortiz family was extremely wealthy, and years later a letter from an attorney arrived announcing that a considerable inheritance was waiting to be claimed.

Mary had an older brother, but he couldn't be relied upon to go through the legal intricacies of the case. The family decided that Mary was the only person who could handle the situation. She moved to Mendoza, and what everyone thought would take a few months to solve became years of frustration, negotiation, and bickering. Finally her lawyers advised her to request an appointment with President Perón. So she journeyed to Buenos Aires and asked to see him.

Mary told me about her meeting with him, and later with his famous wife, Evita.

"He was so gracious and charming that he made me feel at ease immediately. He would be a handsome man if it were not for his pockmarked face. He was aware of the political situation in Chile, and since politics is one of my main interests, we were able to discuss the Chilean Popular Front, and I enjoyed the fact that he was not patronizing. At times he would agree with me, but he also laughed sometimes and said that I was naive. He talked about his own populist regime, then suddenly veered to the case of the Ortiz inheritance. He knew about the problems I had in claiming it, and with a smile he advised me to see Evita."

"'She will tell you about the many charities she supports. You'll be impressed. Two beautiful women like you and Evita should find a common ground.'"

"So it came about that I visited Evita, whose cordiality didn't match that of her husband, not even after I handed her a generous check," Mary told me. "But after I returned to Mendoza, my attorneys were delighted to tell me that every obstacle to the release of the inheritance had disappeared, and the judge had signed all necessary documents. I did not mention my very expensive visit with Evita."

Mary concluded this tale with a wry smile. She considered the whole incident as a lesson in practical politics.

Working at *Ercilla* magazine I'd learned a lot about my editor, Manuel Seoane. His father had been a diplomat, and he was a leader of APRA, a fact that set an abrupt contrast between father and son. Manuel had been exiled for years, first in Argentina, later in Chile. He was married and had a daughter he adored, who currently lived with him in exile. One of Manuel's brothers, Juan, had been arrested and languished in a Peruvian jail. Juan was not a member of APRA, and there was a suspicion that he was held as a hostage in the hope that Manuel would yield to pressure and return to Peru. A manuscript of Juan's book, written about his experiences in jail, had been smuggled out of Lima. Manuel asked me if I would translate it into French. I did.

The narrative was at times so harsh, describing tortures and incredible abuses of the prisoners, that I often stopped my work to cry. The story is as relevant today as if it had been written yesterday. Political prisoners all over the world still linger in prisons and are still brutalized. I knew that the fact that Juan might be in jail as a hostage tormented Manuel. So when a telephone call came from him saying that the ordeal was over and Juan had been released, I knew what it meant to him. Juan was in Santiago and wanted to see me.

We met in a park near my home. Ximena was with me because I never left her behind. Juan kissed me on the forehead and then sat on a bench and pulled Ximena onto his knee. I couldn't find anything to say. I stared at Juan, thinking about what he had been through and how little of his suffering showed on his face. Manuel guessed my thoughts, squeezed my hand, then hugged me and said in a voice broken by emotion: "We'll get together again. Juan will be here a long time." They left, but I never saw Juan again.

CHAPTER 13

The small house where we lived right after our wedding was one that Enrique owned, but when Ximena arrived, I suggested and then insisted that we move elsewhere. His mother and five brothers and sisters lived in the second floor. Our quarters on the first floor were inadequate for us.

"Let's sell this house. We'll find another to accommodate the whole family. We all need more space," I argued.

Enrique said this was impossible as it had been built with a loan conditioned on keeping the property for five years, and they had only lived there for two years. I soon became obsessed. Who was the top man of the institution that financed it? I found out and made an appointment to see him. I explained the situation — where a family of eight and a baby were crowded into four small bedrooms.

"Don't you know that some people live eight in one bedroom and take turns to sleep?" the official said after listening patiently.

"Who are they? Are you talking about slum dwellers? In my case we are the Tagle Zañartu and Lorcas. You can't expect us to live like them, just because of a regulation that forbids my husband to sell the house for another three years!"

"We can't make exceptions."

To lighten the tone, I described the ridiculous situations caused by the room which had been planned as a small office and later turned into our bedroom.

"The bed and the crib fill the room completely so there's no space to walk around. To reach my child for feeding or changing her diaper I have to walk over the bed like it was a trampoline. I'm past the age when jumping on beds is a delightful game," I complained.

This raised a laugh, and the man offered: "Let me see what I can do. I'll call you." Soon he authorized Enrique to sell the house.

My parents had also sold my grandparents' home, where we had lived since returning to Chile. That house was so full of memories that we all hated their decision to move into a more modern place in a more fashionable neighborhood. Over the years, the old house had been remodeled several times, with each architectural intervention coming under Mother's jurisdiction. This had slowly transformed the original structure we had known and loved in our childhood. A second floor had been built over the courtyard where Grandmother used to grow her favorite flowers. Where the stables once were had become a garage and parking lot later sold to a smart entrepreneur. But even the dismemberment of our grandparents' property couldn't efface the memories it held for us. We mourned the sale as we would the death of a dear friend. Later in its degraded life, it became a Hungarian clubhouse. Betty, Eugene, and I asked the new owners for permission to walk through the rooms. So much good and bad was held inside those walls. To our ears, laughter and sobs echoed in our memories in equal measures.

In 1942 Helmuth Gottlieb had left with the highest references. A return to Germany was out of the question. Father kept in touch with him for a while, and the last we heard indicated that he was trying to get a visa to the United States. As he was Danish by nationality, he probably didn't have any difficulty.

Meantime we were to vacate our house, and since my parents had rented a large villa in Providencia, Father persuaded Enrique and me to move in, arguing that the house was too big for the two of them. We could live there while we looked for our own home. The rented house had a big garden where Ximena could play safely, and though I wanted my own place, Father's proposal seemed reasonable.

As it turned out, the villa was not a happy place. Betty's marriage was definitely going sour. After every crisis she sought refuge there, arriving with her son and a small suitcase. A telephone call from her husband usually lifted her spirits, and she departed again, only to return two or three weeks later. There seemed to be no end to this situation, until she became pregnant. Father then insisted that she remain in the house until childbirth.

Mother was to have a mastectomy, brutal as they were at the time. Her physician was our cousin Eduardo, who had become one of the outstanding surgeons in Santiago after long training abroad. As was the custom, the whole family waited outside the operating room for news, good or bad. Eduardo finally emerged in his whites, with his sterile mask hanging from his ears. All eyes were glued on him as he pulled off his still-bloody rubber gloves. He strutted about like a movie star, and picked up a small package from a nurse's tray and handed it to me.

"That's for the pathologist," he said.

Feeling the small soft, still warm contents, I suddenly realized what it was. Eduardo's idea of a joke. His sense of humor was lamentable. I knew that he expected me to scream and insult him, but I wouldn't give him the satisfaction. I stood silent, holding the package until a nurse walked by. Then I handed it to her.

"This is for the pathologist. The name of the patient is Rosa Bunster de Lorca," I instructed her.

Mother's recovery was long and painful. A nurse visited her daily to change her dressings and administer painkillers and sedatives. I spent much time with her, screening the visitors she didn't care to see, or when she felt too poorly for social graces. Often I tried unsuccessfully to hold conversations that would take her mind off her suffering. It seemed an endless convalescence. It hurt me to see a proud, unyielding woman like her broken in flesh and spirit by this terrible mutilation. How would she look once she could wear a dress?

Like most women who are not beautiful but must rely on ingenuity to enhance their best traits, Mother was vain. She had managed to hide her receding chin by holding high her head, and her bad teeth by rarely smiling. But how could she hide this cavern in her chest? She hadn't dared look at her scar. The idea of a prosthesis was revolting. I was the only person she could confide in because I had asked her directly about the reasons for her distress after the worst of the pain subsided.

Eventually she made it back to her normal self, and I felt that I didn't need to hover over her all day. I started to accept invitations again, and with Ximena always at my side, I attended teas and other simple social occasions. My unusual habit of having Ximena always with me led to a nickname I joyfully accepted: Lillian and her papoose.

Rebeca, the cousin who conquered Hamburg all those years before when she stayed with us, was a compulsive hostess. Any pretext was good enough to throw a party. She was a superb and imaginative cook, while her Austrian husband knew more about wines and drinks than anybody I knew. This ensured the liveliness of their parties.

In the midst of one of these gatherings, I received an urgent call from home. One of our maids begged me to return immediately. Mother was starting a bonfire with all the drawings Roberto Matta had left me, including two of his oils. Rushing home, I found her stacking up my drawings, my portrait, and a smaller painting on top of a pile of rags, old clothes, books, and newspapers.

"What are you doing?" I cried, hardly concealing my outrage.

"I'm tired of seeing these things around."

"Mother, you don't have to look at them. They are in my room."

Taking the box of matches from her unresisting hands, I led her away, sensing that she felt relieved that I had stopped her from such an inconsiderate action. The next day I took the drawings and portrait to a friend's house. The other oil, a Nativity, I gave to Roberto's brother, Sergio. Then I started an intense campaign of house hunting. This time I was successful.

The house I found was small but appealing and had everything we needed. It had a garden in front and back, planted with bulbs and bushes that required little coaxing to bloom with every season. At the end of an ivy-covered wall was an arbor, which supported several climbing bushes that burst out with magnificent, fragrant red roses.

Ximena had her own bedroom, with a desk to do her homework and all the frills that little girls love. Her room was strategically located near the entrance door so she could find quick refuge from the neighborhood boys who chased her with raw homicidal intentions. Yet again she had kicked their ball into a yard where two vicious Doberman Pinchers stood guarding the premises. The owner refused to return the ball unless a parent pleaded for it, which meant that the game was over for the day.

Rosa meantime was demurely walking around the block with the maid's daughter, modeling dresses I designed for her. Pinafores were her favorite style. She pulled softly at the embroidered shoulder straps, and in her scant vocabulary said "Angel?" That was what she looked like, all soft, fluffy, her eyes dreamy, her very light blond hair like a gold helmet on her head.

This was a happy time for me. Enrique's gambling did continue, although mostly at home, which meant there was some control and our

Enrique Tagle Zañartu.

guests were trusted friends not out to fleece him. It seemed as though I had good reason to relax and enjoy life. But as ever, I was being too optimistic.

A change of government, a new finance minister, different bank policies, and the tightening of easy loans soon spread panic among chronic borrowers, Enrique among them. It seemed that I would need to work. José María Souviron had returned to Spain and translations were scarce. Trying to work in a business office, I found that my skills were not up to the standard of a first-rate secretary. My work was sloppy and I knew nothing about filing, so I was fired.

Enrique also found a job, but one afternoon he returned home unusually early, and I didn't have to ask what had happened. After a minute of silence, he said: "At least I saw it coming and resigned."

Despite the seriousness of our situation I couldn't help but laugh at this. So he had saved face, whereas I still had egg all over mine. I finally landed another job as a translator at the Bacteriological Institute of Chile. As it turned out, translations were the least of my work. I was also secretary of the newly created Epidemiology Department, under the supervision of Dr. Abraham Horwitz.

Ximena (below) and Rosa (above), our daughters.

Ximena's name was so often mispronounced that she decided to change it to Monica.

Mary Lorca de Mujica, Hernán's mother and my greatest friend.

From the very beginning we got on well. He gave me a meticulous briefing about what I would have to do in Epidemiology. Filing of data and reports was a must. Luckily I remembered that in San Francisco Father had learned about a new filing system, which he later introduced in government with great success. He was delighted to teach it to me, and as a result I was able to perform brilliantly. Delighted with my work — for I had always been interested in medicine — I found myself collaborating with scientific researchers, which gave me a vicarious thrill.

I often explained to Mother what our aims were. She had written a book on child care and I thought she might be interested in the work of scientists at the institute. Inviting her to visit my office, I promised to introduce her to some of our outstanding researchers. But she refused. She wouldn't set foot in the place where her daughter was working. She resented Enrique for allowing such embarrassment to the family as having a working wife. Moreover, she bluntly said that Enrique was no longer welcome in her home.

Enrique had again found a suitable job and decided to stop seeing his gambling friends. Returning home early each day after work, he sat with Rosa cuddling up to him, whispering long stories into his ear until she fell asleep in his arms. On weekends we attended concerts in the park, visited the Museum of Fine Arts, or drove into the country for lunch at rural restaurants. We walked about enjoying the scenery and cutting wildflowers, Rosa always on his lap or his shoulders and Ximena running constantly, talking to strangers, teasing children or challenging them to a race. Tireless, noisy, boisterous, laughing Ximena.

"I never thought I could enjoy all this so much," Enrique said once, listening to an open-air concert on the San Cristóbal hill. I felt proud, so deeply happy that I wanted to cry. I loved him.

Six months went by with no clouds in the sky. I didn't need anything else out of life. Enrique and I were deeply satisfied. The girls were growing splendidly. Father would visit, but not Mother.

Eugene and his wife kept much to themselves with their growing family. Betty, after her second child, rented an apartment and started working. Rebeca, Nana (the matchmaker), and a few other friends were always around. Our contentment was so obvious that they felt almost intrusive when visiting, they said.

The telephone rang on a Saturday afternoon. One of Enrique's closest old gambling friends was on the line. He said: "I know that you don't want Enrique to see us, but we miss him very much. We understand why you want him to stay away from us, his old friends. But tomorrow we leave for the beach, where Raul Magallanes' house needs repairs. He must supervise the work. We hope that Enrique will come with us. And we promise you that there will be no drinking and no gambling. We'll return early. We leave tomorrow at nine from the Providencia Church. We'll wait for him there."

I gave Enrique the message. He was glad to hear that he was being missed but didn't say that he would join them. The next morning we woke up at eight, and I asked him if he planned to meet his friends. He hesitated, then suddenly decided to go. I reminded him that we had guests for dinner.

"I'll be back in time," he answered and walked out.

That evening I sat talking and laughing with our guests. The girls came in to say goodnight, Ximena teasing her uncles for putting on too much weight, Rosa sliding silently on her slippers, shaking hands politely with our friends. Just after eight, the telephone rang. The maid said somebody was asking for me.

"Mrs. Tagle, there's been an accident. The doctors want to keep everybody under observation tonight. Nothing serious!"

"Where are you calling from?"

"The hospital in San Antonio. It's nothing to worry about."

"I must speak to the doctors."

"They've already gone home."

"Then I must speak with my husband. If it's nothing serious he can answer the telephone."

"The doctors have ordered full rest. He mustn't be disturbed."

Ending the call, I reported it to my guests. Then I decided to call the hospital.

"I want to speak with the doctor who is taking care of Enrique Tagle."

"He's busy."

"What is the diagnosis for Enrique Tagle. I'm his wife."

"The diagnosis is confidential."

Obviously the first call had been a lie. I had to go to San Antonio immediately. We didn't have a car. But we mobilized our resources, and in half an hour we had transportation. The driver was a physician, Enrique's friend for many years. Gustavo Finat, one of our guests, joined us. We left Santiago in the midst of a thick fog that slowed us down considerably. It took two hours to drive to San Antonio under normal circumstances. Now it stretched to three hours. Gustavo slipped his arm around my shoulders in a protective gesture. A Frenchman who had lived through the London blitz, he could sense tragedy. He suspected that my world was crumbling. He seemed to know what I vaguely feared.

As I rushed into the hospital, I told the receptionist that I must talk with the doctors taking care of Enrique Tagle.

"They have both gone home," she answered.

Turning to a nurse, I asked directions to Enrique's room. As I approached along a corridor, I saw Raul Magallanes' wife, standing with her arms outstretched, trying to stop me.

"What are you doing here? You didn't have to come. Everything is under control," she said.

"Get away from me! I'm going to see Enrique and you can't stop me."

Pushing her aside, I kept walking. A scream of pain came from inside a room. When I opened the door, a nurse was bending over Enrique. He reached his hand out to me.

"You're always there when I need you most," he whispered.

"We're going to take you to Santiago immediately," I assured him. "We need an ambulance," I told Gustavo, who had followed me in. Looking at Enrique's naked body on the bed, we could see how badly hurt he was. Little had been done to help him. He had bruises and wounds all over his body and, though inexperienced, I could tell that his hip was broken. From a room across the hall, a drunken song reached us: it was Raul Magallanes.

Hospital policy forbade the use of its only ambulance before six in the morning, and before departing the service had to be paid in full. Magallanes' brother-in-law provided this information. Dialogue under such circumstances can be harsh and also brutally frank. A suspicion was slowly sneaking in my mind.

"At what time was the accident?" I asked him.

"Around two in the afternoon."

"When were you called — when did you leave Santiago?"

"About three o'clock."

"Why did no one call me? I wasn't called until eight, and even then the caller discouraged me to come."

I received no answer to this. Magallanes' wife had disappeared, and her brother was reluctant to give any help or offer any solutions. Looking through Enrique's clothes, I found his checkbook and filled out the amount necessary for the ambulance. When I asked him to sign, I could see his despair.

"Don't worry. It will be all right. Just sign. We must leave right away. Dr. Abud will be waiting for you at the hospital in Santiago," I said to reassure him. I'd asked Gustavo to call Dr. Abud, a splendid physician. He told us to which hospital we must take Enrique.

When I asked a nurse to give me a flask of chloroform she refused, until I slipped a handful of bills into her pocket. Then she produced what I needed to anesthetize Enrique. I didn't know the extent of Enrique's injuries but could plainly see that only when he was under anesthesia could we move him into the ambulance. Gustavo called both our families to tell them what had happened and where we would be in Santiago. Father must be told carefully, I warned. He had already had a heart attack.

The four hours on the ambulance were agony. Sometimes Enrique seemed to slumber, and I had no way of knowing if he had passed out. Then he would open his eyes, screaming in pain, and I would give him more ether. He squeezed my hand, saying again that I was always there when he needed me. Haltingly, he talked of the children. "Take good care of them," he whispered.

"They will soon be taking care of you!"

But I knew what he meant, and felt his sorrow and hopelessness. I had no soothing words when he described how Raul Magallanes had been drunk since early morning and continued drinking during lunch. When they were ready to return to Santiago, Enrique asked to drive the car, but Raul refused. Later, as he wove and sped along the coastal road, Enrique tried again to stop him, but Raul kept laughing and calling him a coward. Then the car hit the bluff, careened across the road, jumped a railing, and rolled over the rocks by the sea, ending upside down on a boulder.

Enrique was trapped between the back of the passenger seat and the roof of the car. The police had to use torches to free him. As he finished speaking, he said: "Now you know what happened. But I want you to promise that you will never repeat what I told you. It could ruin Raul's reputation."

With great effort I bit back the words "What reputation? Everybody knows he's a drunk and that only his wife's money and influence keep him in his job as an Air Force attorney!" But I couldn't hurt Enrique under the circumstances. We slowly rolled on toward Santiago, dreading each bump that made the vehicle shake and Enrique shout in pain. It was a test of endurance I will never forget. I felt his pain in my own flesh and bones. When he squeezed my hand, I knew that he was trying not to scream to spare me. I had been careful in dispensing the ether, but I managed to put him briefly to sleep a couple of times.

Later I was told that Raul Magallanes had been driving a government car. His wife's only concern — as Enrique lay helpless in the hospital — was to have the vehicle dismantled and the doors with the official Air Force seal thrown into the sea. As an Air Force attorney, Magallanes could have requested a helicopter to pick up Enrique and take him to a hospital in Santiago. It was devastating to finally realize what their manipulations amounted to. My suspicions were correct. I wondered how much Magallanes' wife had paid the nurse who made the first call discouraging me from driving to San Antonio. Had she also arranged for the doctors to disappear into thin air? Did she try to stop me seeing Enrique alive because she feared the truth he would reveal to me?

When we reached the hospital in Santiago, the first anguished face I saw was Enrique's brother Fernando. He linked hands with Enrique, running with the attendants carrying Enrique to the operating room, where Dr. Abud waited. Fernando and Enrique never let go of each other until I lost sight of them.

That morning at the hospital forever remains a blur in my memory. Finally I saw Mother standing in front of me with an expression of such pity on her face that it jolted me to awareness. I heard my own voice rise in despair. "No, no, no!!"

Mother's words answered: "Dr. Abud says he can't understand how Enrique could live so long with such terrible injuries."

We had had only ten years together.

CHAPTER 14

I went to Enrique's funeral, breaking the tradition in Latin American countries that widows do not attend. Standing discreetly at a distance, I felt that I had to share his last rite of passage.

In the days after I returned home, friends began to visit, to present their condolences. Week after week these visits continued, and I couldn't fail to notice that a particular man was there almost every day. Such persistence must have a special reason, I thought, suggesting to him that we go out into the garden to talk. Then the true cause for his presence came out: did I intend to sue Magallanes? he asked.

"Is that why you come into my home every day? Has Raul told you to ask me?"

"Yes. He wants to know."

"Tell Raul that I'm not going to sue him because I want him to live all his life with the guilt of having killed his friend. Money can't pay for what he did."

Then I told the messenger how Enrique had described his drunken recklessness, and how in his last plea he had begged me never to reveal the circumstances of the accident lest it damage Raul's reputation.

"You see, while dying he still defended his friend! Tell Raul that I'm not as generous as Enrique. *I will talk!* So he can never forget what he did."

Coming home from work about two weeks after the funeral, I noticed that Rosa had developed a habit of sitting beside the front door, where she insisted on staying. She refused to eat. Tears streamed down her face until at last she cried herself to sleep. Often I sat with her beside the door, holding her on my lap, trying to feed her. At three, she seemed unable to explain her actions. I knew she could speak, because she did with Enrique, if seldom with anyone else. One day, in the midst of her sobbing, she said, "Papa is not coming home." How can you explain death to a child that small? How do you fill the gap left by a much loved one, except by offering tenderness? I did all that. I rocked her to sleep, but even in her sleep she continued to sob. Sometimes in the middle of the night she woke up screaming and beating the wall beside her crib with her fists.

I had put away a picture of Enrique that I usually had on my night table. Having tried everything to soothe Rosa's anguish, in desperation, and without a clear understanding of what I was doing, I returned the picture to its place. Then I called her into the room and watched her reaction. Her shoulders seemed to relax. She walked straight to the photograph, placed her hands around it, turned, and smiled at me. Later that day she said to me: "I'm grown up now."

She showed what she meant by acting differently. She stopped waiting by the door and started to eat regularly. She no longer cried herself to sleep. She talked to everybody, preferring particularly my male friends and relatives. She would sit by them, asking polite questions or telling them what she had been doing during the day. She often walked into my bedroom and hugged Enrique's photograph.

Ximena also changed, becoming my guardian. She wouldn't go to bed until I did. If friends came unexpectedly, knowing that we would be talking for hours, she fetched a blanket and curled up with her head on my lap. Ximena was nine years old. Transferring her from the American nuns' school to Santiago College, I selected a school where the emphasis was more on English and sports than on religion and financial status. At the convent, soon after Enrique's death, Ximena had asked for a pencil. The nun had answered: "When your mother pays the tuition fee, then you can have a pencil."

This was widowhood in a Latin American country, or is it the same everywhere?

Invitations anywhere were scarce. Somehow most of the family — with some noble exceptions — seemed to have sided with Mother over my insistence to keep my house instead of returning to my parents' home to await a new nuptial candidate. It might be difficult to find a man interested in a woman who held a job, jealously protected her independence, and had two daughters. But that's what I wanted.

Enrique had left nothing but his contract for a partnership with a friend and city councilman. The foreman of this business came to visit and offer his condolences. He was dressed in black, a true Spaniard, self-exiled from the Franco regime. A wide-brimmed Sevillian hat shadowed his handsome features. He handed me a huge bunch of white calla lilies. I mustn't worry about the business. He would come every week with the accounts and money. I asked him to explain to me what the business entailed.

"Don Enrique came every morning to settle the cost of the job with the workers. We empty the silted sand in the canals and sell it to a construction company."

"If my husband did it, I'll do it from now on."

"You'd have to be at the river every morning by seven!"

"I'll be there."

"You'll have to haggle over cost with the workers."

"I can do that."

"If you insist. But I must warn you that I can't assume the responsibility for your safety around the river if you aren't armed. Do you have a gun?"

"I'll get one!"

By asking around, I got a gun, amid much teasing about my stubbornness. From then on I carried this weapon in my purse, though I never came to need it. The workers seemed to like me, after overcoming their surprise at seeing me replace Enrique. The haggling wasn't always easy.

"Why do you ask for more every day?" I inquired. "Surely the canals are always just as deep in sand. And the work really doesn't look that hard."

Handing my coat and purse to the foreman, I jumped down into the drained canal and grabbed a shovel. I pushed it into the wet sand, but when I tried to lift it, I fell to my knees. The workers laughed with me. Reluctantly, the foreman laughed also and ordered the workers to help me to my feet and out of the canal.

One morning the foreman met me at the bus stop. He asked if I could help with the paperwork he must fill out applying for a small loan to buy a house. I said I would be glad to do it, except that at that point my life was in a crisis and I was unable to fulfill my promise. I still regret that I didn't suggest someone else who could offer him assistance.

After supervising the canal workers, I had to rush by bus to the other end of the city, to my work at the institute. The bus was the only means of transportation, until Miguel Labarca surfaced again in my life.

Having heard in Paris about Enrique's death, he returned to Santiago and immediately got in touch with me. I was less than thrilled, but sometimes he made my life easier, although more often than not his domineering personality irritated me. Yet his imagination, his boldness, and his eccentricities amused and fascinated me.

However, I was not the woman he expected. The weak, grieving widow he longed to protect did not exist. I rejected his eagerness to anticipate every wish of mine. He was too demanding of my time, not to mention the affection he craved.

At the institute, my salary had been increased when a young Frenchman representing "L'Alimentation Equilibrée" (Balanced Diet) needed a secretary fluent in French; I was it. Fernand had a face I disliked on sight. His carrot hair and small piercing blue eyes were set over teeth too large for his mouth. His smile was a frightening experience. Instead of amusement it suggested a streak of cruelty.

After we started to work together, he would stand next to me during dictation. I realized that he had never heard of deodorants, which was typical of Europeans at the time. Suddenly I was surrounded with an aroma that reminded me of school back in Brussels and cinemas in Paris. Fresh sweat on clean clothes can certainly be an aphrodisiac. Our vacations in the country had taught me to appreciate the pungent smell of horses' sweat. There wasn't a lot of difference in this situation. A tickling in my nose promptly spread to my most intimate and hungry senses. Perhaps he knew what he was doing to me, for he was soon as electrified as I was.

We started to date, but I couldn't go out publicly with him because of my mourning. Also the children deserved all the time I could give them. Translations were again coming my way, which I worked at after the girls were asleep.

Miguel's presence was becoming a burden. He drove me to the river each morning, waited for me and then took me to the institute. Most evenings he drove me home. I continually had to fight for my independence.

A while later, a friend of Enrique's ran into me when I was shopping downtown. He invited me to dinner and I accepted. After having worked all day for months without respite, except for a couple of hours occasionally with Fernand, I looked forward to a good dinner with Jorge in a restaurant where we might see mutual friends. I was still in mourning, but black can be very becoming combined with some imagination and jewelry. I dressed in my best, using perfume and makeup that I had neglected for almost a year. Explaining to Ximena and Rosa that I was going out with Uncle Jorge and would be back early, I asked Carmen to read them a story and tuck them in.

When Jorge picked me up, my high heels sang a lively tap on the sidewalk. After a dinner of oysters, lobster, and delicious white Santa Carolina wine, followed by a splendid dessert, I was feeling exceedingly happy. I laughed at Jorge's rather flat jokes and waved to mutual friends, who then stopped at our table and complimented me on my appearance. They said how they had missed me and extended instant invitations. Would Jorge be my escort from now on, they wanted to know? This last question put a damper on my mood. I liked Jorge, but not as a permanent escort. This was out of the question.

After dinner, Jorge suggested that we go to a nightclub. Looking down at my watch, I was halted as he quickly put his hand over the dial.

"It's still early. Just a liqueur and a cappuccino, and perhaps a dance, and we'll leave. The children are probably already asleep. Don't worry. We won't stay late."

Graciously, I gave in. The Benedictine was delicious. The cappuccino was excellent. We danced a perfect tango and a waltz. Catching a glimpse of a radiant woman in a mirror, I hardly recognized myself. Jorge was a wonderful companion, but his conversation was definitely dull. He was single, unattached, and wealthy enough not to have to work, except to watch his investments. He had never traveled outside Chile, nor did he want to. He was rather handsome, although his features seemed to blur after one left him. He had always been like that, invisible to memory.

Enrique had liked him, finding Jorge a good listener who rarely missed his amusing remarks. He laughed uproariously at his stories and clearly appreciated Enrique's wit. In his car on the way home, I kept up the conversation, telling him how much I appreciated a marvelous evening. Jorge was mostly silent. I thought he perhaps resented my insistence on going home.

Once there he walked me to the door, took the key out of my hand, and opened it. There were no lights inside the house. Following me into the entrance hall, he suddenly lifted me off my feet and carried me into the living room. It was then that I realized I was facing a different man. Telling him to let me down, pushing him away, I was overpowered by his strength but didn't dare raise my voice for fear of waking up the children. The maid's quarters were too far away. As though reading my thoughts, he put a hand over my mouth, laying me on the floor and with his free hand fumbled with my clothes. At this he was obviously an expert. One of his knees pushed my legs apart. Pinned down, I could do nothing. I heard a hoarse voice saying in my ear: "You want this. You need it. You have wanted me all night. Here, take it! Take it."

When it was over he collapsed on me with a deep moan. Pushing him aside, kicking him furiously, I hissed: "Get up! Go away! Never come near me again!"

As he got to his feet, straightening his clothes, he repeated his refrain of justification. "You wanted it, you needed it."

"You're crazy! Leave now or I'll call the police."

He laughed at the absurdity of my threat. A scandal was all I needed in my situation. At police headquarters a reporter would jot down the incident. I could see the headlines the next day: "ESCORT RAPES WIDOW."

My brief experience in journalism told me that the headlines could even be worse. I had no one to turn to except Hernán, who advised me to talk to his mother, my dearest Mary. But I decided to spare her. Fearing pregnancy, I nevertheless kept my own counsel. I waited, alone, but fortunately for me, a "safe" address was not needed.

Once again, I found refuge in work, refusing all invitations lest I bump into Jorge. The idea of seeing him again revolted me. Work distracted me from my humiliation, the outrage I had suffered at the hands of a man I thought a friend. My relationship with Fernand had also soured. I couldn't tell him about it, for our affair hadn't reached a level that would permit such a confidence. Instinctively I shied away from telling him that I had been raped. I would never know whether my thinking on this was correct. Does a man feel closer and protective toward a violated woman, or is he repelled?

Still Miguel was constantly afoot. His stalking, persecution, and constant surveillance would be considered sexual harassment by today's standards. In the late forties, however, and in a Latin American country, his behavior was seen as that of a man in love, who considered my widowhood his last chance to possess me. Most of my friends — those aware of the situation — considered it romantic. The fact that he was married never entered their minds. They saw no reason to condemn his behavior.

Increasingly exasperated and hopeless, I told him that our friendship would be ruined if he persisted in demanding more and more of me. One day I thought I had succeeded in eluding him, but he had parked close to the house and intercepted me for a pleading session. Putting my hand in my purse, I pulled out the gun I had never used, and pointed it at him screaming:

"Leave me alone! I hate you. You smother me. I don't want you around anymore. If you don't leave me alone I'll kill you and kill myself! I swear I'll do it! I'll kill you!"

I could see passersby looking at us. Miguel started to cry, mumbling incomprehensible excuses. Then he turned around and walked away.

Father's health was fast deteriorating. A few weeks after Enrique's death he had a second heart attack. He held my hand tightly, and when he could speak he whispered: "Poor darling, you are all alone and I may die any day. If only I could help you more."

Assuring him that I would be fine, that he would soon recover and we would see each other more often, I tried to comfort him. Then soon after this heart attack he had to have a cataract operation. A clumsy nurse jolted the gurney he was being carried on, and Father's newly operated eye hemorrhaged. As a result, he ended up with a prosthesis.

One Sunday morning, sitting in my living room, I saw Father walking toward my house. Going out to meet him, I asked if he would stay for lunch. The children would enjoy being with him. Yes, he said, so I sent the cook out to buy empanadas and fruit. He sat down in Enrique's armchair, with Rosa in her favorite place on his lap. Soon she was talking to him in the peculiar whisper she had used with her father. Ximena sat on the floor and explained to him what she was doing for homework. After lunch Father said he wanted to speak to me in private, so I told Carmen to take the children for a walk.

"Lillian, I must ask you for a very special favor. I don't have much time left, and I need you to protect me from your mother's constant nagging. Please, I want you to come and live with us. I know how highly you prize your independence, but now I need you and the children."

Immediately I moved in with my parents, soon learning what Father meant by constant nagging. It was a relentless, cruel prodding.

"Why are you going out? You can't see! The eye you have left is also bad, and your hearing is deteriorating. Just sit down and stop this foolishness about walking."

"Rosa is my little seeing-eye dog," he answered. "She tells me if I'm taking a risk."

"What does she know about risks. She is only four years old and you may be putting her life in danger. Just sit here in the sun. Don't go out."

Probably she meant well, but the way she did it was awkward and insensitive. After agonizing about a second cataract operation and risking total blindness, Father's new doctor — who used to play with us in the square near our grandparents' home and was now an eye surgeon trained in Germany — insisted that he could save Father's diminished eyesight. He had heard about Father's predicament and was eager to offer his help, obeying the traditional close-knit sentiment of a former neighbor in the small society that Santiago still was at the time.

Trusting in Dr. Amenabar, Father entered the hospital again. During his convalescence he told me how much he missed Rosa, how tactful she was in warning him about obstacles during their walks. She would say: "Now, hold my hand tightly, we're getting near the curb. I'm very little and I have trouble stepping down so let's wait for this car to pass. Be careful. Now, let's go!"

When I took the girls to see him in the hospital, I had to cut the visit short because he became too emotional. Mother scolded me for doing it.

Dr. Amenabar said that the bandages would come off Father's eye in a couple of days, and he wanted us all to be there. We had to be present at the unveiling. He was so sure of his success that he wanted us all to enjoy it with him. On the appointed day we stood facing Father's bed as the nurse unwrapped the bandage.

Dr. Amenabar stood holding Father's hand. Father opened his eye, squinted at the light coming from the window, looked around the room, and after a brief hesitation said: "Rosa, Luz, Eugene, Betty, Lillian — I can see you all clearly!"

He stopped talking. His chin quivered uncontrollably. He lifted Dr. Amenabar's hand and kissed it. Then he laughed softly and sighed: "Thank you."

"Don Arturo, you must rest now. A nap will do you a world of good. Nurse, pull down the blinds. Let's all step outside."

We assembled in a small waiting room, where Dr. Amenabar told us that after Father's nap we could take turns to visit with him briefly.

Mother felt tired, so Eugene offered to take her home. Betty, Luz, and I decided to stay.

Suddenly the nurse came running out of Father's room and told Dr. Amenabar that he was having a heart attack. This time he didn't recover. He died of joy. He could see again. He could resume his normal, independent life. But his heart couldn't stand the shock of such a glorious realization. By the time we entered his room, he was gone. His lovely face was serene. He had prepared himself for a healing nap. He just hadn't known how long it would last.

Thus within a short time, the two men I had loved most were gone. Enrique had often disappointed me, and sometimes I thought I didn't need him. Yet when his lifestyle seemed foreign to me, I had offered him alternatives to what he thought he needed, and he accepted them. I loved him for this. However, our time of joy was too brief, his death too cruel and made even more painful by his friend's betrayal. We had no time for the new love born of unexpected, surprising feelings. I had worshiped beauty, power, and strength. I learned of tenderness with him, as a seed blooming into a love more sure and deep. I had only a glimpse of it before it faded.

And Father. During my life he had led me into worlds of visionary horizons, made true by his intelligence and talent. I had witnessed his brave deeds. He had taught me kindness, loyalty, and his unending aspirations for his country's progress. But he was never able to teach me to forgive, as he did. His heart was limpid, but when I saw him hurt I took upon myself the darkness he must have felt. In his last sorrow he had turned to me for comfort. I was proud that he did, proud that he leaned on me, proud that he confided in me. And now he too was gone. I grieved in silence and took care of my own.

CHAPTER 15

After Father's death my friend Picha and her mother suggested I drop by their house any time. Picha is an extraordinary human being. For various reasons she attended only one year of elementary school, where she learned to read and write. She never learned arithmetic. Did she miss it? I asked her once and she replied: "What do I need it for? I have nothing to add, nothing to subtract. I don't like to divide and hope I don't multiply. Enough with one like me in this world."

With these scant academic resources, she later taught herself English and Greek, the latter to travel with her husband to Greece.

As a child she would hang around her Uncle Manuel Eduardo Hübner, a diplomat and writer, who became her teacher. Their schoolrooms were restaurants and pubs, where Picha listened to his heated debates with politicians, other diplomats, and academics. She sat quietly, absorbing knowledge beyond her years, forging her own opinions while munching on a sandwich and washing it down with good Chilean wine. When this "child in the temple" finally opened her mouth to express her ideas, the pillars of society shook so dangerously that she chose to look for a different audience, settling on selected intellectual and slightly bohemian friends.

Her Uncle Manuel Eduardo wrote *Mexico on the Way,* published in 1936, which became the bible of young Mexican revolutionaries. President Cardenas invited him and his wife, Vicha, to Mexico to celebrate the publication of his book. They were invited to several cities, and

Vicha — a master at evoking vivid memories — told how in one city they slowly rode in an open car along a wide avenue flanked by campesinos in their white clothes and large sombreros. Not a voice was heard. No mariachi music. The silence was broken only by the thundering rumble of hundreds of rifle butts pounding the ground.

When the mayor of Guadalajara greeted them, he offered a long package to Manuel Eduardo. Thinking that by its size and shape it must be a bouquet of flowers, he signaled Vicha to accept the gift. The weight of it almost pulled her to her knees. Her phosphorescent blue eyes asked for an explanation.

"It's a rifle," the mayor explained.

"Why?" Manuel Eduardo inquired, smiling.

"You are now a representative in the Chilean Congress. You'll need it."

That was Mexico in 1937.

Picha was for me what Chileans call "paño de lágrimas," a cloth for tears. Since our home was close to hers, I walked over practically every evening after my children were asleep. If Picha hadn't arrived home, I talked with her mother, Inéz, a tireless and lively conversationalist. We shared a love for Valparaíso, where she had spent her married life until her husband had a nervous breakdown and was institutionalized.

Left with two children and an empty bank account, she survived by selling all her fine things. She described them to me, one by one. She could not forget her treasures. Objects of beauty have the power of remaining in our memories forever.

Even if she'd learned shorthand and typing, nobody would have hired her because in those days there was no place in business for a lady. Once her son had graduated from high school he could fend for himself. Picha, her younger daughter, didn't enjoy the privilege of an education. But she was lucky to have an exceptional tutor in Uncle Manuel Eduardo. Much later I was also to count on his friendship and tutoring.

Inéz was irrepressible in her curiosity. She wanted to know about my own life. She had no qualms about making fun of my problems with Miguel Labarca. Inéz liked him. She appreciated his wild ideas, his feverish imagination, and his consuming love for me. So he often joined us when we waited for Picha.

Miguel was a close friend of Salvador Allende and had started working for him during his first campaign for the presidency in 1951. Allende was a physician who had discovered that he could do more for the people by becoming a politician. He promptly won a seat in Congress, and his career as a socialist was launched. Campaigning for Allende, Miguel invited me to join him when he addressed groups of workers.

Miguel was a fiery orator. He was able to arouse the enthusiasms of his audience, to spark their interest. Those modest men and women were used to listening meekly, never asking questions. Miguel encouraged the people to express their feelings and ideas, thus giving him instant feedback on his own performance. He was no longer the backstage operator I had known as an assistant to Santiago's mayor years earlier. He had matured. He was boss. He was stimulating and challenging. I was proud of him, but that wasn't what he wanted. He demanded love and devotion that I could not give. I stopped attending the rallies. He talked to Salvador Allende about my withdrawal.

One evening at Picha's, Miguel complained that I was failing on my job at party headquarters, where I did the small tasks that today's political groupies do. Inéz understood what was going on and sided with me, telling Miguel that I mustn't return if I did not feel comfortable. He left in a huff and disappeared for a couple of days. Then one afternoon, when I was sitting with Mother and the girls in the living room, the maid announced that Miguel Labarca wanted to speak with Mother. She threw me an inquisitive glance, and I shrugged my shoulders, totally ignorant of Miguel's intentions. He walked in, bowing slightly to both of us. He wasn't tall, and bowing made him lose still more in stature. He dressed poorly and often forgot to shave. Looking at him through Mother's eyes, I judged him a pitiful mess. The fiery orator had disappeared. The imaginative and creative man who so often entranced me had vanished.

I told Ximena to take Rosa into the garden and wait until Miguel was gone. I was right. The dialogue between Mother and Miguel would have thoroughly confused them.

"Doña Rosa, I'm here because I want to avoid any misunderstanding. I have loved Lillian since I first saw her in Ecuador as a teenager. Now she is free, and I want to marry her. I would like to have your permission."

Mother didn't show any emotion and in a calm voice answered: "Miguel, it's very nice of you to ask, but I understand that you are married."

"That doesn't matter at all. It can be arranged."

"How, Miguel? There is no divorce in Chile."

"Marriages can be annulled. We have already talked about this with Lillian."

Mother turned to me, and I rushed to explain: "His wife's name is also Lillian."

"How interesting. Tell me, Miguel, how would you get an annulment? It's a long and costly process. Can you afford it?"

"Don't worry, Doña Rosa. I have never failed to get what I want."

Sensing that Mother's patience was nearly spent, I could see an ugly exchange coming up if the conversation continued. I intervened: "Miguel, you have talked about divorce or annulment with your wife, but you have never mentioned marriage to me. It's out of the question. I would appreciate it if you leave now."

"Are you dismissing me?"

"Think what you will. Before coming to talk with Mother you should have asked me, and I would have told you not to waste your time. Please leave."

He walked out, but I knew he wouldn't give up. I stopped visiting Picha and her mother. Miguel had gotten into the habit of dropping by too often.

Instead I visited Hernán and Mary, his mother. I needed to fill the nights with company. Since Enrique's death I was unable to sleep until past midnight. Their company was soothing. Our friendship had reached that wonderful stage when it's not necessary to sustain a constant conversation. We could just sit reading, commenting occasionally. Perhaps a friend of theirs would drop by. Hernán usually walked me home, since it wasn't safe to wander about alone at night. I might be taken for a prostitute, he teased.

Every Friday, Mother had an open invitation to dinner for the family. The grown-ups would sit at the table in the dining room. The children had tables set in the living room or out on the terrace in spring and summer. One unforgettable Friday, Mother asked Carmen to place an antique high-backed, carved Spanish armchair at the head of the table. The old mahogany and Carrara marble buffet, with a silver tea set on one side and a Rosenthal parrot on the other, was the backdrop. Virgin Mary's visit to her cousin Elsbeth — a beautiful painting attributed to Andrea del Sarto, bought in Italy and registered at the Roman art archives — presided over the scene. Mother's black high-necked dress added a Victorian touch.

Besides Betty and myself there was Eugene, his wife, Luz, and their eldest children, María Eugenia and Arturo. I suspected that Mother was setting the stage for a play. What the subject would be, I had no idea. A fleeting memory of the scene at the Hotel Regina in Paris struck me for a second. After Carmen served the main course, Mother turned to me very slowly, shoulders straight, her neck firmly rooted inside the scarf of her black dress. Her dark piercing eyes skewered me. Her lips moved, and I heard these words:

"Lillian, I want you to leave the country."

Her frozen face and her unyielding, judgmental attitude gave her words the full meaning of a sentence without recourse or appeal. Quickly I took in the family's expressions. Eugene's eyes bulged. Luz' head was down and she covered her mouth with her napkin. María Eugenia's chin quivered distressingly, her eyes moist. This was the child I had cared for when she was little and sick. Betty looked inscrutable, Arturo dumbfounded. Suddenly I heard myself say, sealing my fate irretrievably: "If I leave, I will never come back."

Had Mother expected tears, recriminations, appeals, or promises to amend my ways? I never knew specifically what prompted her decision. Should I have asked? Did she object to my participation in Allende's campaign? To Miguel's constant presence around me? Surely my last conversation with him, in her presence, should have been enough to indicate that I wanted nothing to do with him.

That night I couldn't sleep. Where would I start? Although I earned sufficient income at the institute, I hadn't had a chance to save because I also helped with expenses at Mother's home. Father's inheritance was modest. I had convinced Betty and Eugene that we give it all to Mother so she wouldn't have to give up any of the comforts she was used to, like a live-in maid and a cook. When we visited Father's executor he took me aside and said: "This smacks as being your idea. You must be crazy."

When all documents were signed and sealed, Mother decided to give everything to Eugene in exchange for a monthly pension allowing her to keep her lifestyle intact.

All of this meant that I had no money for an airplane ticket to the United States. Betty snapped out of her initial shock and mobilized all her resources to find the least expensive transportation: a cargo ship with limited accommodations for passengers. I signed up for passage on a nitrate ship. It was a Swiss ship with an Italian crew. A retired nurse and

myself were to be the only passengers. I was asked to sign papers re-
nouncing any claims against the shipping company, because the cargo
was highly explosive. When I told Mother what I'd arranged, she asked
me to give her all my jewels: my gold watch, my engagement ring, a
pearl necklace, and a small solitaire she had given me herself. I never saw
them again.

Betty was helpful. Besides arranging the transportation, she got my
passport and made an appointment for me with the American consul.
My Chilean passport revealed that I was born in California. The consul
said I should have an American passport, then she asked: "Did you vote
in the last election?"

"Of course. I actively campaigned for the women's vote."

"Sorry, you lost your citizenship!"

Instead I was given a permanent visa and advised that if I would be
job hunting in the United States I should wear brighter clothes! I was
still in mourning, and this was a problem I had not considered. But
I had my ticket, my passport, and a permanent visa, courtesy of the
American consul, who could afford such generosity in 1952. I was ready
to leave, but even with the few pesos I had, I was unable to buy dollars.
The exchange offices were not selling them. Again Betty came to the
rescue, discreetly passing word around about the dollar situation.

On my last evening, before a short flight to Antofagasta, where I'd
board the ship, friends started to show up. Each had in an envelope a
small number of dollars. Tens, twenties, fives . . . it added up to a final
count of $150. Word had also gotten about that I needed clothes. Three
years of strict mourning made my wardrobe useless, so when I packed
there were many sizes and colors filling my suitcases. One carried all
the books I'd translated, hoping they would help me find a job. Manuel
Seoane, my mentor in journalism, arrived late with a small white envelope in his pocket. He pulled me aside: "Why the United States? Why
don't you go to Europe? America may become a nuclear target. Come
back if you sense danger. I will also warn you. You must send me your
address when you settle down."

Ten years later, when the Cuban missile crisis brought terror to
America, his prediction almost came true. Manuel's brilliant mind could
project into the future. His *Six Dimensions of the World Revolution,* published in 1960, is still relevant today. Among his predictions was the fall
of the Soviet Union and end of Communism.

I was ready to leave, with minimum financial backing and a secondhand trousseau. I would just be another poor immigrant, hoping for a job and a secure future. The children were to stay with Mother until I found a job. Hugging Ximena and Rosa, I explained that I was going away for a short while and would send for them very soon. We would live in the United States. I'd be in touch constantly, telling them what I was doing.

As I took my seat on the plane, I felt overwhelmed by the enormity of what I was doing. Suddenly a flood of tears rolled down my cheeks, my neck, my dress, as I thought how long it would be until I saw my beautiful girls again. What was I doing? Couldn't I have found an alternative to Mother's edict? Had my pride locked me into accepting it submissively, like a stupid lamb? What kind of destructive pride ruled me that I had sealed my fate by stating that I would never return?

A woman seated next to me handed me her handkerchief. "Come now, you are going to make yourself sick. Let me hold you. Calm down," she cooed.

She slipped her arm around my shoulders and started to rock me like a baby. Sobs and hiccups wrenched my chest painfully. Somebody handed her a glass of water, and she forced me to drink. She made me lie down and covered me with her shawl. She made me rest my head on her lap. Incredibly, I dozed off. When I woke up we were already at the Antofagasta airport, and the woman had disappeared. In my distress I hadn't even looked at her face or asked her name. This wouldn't be the first time in my life that the tenderness of strangers would help me back from despair.

I stepped down onto the tarmac, where a car waited from the hotel where Betty had made reservations for me under an assumed name, in case Miguel discovered my flight. It took me through the most desolate landscape I had ever imagined, which certainly matched my mood. Not a cactus in sight, not a stone, not a bird in almost an hour's drive through the desert.

The hotel, located in the middle of the town's single street, had ramshackle buildings on one side and docks and warehouses on the other. It offered little to improve my first impression of the area. At the hotel's desk I inquired when the ship was scheduled to leave. I was told that a stevedores' strike had indefinitely postponed its departure. I went to my room and cried myself to sleep. When I woke in the middle of the night, I could hardly open my eyes. I grabbed a rough towel from the night table, found my way to the bathroom, wet the towel with cold water, and placed it on my eyes in the hope of reducing the swelling. But wakefulness brought back my pain, and I cried again.

The next morning the desk clerk asked if I wanted to meet the other passenger on the ship. No, I said excusing myself. But she soon knocked on my door. "There isn't much in this God-forsaken place," she said, "but we can go to the movies and eat at a seafood restaurant. You might have seen the movie they are showing. I haven't. And if the restaurant doesn't have good seafood, we'll make a scene!"

As I debated what to answer, she added: "The movie might not be good for those swollen eyes. Let's just go to the restaurant. The shipping company foots the bill for lodgings and food, as long as the strike lasts. We pay for the movies, but it's just a couple of pesos. Let's go."

I hadn't eaten for more than twenty-four hours and thought I wasn't hungry. But the smell of cooking when we opened the restaurant's door started my digestive juices flowing. I devoured everything they put in front of me. Later, over grapes and coffee, my companion and I talked.

"Why are you going to the United States?" she asked.

"I must find a job."

"Why were you crying? Man trouble?"

"No, I left my two little girls behind. As soon as I find a job, I'll send for them."

My eyes started to smart again, thinking of them, and I dried my fresh tears with a paper napkin.

"I'm a nurse, and I've worked and saved for this trip for years. I'll go to New York and buy all kinds of cheap stuff for resale in Santiago. That's all I want to do. What kind of a job are you looking for?"

"Anything that will allow me to send for the children."

"Do you have pictures? Cute! The little one is cute. The other one is gorgeous. You must take good care of her. I mean, keep an eye on her and a tight rein. What can you do as work?"

"Write, translate . . ."

"High-brow stuff. Good luck."

The last two words rang ominously. She seemed to be saying that she wished me luck because I would sorely need it in my line of skills. I would find out later that the easy money was in far more modest occupations than what I wanted to perform. After satisfying our appetite, we decided to go to the movies. It was *For Whom the Bell Tolls,* which I had seen before. Once more I cried. My companion seemed upset by my easy fluidity: "Are you always such a constant crier? You will ruin your eyes," she said.

Two days later we left Antofagasta. I sighed with relief. Miguel hadn't caught up with me. His incredible talent for tracking me down had failed him, and I was free to start a new life. I quickly tired of my companion's monotonous and mercenary conversation. I told the captain about my problem and asked him to put me to work. If I must continue to listen to this woman, I told him, I'll throw her overboard! He laughed and assigned an officer to teach me how to paint the railings on the ship. He was very thorough in his instructions and apparently felt that I would learn faster if he took my hand to direct the brushing movement needed for a good job. His concern was rather sweet.

After briefly touching on a couple of Peruvian ports without going ashore, we reached Panama. I had been through the canal before, but didn't realize how important it was, nor understand what it meant to the country, not only economically but emotionally, to the deepest fibers of its soul. The young Panamanian who opened my eyes and branded the story in my mind was a tall mulatto, boss of the team that pulled the ship through the locks. The minute his green eyes met mine, and his deep voice reached me, we bonded.

"Do you want to know how all this works?" he asked.

"If you don't mind. I'm sure that you will find me very ignorant."

"That's good. I can tell you anything and you'll believe it," he laughed. His snow-white teeth sparkled in the sun. He gave me a step-by-step explanation in very technical terms about how the locks moved, how the flow of the water was kept in exact proportions, the levels it reached while slowly carrying the ship through the width of the isthmus. He excused himself to shout orders to his men. He returned and was silent for a while. I looked at the lush vegetation on both sides of the canal. The jungle was teeming with animals and birds, yet we couldn't hear them at all, only the sluicing sound of the keel cutting through the water. We passed the locks of Miraflores and headed for Pedro Miguel. My unexpected instructor broke his silence and inquired:

"Do you want to know how I feel about all this?"

"I certainly do. Proud, I'm sure."

"I would feel proud if it were ours. But it isn't. It's a tumor in our hearts. Granted it's a prodigious work of engineering, but it tears into the flesh and bones of our nation. All the riches of the world sail through this canal, but our children still go naked, their bellies swollen by parasites and malnutrition. Proud of what? Filling with gold the pockets of faceless businessmen while our own people live in squalor?"

"I can understand how you feel."

"Can you really understand?" His green eyes scrutinized mine.

"Yes, I think I can. You are very eloquent."

"Can you also see that we are doomed? Nothing will ever change, because the system has the approval of the Americans, and that's something we can't fight."

He was mistaken. In 1978 President Carter reached an agreement for the return of the canal to the Panamanian nation in 1999. A second document granted the United States the right to defend the canal if it were necessary. I covered the signing ceremony at the Organization of American States as a correspondent for the *Voice of America*.

My new friend wanted to know where I would be in the United States and would I allow him to write to me. Where?

"At the Chilean Embassy in Washington, D.C.," I told him.

Mother had sent me a letter through the Chilean Consul in Panama saying that I must stop at the embassy in Washington, because the ambassador was an old friend and former colleague of Father's. She had written to him announcing that I was on my way and would soon present my respects.

CHAPTER 16

Traveling by Greyhound bus from Wilmington, North Carolina, I made my way to Washington, D.C. The YWCA on 17th Street provided me with reasonable lodgings, and I was fully aware that I must carefully budget my $150. The Chilean ambassador was a friend of Father's so the next day I called to make an appointment.

Reviewing the dresses Rebeca and Nana had given me, I wore the one that fitted me best to go shopping for something more suitable. I had a brief conference with the reception clerk and asked where I could find inexpensive clothes. She directed me to Lehrner's on Connecticut Avenue, just a few blocks away. There I found what I needed for my meeting with the ambassador.

Before going to the embassy the next day I decided to get acquainted with the city. Map in hand, I found the White House, marveling at its almost humble beauty. I passed the Executive Office Building and proceeded to the Corcoran Gallery, where I was awed by the majestic proportions of the central hall. Workers were preparing an exhibit, and I decided to stay out of their way, promising myself to return for a look at art that, as usual, attracted me like a magnet. From the Ellipse, I stared at the Washington Monument. Later I sat on a bench contemplating the Capitol's dome. It struck me that the dome and the obelisk had a definite sexual symbolism.

Exhausted and hungry, I returned to the YWCA for lunch at the cafeteria, then took a shower and slipped into my new dress. A look in the mirror gave me the self-assurance I needed. After years of mourning for

Enrique and Father, I was finally dressed in a pastel print that enhanced the healthy suntan acquired on the ship.

A couple of questions helped me locate the embassy and I decided to walk. Big mistake! I had been directed to the Chancery on Massachusetts Avenue. The residence was on the same avenue but blocks away. I took a cab. When I rang the bell at the residence and entered the hall, I felt I was back in Chile. The doorman was typically Chilean, of medium height with black straight hair growing practically from his eyebrows and having a golden complexion. I said the ambassador expected me and gave my name. He pointed to a small salon, asking me to wait there. But I didn't have a chance to follow his suggestion.

On the first landing of the central staircase, his white hair lit by the sun streaming through a tall window, stood the ambassador in his navy silk robe. He greeted me in a loud voice:

"Lillian Lorca de Tagle! I received your mother's letter. What brings you here? If you are planning to get a job, don't expect me to help you. I'm tired of all the women who come to Washington and then complain that they don't have maids, cooks, and butlers. Have some fun and go back!"

As he talked I had been climbing the steps until I stood with him on the landing. He didn't look so impressive at close range. Besides I realized that he wasn't really angry. He was putting on an act. A twitching of his lips gave him away. I took his hand, shook it lightly, smiled, and said, "Why don't we sit somewhere and talk for a minute."

He laughed: "You really have some cheek."

"I hope so. It hasn't been easy. I need it."

"It might get worse."

"I'll survive. I know it."

When I told him that I had two girls, twelve and six, he jumped out of his seat. In a booming voice he said, "Go back to Chile. You don't know what you are getting into. If you have any problems, I wouldn't even know how to help you. Whoever encouraged you to come?"

"I'll try never to bother you with problems. I'll get ahead by myself. I can't give up at this stage of the game."

"All right. But don't say I didn't warn you. Let me introduce you to my deputy chief. If I'm not mistaken you are second or third removed cousins on your father's side. Mario, meet Lillian."

As we walked down the steps, Mario said, "Don't take him too seriously. Tell me what you can do. What's your working experience?"

I told him that I had done many book translations from different languages and some journalism.

"Meet me at the Chancery tomorrow and I'll introduce you to our press secretary. He might have some ideas. And if you are not busy this evening, I'd like you to have dinner with us. You must meet my wife and children."

Next morning I met Carlos Reyes Corona, press secretary at the embassy. He was of medium height, with blond hair and dark eyes. He was also so nervous that one felt impelled to hold him down. I would discover later the reason for it and tried to help him overcome it. As we talked about my work in Chile at *Ercilla,* ZigZag, and the institute, he asked about my immediate plans. "I must go to New York," I told him. I had a letter to a Chilean editor at *Vision* magazine, a sort of Spanish *Time.* I also mentioned Carlos Dávila, the president of the 100-Day Socialist Republic in Chile in 1931. The contact was old. Would he remember the teenager he had met twenty years ago when our family was on its way to Ecuador? Anyhow, Carlos Reyes seemed impressed.

"If I hear of anything interesting while you are in New York, I'll call you, send a message," he promised.

A trusty Greyhound bus carried me swiftly to New York. For the first time I felt the thrill of anticipation that grabs me every time I approach this unique city. Two of my cousins, Eliana and Esther, were waiting for me at a women's hotel on 6th and 44th. It was almost as modest as the YWCA, but it was clean and inexpensive, if crowded and noisy.

I made appointments for the next day. My cousins took me that evening to Coney Island. It was a crazy, wild evening. We couldn't stop laughing. We went twice on the roller coaster, twice on the ferris wheel. It was evening dusk, and the profile of the skyline was dazzling. The last light of the sun covered the horizon in all shades of red, as the skyscrapers turned on their nightly displays. I needed this taste of childhood. Boarding schools and playing "Heloise at the Plaza" in Paris, Wiesbaden, and Nice never gave me a chance to enjoy games and fun fairs.

The next morning I had my appointment with the man at *Vision* magazine. He greeted me with typical Chilean effusiveness, kissed me on both cheeks, and put his arm around my shoulders while leading me into his office. When we sat down he said, "You must return immediately to Washington. Carlos called. You may have a job at the *Americas* magazine. The director is supposed to interview you early tomorrow."

At this I dashed back to pack suitcases and rushed to the Greyhound terminal, and that night I slept again at the YWCA. I called Carlos, and he gave me directions to the Pan American Union and instructions to meet Kathleen Walker, director of *Americas* magazine.

Five days later I was signing forms for a five-year contract, at an amazing salary as assistant editor of the Spanish version of *Americas* magazine of the Organization of American States.

The offices were on the second floor above a garage. It wasn't plush, but the location, within the grounds of the Pan American Union, and close to the residence of the Secretary General of the OAS, gave the address prestige. I would soon learn about the need for a good address.

Americas magazine was published in three languages: English, Spanish, and Portuguese. Kathleen Walker and her assistant were responsible for the English edition. The Portuguese had three writers and the Spanish two: Alberto and myself.

The most interesting personality on the staff of the magazine was a Venezuelan exile, Raul Nass. He turned out to be a treasure of knowledge of Latin American art, history, and literature. He recommended *Mr. President* by Guatemalan writer Miguel Angel Asturias. My translator's spirit was jolted. I worked on a chapter and sent it to an editor in New York. The answer came soon: "It's not commercial. Sorry." I've always wondered if he realized what he had done when a couple of years later Asturias was awarded the Nobel Prize in literature.

To talk with Raul was like leafing through an encyclopedia, although he was never pedantic or overpowering. After a change in government in Venezuela, he had moved into the embassy of his country in a high position.

Working at *Americas* magazine I remembered Sergio Matta's advice: "If you have to work, make yourself indispensable." Also I wanted to show my appreciation to Carlos and Mario, who had helped me find such a wonderful job, one which would allow me to bring my girls to the United States.

Mario and his wife invited me often to their home, and Carlos made it a point to check in regularly with me to be sure that I was happy. When he invited me to dinner, his extreme nervousness made me uncomfortable. I asked him one evening if he would tell me what bothered him. He said that every evening he was supposed to send a report to Chile about the latest political developments in Washington. This was a hard assignment.

It was election time. General Eisenhower and Richard Nixon were running for the Republicans; Adlai Stevenson and Estes Kefauver for the Democrats. Senator Joseph McCarthy's hearings were beginning. The Korean War was still on, and Eisenhower was promising that he would end it if elected. The Rosenbergs were on trial. Carlos must keep tabs on all this and report daily about developments. I asked if I could help him. We started then a collaboration that fascinated me. He often took me to the National Press Club to watch the hearings on television. He introduced me to well-known American journalists. Carlos would ask me to write about our observations, and he picked up my reports at my office. In short, I became his ghostwriter. The experience was invaluable to me. Carlos taught me to change my style. No editorializing: only facts, facts, facts. When his daily report was on its way, Carlos relaxed and we would talk over coffee. He was a delightful raconteur. Among many of his funny or piquant stories I remember one in particular. I had met a young Chilean diplomat who struck me as lacking in essential social graces. I asked Carlos about him: "You are right. He is a rather peculiar character, and he isn't very well mannered. But he is indispensable at the Embassy. He has a memory short of miraculous. When we attend a conference, we don't need to take any bulky reference books. There is nothing in law, finances, or history that he hasn't memorized and keeps at the tip of his tongue when necessary. He's amazing."

A while later Carlos said this young man had told him that he was a virgin. He was worried because he planned to get married. I had no particular reason to say what I did then. It was rather intended as a joke: "If he loses his virginity, he will lose his memory," I said.

And that's exactly what happened. From then on Carlos called me a witch.

If I had been a real witch I might have anticipated what happened a few months after my arrival in Washington. One morning I arrived at my office and found Miguel Labarca sitting at my desk.

I wanted to scream, run away, gouge his eyes out. My girls were supposed to arrive shortly. I didn't want him around. Neither did I want them to find me a nervous wreck.

His presence in Washington made me fear he would again act as a lunatic. Declining invitations, concentrating on my work, I stopped my collaboration with Carlos. Miguel's presence in Washington terrified me. I had to find a way to make him return to Santiago. He must leave, and the sooner the better, I told him. He promised he would return to Chile within a couple of days. He only had an important meeting with a businessman interested in making investments in Chile. He asked if I would act as his interpreter. As long as it would hasten his departure, I agreed.

The meeting started on amicable terms. But after a few minutes the atmosphere changed as Miguel told me to tell the man that he was a bastard, a thief, and an exploiter of small nations. Turning to the businessman I translated his words as: "Mr. Labarca says that you don't seem to understand Chile's situation. The people are now determined . . ."

The businessman interrupted: "I know a little Spanish and you are not translating accurately. You are softening Mr. Labarca's expressions. Tell him that I admire his patriotism, but it's an argument that has no value in business."

I stood up and took my leave as politely as I could. I had never felt so embarrassed. In the street I hailed a cab and went to my office. Miguel called me in the evening to apologize. I answered that all I wanted to hear from him was that he was leaving within hours.

The children's arrival was imminent. My cousin Nana was coming from New York to meet them with me at the airport. She and I had been shopping for everything that the girls might find attractive. Clothes for twelve-year-old Ximena, games and toys for six-year-old Rosa. I was delighted to have Nana with me. She was outraged when I told her that Miguel was in Washington. I finally had someone to talk with about it and discharge my anger. The wait for the children was excruciating. Mother had made a last effort to keep them in Chile, and I couldn't be sure that she had given up until the moment I saw them at the airport. My fears were unfounded. Mother had given up, and the children arrived on schedule.

I was renting a charming apartment on upper 16th Street belonging to two archeologists — Clifford Evans and Betty Meggers — on a Smithsonian assignment in Brazil. We spent a week with Nana taking the children around. It was fall, and Rock Creek Park was glowing in a magnificent palette of colors.

There was a parochial school in the neighborhood, and I registered the girls there. The nuns had no objection to them starting in midsemester. They tested Ximena's English and were glad that she needed little tutoring. Rosa would have to start from scratch. Nana returned to New York, and I resumed work at the magazine. The girls would have to fend for themselves and start adjusting to new circumstances, a process that was at times more painful than I had ever expected.

One afternoon we arrived at the apartment to find a mountain of gifts, flowers, and candy piled up by the door. The girls were delighted, opening boxes and gorging on candy. I was devastated. There could be only one explanation: Miguel hadn't left as promised. He would soon show up.

The next day was a Saturday, and he called to say that he had rented a car and would pick us up for a ride to the beach. I refused and took the girls to a park nearby. Next day, Sunday, he tried again to take us out. He arrived at the apartment with a picnic basket. I said we had plans and couldn't go with him. Suddenly Ximena stood in front of him, pale, with her hands clenched: "Can't you understand? We don't want you around. Leave us alone. Go away!"

He did. He flew back to Chile. Except for a couple of whining letters, I never heard from him again. The grapevine told me that he had returned to France, only traveling to Chile to campaign for Salvador Allende each time he ran for the presidency. When Allende was finally successful in 1970, he appointed Miguel Under-Secretary of Mining. He presided over the nationalization of mines and had to struggle with discontented workers whose demands were outrageous. Typically, one day Miguel slammed the door to his office, ordered his secretary to tell anyone who asked for him to go jump in the lake, and returned to France, where he died years later.

Hernán called me unexpectedly shortly before the girls arrived. He was in New York and wanted to see me. We decided to meet over the weekend. He gave me the name of his hotel, and Friday evening I took the train that delivered me to Penn Station and his arms.

We walked down Fifth Avenue, turned onto 57th Street and then Lexington Avenue, and had dinner at a small restaurant.

It was 1952, and it was no problem at the time to get tickets for a Broadway show — nowadays one has to wait six months after a considerable investment for a couple of seats. I don't remember what we saw, but I'm sure it wasn't the greatest, since it didn't stay in my memory. By the end of the show we were both exhausted and walked to the hotel, where Hernán had made reservations for me.

He took me to my room, and in spite of our fatigue we found out that we still had much to talk about. The room was very small, and we sat on the bed. It wasn't long before I saw his eyes soften into a significant stare. His hands took mine and he silently pulled me closer. His lips on mine were soft and warm and tasted like sweet milk. He didn't smoke. His hands started to move over my body, tentatively caressing my breasts, my waist, and my thighs. He lay me down next to him . . . and then the bed collapsed!

"I think I get the message from high above," he said, laughing. "This is not meant to happen."

"You are right. We really don't need it," I replied, also laughing. "Our relationship is rich enough without it. I love you."

"I don't have to tell you, but I love you too," he asserted.

Back to the magazine, now sure there would be no more distractions, I concentrated on excelling at my work. During our daily meetings I submitted ideas that Kathleen Walker, our director, usually approved. *Americas* was supposed to please and inform three different audiences. English was addressed at the American readers and therefore must have features on the Latin American countries: their personalities, culture, and customs. Spanish and Portuguese readers wanted to know mainly about the United States. It was imperative that we reach an equilibrium, a balance where all three of our magazine's versions would satisfy quite different audiences.

I argued that having so recently arrived in the United States I would like to reflect in my writing what most attracted my attention as typical in the country. I focused first on New York, the city of superlatives. But I wanted to show its creative spirit in industries and entertainment. So I wrote about José Quintero, the Latin American director of the Theatre in the Round. His interpretations of O'Neill's and García Lorca's plays were refreshingly new. New York's world of fashion was successfully competing with Paris and Rome. I must report on this industry that was growing by leaps and bounds. Few countries in the world have as large a toy industry as America. Christmas was around the corner, and I made arrangements for several interviews with manufacturers. One of them gave me the secret of his success.

"I make dolls and always attach a label that says: *free* hat, *free* shoes, *free* wig. The word *free* is stronger than sex."

I traveled to New Orleans to interview the president of the Latin American Chamber of Commerce, whose goals were similar to those of the OAS although with a definite emphasis on regional trade. The ship that had brought me to the United States was in port, and I was able to meet again the young officer who supervised my work when I painted the railings.

An envelope from *Reader's Digest* arrived regularly, containing a check and a letter indicating that my stories were being printed in the magazine. Raul Nass congratulated me on my success. He continued to be the greatest influence in my work and the best of friends.

A year later, when I met the man I would eventually marry, I introduced him to Raul. His opinion meant much to me, but his words shocked me: "There's nothing there for you. He is probably a great guy, but you are totally different in temperament. Do you really, truly love him? I'll never understand women! What's the rush? Aren't we helping you enough with the girls?"

This was true. Every Saturday, Raul Nass and José Gomez Sicre, OAS Latin American Art Museum Director, took over my kitchen and cooked an enormous cauldron of food heavily seasoned à la Caribbean. After savoring their creation at lunch, they would leave saying: "There, now you have enough food for the whole week. The girls will have in it all the vitamins and minerals they need. We won't have to worry about them getting pellagra for lack of the proper nutrients."

As to my own social needs, Dr. Abraham Horwitz, reelected three consecutive times to the directorship of the Pan American Health Organization — PAHO — invited me often to concerts. I enjoyed them but couldn't match his familiarity with scores. I would turn to him entranced at a passage, and he invariably shook his head hopelessly. Would I ever learn? Didn't I notice that the first violin dragged during the scherzo and the cymbals rushed in too early? We laughed at my mistakes, but it took a while for him to forgive me when I applauded at the wrong pause.

Armando was another delightful friend. He arrived from Chile shortly after I did and also worked at the OAS. He joined the Department of Economics and started a meteoric career. He would often pick me up after work, and we would spend a couple of hours together. Then we went home to see the girls. He scolded me for dressing Rosa so poorly in mismatched colors, often in sizes too big allowing for growth. He nicknamed her "Miss Butterfly." My feelings for him were lighthearted. We never considered a future. He left on an assignment in Brazil. When he returned I had married and moved to Tennessee.

CHAPTER 17

I've never been proud or even reconciled with what I did, but important factors weighed in my decision. I would finally be able to be close to my children and to be with them full-time. Sidney was a widower, also with two children almost the same age as my own. My only occupation, if we married, would be to make a home for my girls and his children, he said insistently. His sister, Anita, had been my best friend since I arrived in Washington. My future in-laws had visited me, and I felt good about them from the minute we met. Sidney asked me to Chattanooga to meet his children and to hunt for a house. Doris, thirteen, and Morris, eight, seemed curious about a woman from a country they had never heard of. They asked many questions and wanted to see pictures of Rosa and Ximena. Everything looked promising, but I was heading for some surprises because of differences of temperament that soon surfaced.

During our long-distance courtship, Sidney had said he loved and needed my zest for life. But after I moved to Chattanooga into the new house we had selected, I noticed a change in his disposition. He returned to his previous routine, working doggedly, even on weekends. My father-in-law financed the purchase of new furniture as a wedding gift. The selection of everything needed for the living and dining rooms was left to his wife, Addy, and I. Sidney didn't have the time or the inclination for such frivolities. During our year's long-distance courtship, in his sporadic visits to Washington I never detected his deep depression. Parties and outings with Anita, her husband, and their friends helped camouflage this condition.

We had figured that the children's closeness in age would be a positive factor. We were wrong. The jealousies between the teenagers were a cause of constant anxiety. I turned to Sidney's mother for help and advice, and she begged for patience: teenagers were all alike, bellicose and competitive, she said. Time would take care of it. She was an intelligent and sensitive woman. She had emigrated from England and had the hardest time adjusting to the small Southern town. Her husband, Abe, made a fortune with a chain of department stores, but lost everything in the Depression and had to start again from scratch. Addy took it all in stride. She was not a pretty woman, but handsome with perfect grooming. Her main attraction was her intelligent and sparkling conversation. Abe, her husband, was a kind, warm optimist. His son was exactly the opposite.

With members of the extended family, Sidney now headed the main department store in Chattanooga. It didn't take me long to realize that he was a penny pincher. I said I would have to find a job since he resented my girls' expenses. He offered me a position as a buyer in the family business. I accepted. We traveled together to New York on buying trips, and I noticed that the man in Washington who had attracted me surfaced again in the big city. We worked during the day, and evenings were spent at fashionable restaurants and Broadway plays. This didn't last long though. After a while he decided that I should travel alone.

Our good friends in Chattanooga were Senator Estes Kefauver and his wife, Nancy. We had met them through my brother-in-law, Sydney Shallet, the senator's editor. Nancy was a beautiful woman who couldn't deny her Irish ancestry. Very tall, with bright red hair and striking green eyes, she reminded me of my sorely missed and beloved cousin Nana. She had a keen sense of humor and when during a party the senator ordered the lights dimmed to put an end to the reunion, she pulled us into her private salon, well provided with candles, to finish our drinks and exchange the latest gossip. She liked to tell anecdotes about her husband's colleagues in Congress and often about Estes himself. Apparently he was extremely absentminded and on one occasion, during a rally, he worked the crowd, shaking hands and talking briefly with everybody. He approached a young man he seemed to recognize and asked him about his father.

"He died three years ago," the young man answered.

The senator mumbled condolences and went on to greet other constituents. After a while he came upon the same youngster and once again asked about his father.

"He's still dead," he replied.

Years later Nancy was extremely gracious in making my second stay in Washington easier and more interesting.

For eight years I tried everything I could imagine to make my marriage work. The idea of a divorce was repulsive to me. Finally I realized that there was no other way to save my sanity and allow my children to breathe in a healthier atmosphere.

The divorce proceedings dragged for six months. During that time Sidney's daughter, Doris, married her sweetheart. Ximena became engaged to a young district attorney, Douglas Meyer, whom she married shortly before I left for Washington with Rosa.

Sidney's sister, Anita, called one day to say that she was in Chattanooga. She wanted to see me on condition that we didn't speak about Sidney and the divorce problems. She'd spend the day with me just like old times. Those hours were heartbreaking to me because I knew I wouldn't see her again. During our secret farewell she said that I should return to *Americas* magazine. Kathleen Walker had left, but the new director remembered me and wanted me to return and work with her. Anita had even made arrangements for me to have a job upon my return to Washington.

If anybody made my stay bearable in Chattanooga it was Rosalind Solomon. At first encounter I saw a woman apparently shallow and very tense, trying hard to fit into a straitlaced Southern community. She was from Chicago, and the adjustment to Tennessean society was as difficult for her as it was for me. What was a Chilean Catholic woman married to a Jewish businessman doing there? What did a Jewish sophisticate Chicagoan have in common with the Daughters of the Confederacy?

That first impression of Rosalind happily did not last. We were soon talking passionately about projects we wanted to tackle. After graduating from Goucher, Rosalind had traveled to Belgium with the Experiment in International Living. Then she found out that the Experiment was bringing international visitors to the U.S.A. and she contacted Gordon Boyce, the director, to express our wish to participate in the programs.

Rosalind was a natural public relations person. She always knew what had to be done, whom to contact, and what to say to get the ball rolling.

I learned with her how to persist, how to present a project, how to use publicity effectively.

As the traveler who has once been from home is wiser than he who has never left his doorstep, so a knowledge of one other culture should sharpen our ability to scrutinize more steadily.
— *Margaret Mead,* Coming of Age in Samoa, *1928*

The first group of Experimenters in International Living to arrive was from Chile, as a courtesy to Ximena, who had taught Rosalind Spanish. The visit was an unqualified success. The host families never stopped talking about how much their guests had taught them about their country.

I lived in awe of how much Rosalind could achieve. Next we decided to try another phase of the Experiment. They offered us a girl from Kenya as Community Ambassador. Rosalind and I looked at each other. It was 1961. The civil rights movement had started. Activists had already been in Chattanooga. If the girl was from Kenya, she must be black, but we did not want to inquire about this. Deciding to tough it out, we were surprised that we had no problem finding host families for her. She turned out to be a charming Hindu girl. At Ximena's wedding she stole the show by marching down the aisle of the church in a gorgeous sari enhanced by magnificent jewelry. We had found out that she was the daughter of the Agha Khan's Minister of Finance. Now divorced, I had the pleasure of seeing all my friends in the church, as well as Rabbi Feinstein and his wife, with whom I had developed a sincere friendship.

When the Experiment in International Living offered Rosalind the job of National Public Relations Director, her husband, Jay, balked at the idea of her commuting between Chattanooga and New York, and she, fearing a divorce, turned down the job.

After I left for Washington I lost track of Rosalind and Jay. I knew that she had branched out into an AID program that recruited outstanding black graduate students from different universities. I had joined the *Voice of America* and was concentrating on mastering new skills. In 1977 an assignment took me to the White House for a swearing-in ceremony. Jay Solomon was being sworn in as head of the General Services Administration under President Carter. Rosalind and I were reunited.

When Jay resigned his government appointment we lost track of each other once again. But somehow news about them always reached me. I heard that they had divorced and Jay returned to Tennessee. Rosalind was living in New York and had become an art photographer with exhibits at the Museum of Modern Art and the Corcoran Gallery. She has also exhibited in England, France, Japan, Italy, Peru, and Spain. She is at present about to publish a book with the best of her work. During a trip to New York I tracked her down, and we were reunited for the third time. We keep in touch regularly now.

I also keep in touch with Dr. Morris Effron, my stepson. After the divorce I wrote to him several times, but I was told that my letters upset him, so I decided to refrain from my desire to communicate with him. Several years later we found each others' addresses. I was in Washington, and he had moved to Maryland. We were very close, and I visited him in order to meet Kathy, his wife, and their first child.

During one of our calls, I told him that I was writing my memoirs. I asked if he would contribute his impressions of his first encounter with his stepmother, me. Shortly afterward I received the following letter:

Lillian never had a son until she met me. In the winter of 1954, when I was eight years old, she married my Dad. And on the day we all moved in together, I showed her my decaying tooth with a hole big enough to throw a cat in, the wart on my left hand bleeding from where I picked at it, and on my right foot, an ingrown toenail from which I could squeeze yellow pus. She surveyed all this as I stood under the bathroom light in my briefs, having just thrown up the green beans from supper.

"Can I call you Mom?" I asked hesitantly, folding my arms protectively in front of me. I was scared. I never had to ask that of anybody before. My Mother had died when I was three and I hardly remembered her. But her leaving left me feeling alone and now, fearful of being rejected, I kept my head tilted to the side, but never took my eyes away from Lillian's face.

Lillian was bending over the toilet, dunking my clothes to clean off the vomit. We had just come in from her first supper with my grandparents, her new in-laws. Yet she was composed and didn't seem to mind the odor or the occasional splash onto her black party dress. She had viewed my various afflictions with appropriate concern. Only the dampness along her upper lip betrayed any sense of her feeling stressed.

"C-C-Can I?," I whispered carefully, now looking away.

She spread the dripping clothing over the bathtub and dried her hands. Turning toward me, she knelt down bringing her dark brown eyes level with mine. Gently Lillian unfolded my arms, still tightened across my chest, and took my hand in hers. For a moment I could hear only the thumping of my heart. Then, with the softness of a smile but with the force of a church bell ringing, her answer came.

"Yes." Unequivocal. No hesitation. Direct. Without reservation. Surrounded with love. "Yes, my dear, of course you can. You are my son."

I dropped my hands and fell against her shoulder, wrapping my arms around her neck. Too scared to yell, too happy to cry. I danced about on my bare feet, hugging this wondrous stranger who now was my mom.

I left Chattanooga when he was sixteen, and I treasure many memories of Morris during the years when he was growing into a handsome, charming, typically mischievous teenager.

Doris also had ingrown toenails and was overweight, and all that was taken care of. She surfaced a beautiful girl: slim and elegant, although less cordial than Morris.

When I returned to Washington in September 1962 with Rosa, I faced unexpected problems. Wisconsin and Massachusetts Avenues were areas I knew well, having lived on Cathedral Avenue. I made the rounds of apartment buildings but was turned down as soon as I mentioned that I had a teenager with me. I finally sublet a flat, temporarily left vacant by a Chilean friend, and kept looking until I found a sympathetic manager on Wisconsin, across the street from Alban Towers and the Cathedral. On our previous stay, Rosa had attended the Holy Trinity parochial school in Georgetown. She was accepted there again and returned to classes, where she found some old friends.

The job that Anita thought I could have at the OAS *Americas* magazine didn't work out. During my eight years' absence much had changed. Raul Nass had returned to Venezuela, where he held an important position in government. Alfredo had retired. The Brazilians were dispersed, and the new director who had talked with Anita about having a job for me had left on a long tour of Latin America and forgotten to leave instructions about my reinstatement.

So I was back at the beginning again, reading the want ads and calling for interviews. One woman looked at my resumé and returned it to me saying: "I'm sorry, you are overqualified for this job."

"What do you mean? The ad says that you need a secretary with a knowledge of languages. I speak and write Spanish, English, French, and some German."

"I don't want to offend you. I would never feel comfortable with you around. I wouldn't be able to shout and curse. You are a lady. I need a simple girl with some skills."

I found similar reactions in other places. I felt embarrassed to look for old friends and ask if they knew about openings. Then I decided to try the language offices at the State Department. To my horror I failed the translation test. The man supposed to read and rate my work tore it up without even looking at it.

"Why did you do that?" I asked.

"I gave you two hours for this test and you came out of the room in one hour. We expect perfect work from our translators. Our material is often highly sensitive."

On the way out I saw a sign: Interpreters Department. Why not try? At the test next morning I interpreted from English to Spanish, Spanish to English, and French to English, English to French — and passed both!

"When can you take a two month assignment?" asked Don Barnes, the chief of interpreters, as we walked out.

"Give me a week."

The apartment problem had been solved. The school for Rosa was going well, and she seemed happy, except for some nostalgia for her friends in Chattanooga. Her Tennessean boyfriend was at the Naval Academy in Annapolis and would soon be able to visit on a few days' leave. But I couldn't take a job traveling around the United States and leave her alone. I must find someone reliable to keep her company and take care of her. A young Argentinean concert pianist with a lodging problem appeared and immediately moved in with us. I called Don Barnes and told him I was ready.

"That's good. You must meet your grantee at the Hay Adams to-morrow at 10 A.M. He is anxious to meet you, but I must warn you that he is not the easiest person to get along with. He has refused interpreters before. But we can't let him travel alone for two months. His English is very poor and his wife doesn't speak a word. Do your best. And good luck."

At the hotel I asked for Mr. Cesar Alvarez Barba. He was an Ecuadorian senator. Finita, his wife, was a lovely woman, and we became fast friends. I didn't talk about the trip we would take together. Having lived in Ecuador as a teenager, I asked for the friends that I remembered. They both relaxed. We had mutual friends, and they brought me up to date on the latest Quito gossip. We laughed together at some of the stories.

They had an appointment next morning for a tour of the White House. I was a little late starting from home, and driving down Massachusetts Avenue I was stopped for speeding. I was devastated. I was going to be late for my first job. I showed my registration and driver's license to the policeman and then begged, "Please write the ticket as quickly as possible. I must pick up a foreign dignitary and take him to the White House, where he is expected."

I didn't let him know that it was only for a tour. The policeman thought that the meeting was with President Kennedy and rushed writing the ticket. Handing it to me he said: "Just follow me. We'll be there in no time."

Turning on his siren, he sped down Massachusetts Avenue, turned on 16th and screeched to a stop at the Hay Adams Hotel. Cesar and Finita jumped into my car and following the police car we arrived at the White House in a matter of seconds. Waving enthusiastic thanks to the policeman, I muttered to Cesar: "Don't ask now. I'll tell you later."

Both Cesar and Finita thoroughly enjoyed the misunderstanding.

During lunch Cesar revealed his greatest interest in traveling through the United States: "I want you to know what I must learn from this trip. You know Ecuador. Those mountains don't grow wheat, but we have a surplus of potatoes with which we don't know what to do. I've been told that in the United States bread is being made with potato flour. I must find out how it's done for my country's sake."

This plea reminded me of Father, always looking for something new to solve Chile's needs. I vowed to investigate the manufacture of potato bread for Cesar and Ecuador.

As we departed the hotel I read the headlines on the newspapers. The Soviet Union was transporting nuclear missiles to Cuba. President Kennedy had to find a way to stop the progress of the ships.

At home Rosa was expecting me with her own news. The nuns at Holy Trinity had ordered the students to take pillows, blankets, and canned foods to the school. The students had been drilled on what to do if the Soviets attacked Washington. I made several calls and realized that panic was spreading. The comments I heard were that Kennedy was such a young and inexperienced President, could he stop the Soviet ships from reaching Cuba? If they did unload in Cuba, how long would it take before they attacked the United States? The speculations were frightening.

My personal dilemma was tearing at my heart. The first time I arrived in Washington I found a job within ten days. Eight years later it had taken me two months to find work. My divorce cash settlement was dwindling fast. Could I risk giving up this assignment with Senator Alvarez in order to stay with Rosa? In spite of the spreading panic, I trusted that nothing would happen. I believed that Kennedy would find a way to defuse the crisis. But even the remotest possibility of an attack was dreadful.

Scheduled to meet the senator and his wife the next afternoon at the Waldorf Astoria in New York, I debated all night what I should do. I shied away from talking with Rosa less I frighten her more. Once I had made up my mind, I asked her to sit with me and listen. I would go to New York and start on the assignment. We shouldn't give in to panic. I went on with other arguments until Rosa, with her usual serenity, interrupted me: "You know what you have to do. I'll be fine. Just keep in touch as often as possible."

The next morning I left for New York after she had gone to school. At the Waldorf Astoria I found a message from the Alvarezes saying that they were with friends and wouldn't see me until the next day. I called a friend, who invited me to a party that evening. Dozing off, catching up on the previous sleepless night, I later showered and dressed. Before leaving I called Rosa. She was doing her homework. No problems, except that the woman who was supposed to take care of her was hysterical and it was Rosa who had to calm her down. She laughed at the irony of the situation. I gave her the telephone number at the hotel and my room, also the telephone of the friends I would be having dinner with. As I reached the lobby I heard loud voices and laughter. People were embracing, the men vigorously slapping each other's backs. In the street a passerby lifted a newspaper for all to see. The headline read: SOVIET SHIPS TURN BACK.

My knees buckled. I started to cry uncontrollably. I felt dizzy and called a cab. I couldn't speak. The driver turned around and realized that it would take a while before I could give directions. He said: "I can wait. Take a deep breath. Nobody deserves that you ruin your eyes for him."

"You are mistaken. I'm crying from joy and relief. The crisis is over. No more fear. Haven't you heard? I was so afraid. I had to leave my daughter Rosa alone in Washington."

But the sobbing started again. The driver turned around:

"Rosa, Spanish name, also Italian. Now I understand. Let me tell you. Come home with me and my wife will give you a nice warm soup and you both can talk together about what worried you. I picked you up as my last passenger. I was on my way home. I'm serious, you must meet my wife and forget all your troubles."

So, I went with him. He was right. Anna was sympathetic and generous. I called Rosa to tell her where I was. She hadn't heard that the menace was over. She was as happy as I was, and I let her talk with Anna and thank her for her hospitality.

That was New York in 1962.

Meantime in Washington President Kennedy released a statement on television saying:

Yesterday a shaft of light cut into the darkness. For the first time an agreement has been reached on bringing the forces of nuclear destruction under international control.
— JFK TV address, July 26, 1963

That trip with the Alvarezes was the happiest of all my experiences as an escort interpreter. Other assignments were educational, and I will never forget how much I learned about the United States and its institutions. Also about human beings when facing a different culture. Situations can become potentially explosive, and it requires the patience of Job to explain American ways that often shock persons who have usually been pampered in their own country because of their social or professional status.

The Alvarez Barbas were different. Cesar was a senator and his wife lived in Paris, visiting Ecuador only occasionally. Yet he never pulled rank and neither did she act as a prima donna. Besides following the program set for him — visiting factories, chambers of commerce, mayor's offices — he invariably asked about the bread made out of potato flour. We crisscrossed the country, stopping at large and small cities until we reached Los Angeles. I gladly escorted Finita on her shopping sprees. She was a compulsive buyer and always found an excuse to buy, not only for herself but also for friends, children, and relatives in Ecuador. I knew that Cesar often liked to be by himself, to roam around and try his luck with his insufficient English. This gave him a breathing spell, for like most Latin American men he tired of women's company easily.

One morning Finita called me unusually early: "Lillian, Cesar is gone."

"What do you mean? Where do you think he might be? I'll have to call the State Department and tell Don Barnes about it."

"Don't do anything yet. We'll have a day to ourselves to do whatever we please. I'm sure that he's all right. Let's go to the beach."

"If he's not back tomorrow, I'll have to call State."

"What will happen if you call? Will the FBI hunt him down and bring him back in handcuffs? That would be funny!"

He did return, confessing that he had gone to Seattle because somebody gave him a tip about a baker who used potato flour. Finita burst out laughing. She didn't believe him and neither did I. But we didn't press him for the truth. That evening he took us to a fine restaurant and a nightclub to dance la bossa nova. Latin American men's acts of contrition can be much fun. A man invited me to dance. The new rhythm was irresistible. It carried one away like in a stream of sensuous sound. It rocked the body, which responded as if to a magic spell. We danced for almost an hour until I remembered that Cesar and Finita were waiting for me. Cesar never believed that the man hadn't followed me to the hotel and knocked on my door: "I heard him knocking, Lillian. Did you open . . . the door, I mean," he teased me.

So we were even: I didn't believe Seattle, he doubted that my dancing partner hadn't followed me.

Next Cesar insisted that I call Don Barnes and ask him to authorize a stop in Las Vegas: "Tell him that I must see the Hoover Dam."

"Cesar, you know that during this tour your program is based on what you can apply in Ecuador. Where do you think that your country can afford to build a dam?"

So I called Don anyhow and Cesar got Las Vegas. I thought that he wanted to see the glitter of the shows and look at the chorus girls. No one had warned me that he was a compulsive gambler. As he sat at the tables, winning and losing, Finita and I walked, shopped, had fabulous dinners, and did enjoy the shows.

We missed four flights before I was able to get Cesar away from baccarat and roulette. My final argument was that New Orleans — our next stop — was as attractive, exciting, and naughty as Las Vegas, with a European flair. I had been twice in New Orleans and knew what I was talking about. Both he and Finita loved it. At the end of Cesar's State Department tour, they left for Quito. I felt sad to part from them. I liked Finita very much, and in those two months we had become very close. Cesar was at times a genius and could also play the fool if it suited his purposes. His aristocratic family background and his wealth had taught him that he could always have anything he fancied. In my report to State I said as much: "If Senator Alvarez Barba sets his mind on being the President of Ecuador, he will be President."

He chose instead the ambassadorship in Paris and got it. Finita invited me to join them, but I had started working at the *Voice of America* and couldn't leave. I have always regretted declining their invitation.

Fatigue caught up when I returned to Washington. Two months of shepherding the Alvarez Barbas from New York to Chicago, Indianapolis, Sacramento, Los Angeles, Las Vegas, New Orleans, and points in between, had been interesting and fun, but I was exhausted and in dire need of relaxation. Rosa was spending the weekend with friends, and I was determined to put some order into the new apartment I had rented. We had hardly any furniture, so this presented few problems. Then I sat on the couch to read a magazine and fell sound asleep.

A knock on the door woke me up. My first thought was that Rosa was early. I opened the door, and Manuel Seoane was standing there, his peculiar crooked, mischievous smile showing how much he enjoyed my surprise and bafflement. I could not believe my eyes. We hadn't been in touch for a long time. Nevertheless I was aware of events in his life in the last few years. After his daughter Nora's death, following childbirth in Paris, I had written to him in Amsterdam, where he was Peru's ambassador. At his next diplomatic appointment in Chile, I had asked him to call Ximena, who was spending some time with the family in Santiago. On his return to Peru, he campaigned for the APRA ticket for the presidency with Haya de la Torre. They won the election, but a coup annulled the people's will, and he was subsequently appointed roving ambassador to the Organization of American States with residence in Washington, D.C. But I had no idea when he would arrive.

Stepping back to let him in, I was laughing half in surprise, half in embarrassment. I knew I looked a mess. He laughed also. It was good to hear him laugh. I will never remember what I said, or perhaps I didn't say anything. How many years since last I'd seen him? I didn't recall how tall he was, or was it that I had no shoes on? I raised my arms to run my fingers through my hair.

"I hope you know that I'm going to need you a lot," he finally said. "Whatever your schedule is, you will have to make time for me."

I don't know what my answer was. I was laughing for joy.

"You are glad to see me?" he asked, and he knew the answer.

"Fine. I was afraid I might find you with a boyfriend," he teased.

"I haven't had time to find one. Besides I'm just divorced."

"So you are free. Good. You will have time for me. I really need you. This city frightens me."

"I can't believe that. Nothing frightens you."

"Believe it. Washington is unknown territory to me. I'm appointed to the OAS which I have often attacked in my writings, calling it the Department of Colonies. Now I will have to find its more palatable aspects. You worked at the OAS once. What can you tell me?"

"I wish you had been appointed when Carlos Dávila was Secretary General. He was a socialist, like you. That should tell you something about the OAS. You'll have to deal with some sacred cows, like Ambassador Sevilla Sacasa, from Nicaragua. How much do you know about Central America? In the Southern Cone we are usually quite ignorant about the area. I speak from personal experience, but you probably know more than I did. I had to learn fast. Like the UN, the specialized agencies of the OAS do a splendid job. Dr. Horwitz, Director of the Pan American Health Organization, can give you valuable information. He will invite you to the exclusive Cosmos Club to meet outstanding Washington personalities."

"I have a meeting next week at the Brookings Institution. Will you go with me? I may need an interpreter."

He didn't need one. Everybody spoke fluent Spanish. The Seoane charisma was in full force. He gave a brief history of his party in Peru, speculating on what the recent defeat might mean to its survival. He went on to elaborate on his present appointment, how he expected to perform and use his diplomatic and political experience to solve conflicts and negotiate accords. He was asked if he believed in the success of the regional common markets. He was cautiously hopeful of their achievements.

When Rosa arrived home that evening, I told her about Manuel's visit.

"I hope this will make you buy some furniture," she teased me.

Next day we went shopping and bought a truckload of everything we needed to make the apartment more homey. Once our acquisitions were delivered, we threw out the crates we had been using as coffee tables and TV stands.

On weekends we would go to the beach at Rehoboth or to the mountains in West Virginia. We visited Baltimore, Annapolis, and the quaint small towns along the Chesapeake Bay. Manuel was working hard and needed to relax at the end of twelve-hour days of stressful toil. He complained that I had allowed Rosa to forget Spanish. He tried to communicate with her, but his English wasn't good. Rosa was six when she came to the United States. Once she had learned enough English to get by in school, she refused to speak Spanish. Now when she was sixteen years old, English was her only language.

"I don't plan to marry again," Manuel said one evening after one of our excursions.

"Neither do I," I remarked, and we both laughed. It was such a pleasure to understand each other so perfectly, to be able to be comfortable in each other's company.

Don Barnes called me for an assignment. I asked Manuel about his plans. He was supposed to leave for Bolivia. My cousin Nana was in town and would stay with Rosa. So I accepted an assignment to interpret for a group of Latin American businessmen, partly in New York, partly at a Rockefeller's estate in upper New York State.

As we ended the assignment I knew that Manuel had returned from La Paz. Looking forward to seeing Rosa and introducing Nana to Manuel, I thought it would be fun to see them react to each other: Manuel the writer, politician, and diplomat, and Nana, the beautiful redhead, irrepressible flirt, typical Chilean social butterfly with a heart of gold.

It was late. We had had a particularly stressful day with lectures, meetings, and speeches. Even my companion interpreter was tired, although he was a master at the trade, usually performing effortlessly.

I was getting ready for bed when I was called to the telephone. I heard Ximena's voice: "Mother, please don't get too upset. Manuel had a stroke. He is dead. Come back as soon as possible. Carlos Vidal is here in Washington and he wants to speak with you."

Carlos Vidal, the loyal friend who had introduced me to Manuel. Not finding me in Washington, he had traced Ximena in Chattanooga and asked her to call me with the painful news. He had also advised her to meet me in Washington.

I couldn't sleep that night. I cried, remembering Manuel's tragic life. He was always apparently successful, yet his ideas and convictions forced him into exile for many years. His political aspirations had to wait. Reaching an agreement with the Peruvian government, he returned to Lima, won a seat in Congress, and then was appointed ambassador to Holland and later Chile, which amounted to honorable exile. When at last he returned to his homeland to lead APRA to power through elections, a coup deprived him of his victory. Then came his appointment to the OAS. Once more he must leave his country. And on his first mission, had the La Paz altitude brought about his death?

In Washington Ximena and Rosa were waiting for me. Ximena called Carlos at his hotel, and he rushed over to see me. We sat together reminiscing and lamenting the loss of an exceptional friend and a brilliant mind, whose disappearance might set back the political evolution of all of the Americas.

"I want you to write about Manuel," Carlos said. "We always admired you as a talented writer. You knew him well. Write about his life." But I couldn't do it.

Carlos' request made me realize that there were troublesome gaps in my knowledge of Manuel's life. The most significant and influential events in his life had been so painful that I never dared probe into them. How could I ask him to reveal his innermost feelings about his long exile, about his brother's imprisonment as a hostage, his beloved daughter's death, or the loss of the election to a cunning opposition led by a prominent member of his own family? (according to rumors) How could I reveal his wounds? He knew how much I wanted him to trust me with his confidence, but it had been up to him to decide when the time was ripe. After his death I could only regret having been too cautious and tactful. But I sensed that it was what he appreciated and wanted from me.

CHAPTER 18

On my last assignment as an escort interpreter for the State Department, I received a call from the *Voice of America*'s personnel office saying that I must join their ranks immediately. I had been waiting for this call for almost a year, but I explained that I had made a commitment to the State Department that I could not break. It was December, and I knew that at that time of the year it was very difficult to find replacements. Having traveled much of the year, escorts looked forward to spending the holidays with their families. Don Barnes, Chief of the Interpreters Department, had been extremely helpful to me, and I felt I mustn't burden him with a problem. Rosa was spending the holidays in Chattanooga with Ximena, which left me free to accept an assignment with a group of fourteen Latin American professional women. The assignment would take a month, and I would then be able to answer the *Voice of America*'s call. It would just have to wait.

On January 13, 1964, I presented myself at *VOA*'s personnel office, filled in their forms, got sworn in, and shook hands with the acting official, who congratulated me warmly and gave me his set speech on excellence of performance. I was so excited by this new stage of my life that I forgot to ask questions, whose answers I would find in the orientation courses we attended later. The *Voice of America*, with over 2,000 employees in the USA and overseas, functions under the umbrella of the United States Information Agency together with foreign service, cultural affairs, scholarships, USIA-TV, press, and movies. It was a wide field to cover, and once a member of this institution I would learn much more about the scope of its operations, dedicated to informing the world about the United States, its policies, institutions, and goals.

Done with personnel, I left the temporary World War II building on Independence Avenue, crossed the street, and entered the edifice where *VOA* has its offices and studios. The Latin American Division was located on the first floor toward 2nd Street, S.W. As I stepped into it, the smell of heated typewriters instantly brought memories of *Ercilla* magazine and my work as a translator. Immediately I felt at home, although everything around me seemed rather shabby and crowded. Tiny cubicles housed old desks, editing equipment, a couple of chairs. From the depths of these boxes, suspicious eyes scrutinized me with a curiosity bordering on impertinence. I kept on walking until I heard a voice saying: "Who's there? Lillian Tagle? What shall I do with her? Nobody told me that she would be here today. Where shall I sit her among all these men?"

It was Mel Niswander, chief of the Spanish branch of the Latin American Division. He did have a problem. Only one other woman worked there, and she was well sheltered in a cubicle far away from the all-male staff. I would soon find out the reason for this precaution.

For lack of space I was assigned a desk and typewriter in a larger cubicle already occupied by two of the eighteen Latin American men on the staff. Never having worked in radio or edited a tape, I had much to learn. I had to change my style. Use shorter sentences, or the broadcasters would run out of breath. That was no big problem.

What became a real challenge was the editing of tapes, but by the end of the week — in which I ruined more than one report — I was an expert with the little knife. Then came the most serious test: could I broadcast?

At first try it was decided that my voice was too high-pitched and my reading so fast that my elocution suffered. My new colleagues offered to help. They taught me to breathe properly, slow down — short-wave broadcasting can't handle speed — be assertive. The breathing was the most difficult part of my broadcasting training. Everybody seemed to have a different opinion: fill the top of your lungs, now speak slowly, don't inhale in midsentence. No, fill your diaphragm with air, speak assertively, that's right, very good, much better.

By the end of the second month I felt sure of myself. I would make it. But broadcasting wasn't the most satisfying task for me. I wanted to write again. I did, with a special documentary on the assassination of John F. Kennedy. The script called only for male voices. We had a splendid producer who offered to work on the program. The day it went on the air was memorable for the broadcasters, the producer, and me. The tape was later presented as a gift to the Kennedy Memorial Library, where it has been probably sitting since on a shelf. But nevertheless there it is, and that's all that counts to me.

This program had a secondary effect. I had proved myself a good scriptwriter, so I set out to find a place for myself as such. A daily program was prepared by one of the young men who shared my cubicle. I asked if I could help him with it. We discussed the changes I wanted to introduce, and he agreed to let me write the scripts for a week, so long as he remained the anchorman. He was an excellent broadcaster, and I agreed. By the end of the week I had taken over. It was a bloodless, spiteless coup and everybody was happy.

I bought three small TV sets, and early every morning I turned on all three networks — ABC, NBC, CBS — and took notes from interviews, news, etc. *VOA* routinely recorded the network's broadcasts, and I ordered my own set of tapes that I could cut for sound bites according to my notes. These would be used in the program, giving it a crisp flexibility and life it didn't have before. The broadcasters enjoyed the changes and soon competed to figure in *Issues of Our Times,* as the program was named.

As soon as I arrived at my desk I put on earphones, turned on the editing machine, and cut out the material I needed for the program. I would splice the sound bites together and then sit to write the continuity. *Issues* started at ten minutes. Soon radio stations in Latin America requested it be extended to fifteen minutes, then twenty minutes. It was broadcast in the evening, and the anchorman of the breakfast show repeated the program in the morning, adding or subtracting as necessary for updates.

For six years I wrote the scripts for that show. It featured every important event of the sixties: the civil rights struggle, Martin Luther King Jr.'s assassination, the subsequent torching of Washington, D.C., Robert F. Kennedy's assassination, the demonstrations against the Vietnam War, the unforgettable speech in support of the demonstrators by now Senator John Kerrey.

You know we've had to imagine the war here, and we have imagined that it was being fought by aging men like ourselves. We had forgotten that wars were fought by babies. When I saw those freshly shaved

faces, it was a shock. "My God, my God," I said to myself, "it's the Children's Crusade."
— *Kurt Vonnegut Jr.*, Slaughterhouse Five, *1969*

The space program's successful moon landing was an event that brought special notoriety to our division. A team was assigned to cover all the launchings. At the *VOA* studios in Washington, Enrique Gonzalez Regueira, a Uruguayan, was the anchorman. Carlos Rivas, from Guatemala, was his assistant, and third in line was another Uruguayan, Roland Massa. For the launchings at Cape Canaveral we had Ramon Levy, from Panama — later transferred to Houston — and José Perez del Río, from Mexico.

In a supporting role, I assisted the team in Washington. My job was to keep tabs on every development of the flights conveyed via teletypes and pass on any pertinent information during the actual broadcasts. Some flights required that the team remain in the studio for hours, and it was vitally important that they have enough material to keep the ball rolling with fresh information. I was also responsible for screening long-distance calls from all over Latin America asking to speak directly to the broadcasters. This required tact and intuition. I had to know the difference between the call from a personality, either a politician or a writer, and one from a crackpot. We wanted the calls to keep on coming, but I had to sort out those that I suspected of being from excited spiritualists determined to expound on their theories about the astronauts' endeavors, taking advantage of *VOA*'s wide dissemination to spread their ideas.

Each man on the team had a well-defined personality that came over during hours of work, sustained by a steady stream of coffee. Gonzalez Regueira had the commanding, powerful voice that kept the emotional tone of the broadcast. Carlos Rivas was the poet, the philosopher, the sensitive man who projected the event into the history of humankind. Roland Massa was sound, providing necessary, reliable information. His was the voice to believe. Ramon Levy was the scientist, the man who did his homework with such dedication that in his reports from the Houston Space Center he managed to explain intricate concepts in lay terms. His government in Panama decorated him for his performance. Perez del Rio gave the launchings the excitement of a soccer game's goal. His triumphant launching scream made him famous.

The broadcast of the space program launchings didn't always go smoothly. In my role as an assistant, some staff members believed I could

Leaving the Voice of America *after the breakfast show.*

help them actively participate in the team. They were mistaken. The division and Spanish branch chiefs, in consultation with the team, selected the broadcasters. When I explained that I had no authority in the matter, the soliciting party was resentful.

One incident put me in a quandary. It was very early morning, and I heard the bell ring at my apartment's door. I opened it and faced a deeply depressed individual. Slumped shoulders, pale face, disheveled hair. It was one of the team, and he should have been on his way to the studio.

"What are you doing here?" I asked, surprised.

"I can't broadcast today. No matter what you say, I can't do it. Call me a coward, I don't care. I just can't do it."

I took one step toward him and slapped him so hard my hand hurt.

He turned around and started walking toward the elevator. The back of a defeated creature is the saddest spectacle in the world. I ran after him and faced him.

"You get to that studio fast," I said, and looking at his moist eyes, I kissed him.

When I arrived at the studio, he was sitting in his place. He lifted a hand in welcome and smiled. The incident was never mentioned again.

The moon-landing broadcast brought a formidable reaction from Latin America. Letters and small gifts arrived at the Washington post office in such bulk that the USIA director was asked if this flow of correspondence would last long because the postal authorities had to order special trucks to deliver it. At the *Voice of America* itself, rooms were set aside for all the bags of mail.

When Neil Armstrong made a tour of Latin America, Enrique Gonzalez Regueira, our anchorman, traveled with him. In the San Juan Islands of Panama, the women created a mola with a special design to celebrate the landing. Their interpretation of the capsule's descent on the moon was a fish hovering over the Sea of Tranquillity.

Listening to television today, August 1997, about the mishaps in the MIR Russian space station, I feel the same excitement I experienced during some of the troubled flights of the Apollo program. In the midst of news about ups and downs in Wall Street, scandals, and ghastly crimes, the heroism of the Russian-American crew keeps up my faith in the excellence of human beings. When I say "heroism" I have in mind not the brutish, killing heroism of warriors, but the consuming dedication of scientists for whom no sacrifice is too great to advance the belief in a better world obtainable through science.

Rosa had married her longtime boyfriend from Chattanooga after he withdrew from the Naval Academy. Three years later she had given birth to two little girls, Teresa and Christina, and moved to Northern Virginia, where she had an apartment close to mine.

In Chattanooga, Ximena had her first son, Alexander, and seemed happy. We visited back and forth several times during the year.

My work was becoming more intense. I was asked to take the weekend morning broadcasts, and I enjoyed the overtime money that allowed me to pamper my grandchildren and indulge in collecting antiques and artworks. "Thieves Market" in Alexandria was my favorite hunting ground. A patient search was usually rewarded with unexpected treasures.

My stay at *VOA* suffered from one annoying flaw. The term *sexual harassment* wasn't used yet as liberally as it is today, but it did exist then; nowadays we know about its practice because women have decided to speak up. I had become a most unwilling target. The friends who had helped me learn the trade at the beginning set siege to me: direct invitations that I consistently declined; innuendoes and crude remarks whispered into my ear — all these were daily occurrences. I tried everything to counter it: flatout rejections, humor, anger, or threats.

One particular young man was subtler and less insistent. The seduction game as he played it was more intriguing. I thought that he could understand the term *amitié amoureuse* and took a chance. The honeymoon was brief. He soon turned into a demanding, jealous, domineering master macho. He didn't know the meaning of discretion. I had another Miguel on my hands, much to my regret. In earnest I set out to find a solution that would not only correct my mistake but open other horizons. To my disenchantment was added the nagging thought that although I had done well careerwise, I was still behind because of my eight years of marriage in Tennessee. Now I must catch up.

It was 1965, and the Vietnam build-up had started. I talked with Rufus Phillips and his Chilean wife, Barbara; he had just returned from Saigon after spending several years as an AID officer in the Pacification program. I told him about my idea of volunteering as a *VOA* correspondent in Vietnam. He listened and asked a few questions, obviously probing to determine how serious I was. Then he gave me the name of the recruiting officer at the United States Information Agency. Two days later I had an interview with him.

"Why do you want to go to Vietnam? Why do you think that a

At work in my VOA *office.*

Latin American audience would be interested in listening to a Spanish-speaking *VOA* correspondent in Saigon?"

"Because I believe that a war such as the one in Vietnam might spread to Latin American countries. The Tupa Marus are already active in Uruguay. My credibility would be unimpeachable since I'm known in several Latin American countries. As a correspondent I can point out the destruction and tragedy these conflicts bring to the population."

"Have you told your supervisor about your idea?"

"No, I haven't."

"I must consult my own supervisor about your volunteering for Vietnam. I'll call you as soon as possible with his decision."

When I arrived at *VOA* half an hour later, the chief of the division had left a message on my typewriter asking me to see him immediately. As I walked into his office, he snapped:

"What have you done? Why didn't you speak with me first? You have been recruited to go to Vietnam as our correspondent."

"Yes, I did volunteer. Are you telling me that I have been accepted?"

"Yes, that's what I'm saying."

News spread fast. When I returned to my office a group had assembled and the first verbal volleys hit me.

"What do you think you are doing? I would have never thought that you would approve of the war in Vietnam."

"To report about a war doesn't mean that I approve."

"Do you know what can happen to you? The Vietcong will capture and torture you. They will send back your remains in a paper bag."

"You are really stupid. I thought you were more intelligent. The Yanquis will use you as a spy."

"Adiós, Lillian. Don't deny it. You approve of this war that hasn't even been declared."

This barrage went on for months. It was suggested that I learn Vietnamese, as my French wouldn't be sufficient to communicate in Vietnam. Each day I got up at 6 A.M. to get to my Vietnamese lessons. I had difficulty in pronouncing the right tones for each word. Other students had the same problem. The teachers teased us, saying that a mispronounced word could get us in serious trouble. For example, the word 'get' in English means 'kill' in Vietnamese. They told us the story of a very religious young soldier who asked a cab driver to take him to a church. He mispronounced and ended up in a brothel. Being extremely courteous, he stayed.

Meantime the hostilities and criticism went on unabated at work. A USIS officer serving in Milan was recruited for service in Saigon. He had no alternative but to resign. On arriving in Washington he looked me up. I was in the cafeteria at lunch when he approached my table.

"You are a meddlesome woman. Why do you want to go to Vietnam? I was working well in Milan, then suddenly I'm recruited for Vietnam. When I declined I was told that a woman had volunteered, Lillian Tagle. I had to resign."

"I fail to see the connection. I did what I wanted to do for my own reasons. It has nothing to do with you or anybody else."

One of our *VOA* producers had a son sent to Vietnam. He turned against me in his fear for his young man. One day he said to me: "If it's the money that made you volunteer, why don't you go to Saigon and start a whorehouse?"

I had awaited the order to leave for several months. My supervisor would ask me periodically if I still wanted to go to Vietnam and I would answer in the affirmative. Suddenly a colleague, José Perez del Río, told me that he was leaving for Vietnam on a six-month assignment. After him, Federico Schiele followed. When I asked why was I passed up, the answers were always vague. I gave up the Vietnamese classes and re-solved to look for other avenues of advancement.

It was time for the annual White House Photographer's Dinner at the Shoreham Hotel. The *Voice of America* had assigned me to attend, and I was thrilled. I would have a chance to meet important people in a field difficult to describe for an international radio audience. But I've always been attracted by challenges and I felt ready.

I had seen in the *National Geographic* an article about Chile, and I de-cided that the author would be my first interviewee. I was disappointed. The young photographer was absolutely inarticulate. He proved right my theory that artists' expressions are to be found in their works, be it literature, art, or music. They usually aren't particularly adept at describ-ing their emotions verbally. They do it by practicing their own specific artistic skill.

So I moved on to find another subject for an interview. Senator Edmund Muskie was sitting by an empty chair that I promptly filled. I introduced myself as a *VOA* reporter, and he was most enthusiastic about our work. His deep gravelly voice praised our organization and asked many questions about our operation. I realized that he was turn-ing the tables on me. I must quickly return to my reporter's persona.

I remembered the incident that had so unfairly hurt his chance at the nomination for the presidency: breaking down emotionally at the mention of his wife in a nasty newspaper report, with light snow falling around him on a campaign stop in a northeastern town. I could clearly visualize the scene, run daily on all networks. I told him that if this had happened in a Latin American country he would have won the nomination instead of losing it.

"How come?" he asked, surprised.

"Because it would have never been interpreted as a sign of weakness, but rather as the tender reaction of a sensitive man."

He considered this for a moment, then laughed.

"Never thought about that. Different cultures. How interesting."

He squeezed my hand and said warmly, "Thank you."

I must get a sound bite: "Will you run again?"

"Perhaps in a Latin American country next time," he exclaimed, laughing.

I had my sound bite.

When I was promoted to the position of supervisor of the Spanish branch at *VOA*, I automatically became editor of the evening air show. I had looked forward to this promotion but didn't dream what it would mean and how my relationship to the rest of the staff would be affected. Little anonymous notes appeared regularly on the bulletin board criticizing my decisions. It was important that our broadcasters pronounce correctly foreign names and places. One word in particular became the butt of constant conflicts: *détente*. The broadcasters would pronounce it in Spanish, *detente*, meaning "stop," as in the scapularies. During a meeting I explained that the word was French, meaning a relaxation of tensions. Many Cuban members of the staff insisted that their interpretation was correct as a warning to the devil to stay away, 'va de retro.' I finally prevailed with the support of the division chief, who intervened.

While editing a news report I came upon the translation of a sound bite from Senator Eugene McCarthy, who during an interview said: "To be a politician one must have the hide of a hippopotamus." The translation in Spanish was: "to be a politician one must know all the hiding places of the hippopotamus." I had once the opportunity to mention this to the senator, who thoroughly enjoyed the story, then commented: "It could be a correct translation if it were to mean that a politician must know all the secrets of his opponent."

I was assigned to cover a signing ceremony of documents concerning

Latin America at the White House. President Nixon was then in the Oval Office, and protocol was changing fast.

I arrived at the gate on time for the press conference preceding the ceremony. My *VOA* pass was in order, but the guards asked me to wait while they checked their list and confirmed my identity. This had never happened to me before. I had often attended White House events and my pass was all I needed to be promptly admitted. I was getting nervous as minutes elapsed. It would be embarrassing to arrive late. I might not even be allowed to enter the conference room if the Press Secretary had already started the briefing.

Dan Rather stepped hurriedly into the booth by the gate. We had briefly met on previous occasions. He asked me why I was standing there. I told him the reason. Dan Rather then impatiently addressed the guards: "I know the lady. Let her in."

And they did, on Dan's authority. I was lucky he had come by and helped me break the new rules of protocol à la Nixon.

By 1970 I'd been away from Chile for eighteen years. Both my brother and sister insisted that I visit them. When I requested leave at *VOA,* I was asked to cover a conference in Bogotá on the way back. The Inter-American Commission of Women, of the Organization of American States, was meeting there.

Shortly after I arrived in Santiago, a call from Washington requested that I cover Pat Nixon's visit to the recent earthquake area in Huaraz, Peru. The U.S. Embassy made all the arrangements and I departed for Lima for three days. There I met Philomena Jurey, worldwide English and White House correspondent for *VOA.* It was an extraordinary assignment, and I will always remember how much Philomena helped me. We flew into Huaraz in military planes and helicopters. The First Lady's visit had naturally attracted many correspondents, among them Helen Thomas.

When the sun started to set and the Andean mountain's chill grabbed us, the children of the ravaged town begged aggressively, pulling at our wraps. The helicopters were rushing in and out, evacuating the visitors. Panicking, lest I have to wait too long and miss my deadline with *VOA,* I approached the pilot, yelling: "Please, take me out of here. I'm pregnant."

For a long while after I felt guilty about those who were left behind, among them Philomena Jurey and Helen Thomas. Philomena forgave me. I don't know about Helen Thomas. I returned to Santiago just in time to hear that Salvador Allende was the new president of Chile.

My next stop was Bogotá, and I had to be prepared to send out a series of reports about the discussions over subjects that shook Colombia to the roots of its conservative soul, family planning being the most controversial. Jean Wilkowski was the chairwoman for the USIA delegation and she handled press and CIM's internal conflicts with a cool spirit.

CHAPTER 19

The *Voice of America* was offering civil service employees the opportunity to become Foreign Service officers. I jumped at this chance to change my status and started to look for an overseas assignment. Where in the world did I want to go?

We had a new Spanish branch chief, Richard Knowles. He did what no other officer in his position had ever done, interviewing staff members individually. When it was my turn, he asked what I had been doing; he looked at my job description and realized that there were disparities between it and my report. He probed further. "So you have been writing *Issues of Our Times* for several years now? You've done a good job. Do you have any plans for the future?"

"Now that I'm in the Foreign Service I want to go overseas."

"Do you know what to do about it?"

"Not really. I've asked some questions, but I'm still quite lost."

"Let me see what can be done."

A few days later he called me to his office.

"From now on you will be the Spanish branch supervisor. You must stop writing and get into management and programming. As for your overseas plans, work at this new assignment and when I'm through with my present one, I'll help you."

It wasn't easy. In scarcely six years I had jumped into management. Some of the staff members were resentful; others congratulated me but warned me not to let success go to my head. I regretted giving up a program I'd created from scratch, but set out to find a replacement. No one wanted to take it on under my supervision, until a new staff member arrived from Chile, Máximo Mewe. His family had owned a radio station in Valparaíso, and he was born into radio. He had listened many times to the program and liked *Issues*. He also had some interesting ideas. I assigned him the program and devoted my attention to my managerial duties.

After spending two years in our division, Dick Knowles was appointed public affairs officer (PAO) in Helsinki, at a time when the human rights accords were being discussed. This meant a promotion for Dick, who until then had only worked in small Latin American countries. I congratulated him, and we sat for a special session that was designed to start me on the quest for my own overseas assignment.

He gave me names, described personalities, advised me how to handle them, and assured me that he trusted me to do a good job. He wrote my most commendable officer evaluation report (OER) and departed. A new branch chief took over. The Watergate hearings had started. I supervised the material included in *Issues*. The new chief called me into his office and said that I must not include sound bites from the hearings in the program. The subject had to be treated as sparingly as possible. I argued that the press was reporting worldwide about the hearings in great detail. If we did any less, the *Voice of America*'s credibility would suffer. He walked away, but returned shortly afterward and gave me the green light.

Following Dick's advice to the letter, I visited the Latin American Department at USIA and talked with the director, Dorothy Dillon. She referred me to Mildred Marcy, and the ball started rolling. The first offer I received was for the position of cultural affairs officer (CAO) in Cameroon, on the basis of my French. There were two categories that alternated in matters of assignment: specialist or generalist. Dorothy was opposed to my stepping into Africa because I was a Latin American specialist. So the little ball on the roulette wheel jumped from one slot to the next, from Colombia to Ecuador and finally to Honduras.

I knew little about Honduras, but Mariano Sanchez, a good friend, had lived there, and his family was in Tegucigalpa. I asked him what I'd do for entertainment there. "Have you ever been interested in archeology? You will be living in a Mayan museum. Start with Copán."

He was right. I became an avid student of Mayan culture and collector of artifacts.

I had already left *VOA* to undergo the training I needed to perform

As the cultural affairs officer, I visit an agricultural academy in Honduras.

in my position as a cultural affairs officer (CAO), when the news of the coup that resulted in Salvador Allende's death reached us. I remembered the man I had known years earlier. His death by his own hand seemed totally unseemly and out of character. It was difficult to get reliable news about what followed his demise, but I was soon aware of the chasm brought about in Chilean society by the military regime. After my failed return to Chile three years earlier, I realized that it would be a long time before I could feel comfortable in my family's land.

I arrived in Honduras in December 1973. John Griffiths, the public affairs officer (PAO), was glad to see me. He'd been running the United States Information Service (USIS) singlehandedly for several months. We got along famously once I got the hang of things.

My house was a lovely haunted building where many strange occurrences took place, such as swinging chandeliers and repulsive odors in the middle of the night. When I reported these facts I was told the story of the house. A jealous husband had killed his wife and her lover there. Since then the house had remained abandoned, becoming a shelter for vagrants and petty criminals. At last a fire had almost destroyed it and incinerated a few of the unwanted guests.

Deciding to exorcise the ghosts, I concentrated on the unfaithful wife. I threw a costume party to which I invited the ambassador, Phillip V.

Sanchez, and his wife, Juanita, all my embassy friends and members of other foreign missions. In the middle of the party I disappeared to change from my peasant dress into a flowing white gown, with blood splashed down the front. As I came down the staircase, eerie electronic music played and spotlights followed my descent, as fans blew a mass of white veils around me. These stage arrangements were by courtesy of Carlos Boker and his wife, Pia. The Italian ambassador's wife fainted, but the rest of the guests enjoyed the drama. The American ambassador and his wife wore Cherokee costumes. John Griffiths and Graciela enacted *Madame Butterfly*, he stunning in a white navy uniform, she beautiful in a fine kimono.

Recalled to Washington, I attended a seminar on the management of binational centers. Two were under my supervision: Tegucigalpa and San Pedro Sula. I was met at the airport by Máximo Mewe, who had become my dearest friend. We stopped at Rosa's to hug her and take a look at the girls, who were asleep. Then at my hotel, Máximo and I talked until dawn. All efforts to get him a permanent visa had failed. His contract with *VOA* required that he return to Chile after two years of service. He could request a waiver at the Chilean Embassy, but the new diplomatic officials appointed by General Pinochet had demanded that if he wanted a waiver he must take photographs of Chilean exiles demonstrating at Dupont Circle. Máximo refused. The prospect of a return to Chile under the Pinochet regime was frightening. We decided to marry, and did.

This gave way to another nightmare. Reading the regulations for Foreign Service officers, apparently I had skipped the rules about marriage, a thought far from my mind at the time. When I returned to Honduras, I told John Griffiths what I had done. He talked it over with the Deputy Chief of Mission, who told the ambassador.

Messages flashed between Tegucigalpa and Washington for days. I had broken a rule by not announcing my intention and waiting for authorization to marry. Opinions shifted back and forth, pro and con. I might have to return to Washington, perhaps jobless. Somehow nothing drastic happened. But Immigration suggested it was a fraudulent wedding. My friend Joy Billington arranged for a member of Congress to clear up the situation. Months went by. Then Saigon fell. Vietnamese refugees started flooding into the United States. Comparing their acceptance, often without background checks, with the situation Máximo and I were in, I got extremely angry. One morning I butted into the ambassador's office, over his secretary's protests, and poured out my frustration:

"Mr. Ambassador, my husband and I married a year ago and Immigration still won't clear him to join me. All these Vietnamese refugees are being allowed into the United States without even checking who they are. My husband was invited to work at the *Voice of America* because his credentials are impeccable, as an honorable man and a skilled professional."

Ambassador Sanchez lifted a hand to interrupt me, reached for the telephone, and waved at me to leave. I never knew whom he called, but three days later Máximo telephoned to say that he was free to travel with a brand-new visa. He would be flying to Honduras soon and wanted us to spend his first weekend diving in the Bay Islands.

Nothing has been clearcut and simple in my life. A Chilean FAO officer (U.N. Food and Agriculture Organization) named Hugo had been a devoted friend since my arrival in Honduras. When I told him that Máximo would arrive in a few days, he said: "I have asked my wife for a divorce. She has agreed, on condition I keep our three children. Will you marry me if things don't work out with Máximo, after such a long separation?"

Horrified at the thought of losing his friendship with a blunt negative, I felt that even if things didn't work out with Máximo, I still couldn't consider marriage to Hugo because of his three uncontrollable children, as he had described them himself. A slight suspicion that his wife was playing an astute game crept into my consciousness. I was probably right.

Máximo arrived, and the old feeling that not a day had passed took over swiftly. We went to Roatan, one of the Bay Islands. The accommodations at the hotel were rustic but clean. The food was excellent, particularly the memorable conch soup. Later I asked my cook to prepare it, but she threatened to leave if she had to deal with its complicated preparation.

We remarked to the hotel owner about the beauty of the women and children of the island, many with mahogany-colored skin, blond hair, and blue eyes. "Well, you see, the men of these islands must look for work on the mainland. Many ships stop here for food and water. The sailors roam around, and the women are very hospitable."

Máximo soon had to return to Washington to resume work as a freelance broadcaster with USIA TV, and a small Spanish radio program beamed into the District. I had to concentrate fully on my work as cultural affairs officer, selecting candidates for scholarships, programming speakers from the United States, and looking after the two binational centers.

My social life had also expanded. One new friend was an extraordinary woman, Leticia Silva de Oyuela. She was a history graduate of Madrid's university, owner of an art gallery and bookstore in Tegucigalpa, and an accomplished storyteller whom I nicknamed Scheherazade. Her husband always listened intently to her narrations. I asked him once if he ever tired of listening to her. "Never," he replied. "If you listen carefully the stories are always different. The subject and the characters may be the same, but the narrative changes every time she tells it."

Leticia became an addiction. Almost every evening that I didn't have to attend some official party, I would visit her at the art gallery, which gradually became a place where writers, artists, and academics met to discuss national and international events.

A call from New York from my dear old friend Hernán announced his imminent arrival. Three days later we sat in my living room, bringing each other up to date on family, friends, personal events, and gossip. Hernán had decided that the best way to satisfy his wanderlust was to become a ship's physician. This way he had seen half the world. He confessed he had always envied my chance to see so much of it. As he looked at me I saw not his but Mary's sparkling blue eyes. He spent a week with me. He had a chance to meet Hugo, who was frequently around. It was funny to see both of them bristle like scared animals.

Hernán laughed at my ghost stories, but one extraordinary experience in which he had the fright of his life was sufficient to get him to take me seriously.

"Get out of here," he said, "before the spirits play a dirty trick on you and drive you mad. Besides, the miasma from the river is ruining your health. That's why you have asthma."

I introduced him at Leticia's gallery, where they all greeted him like an old friend. That evening marked a special date in the gallery's calendar. We sent out for food and remained till dawn exchanging stories, discussing politics, laughing, and teasing each other. I was happy that they felt free to speak so openly although I was an American embassy official. Hernán remarked on this later, saying that he was proud that I had been able to establish such a healthy relationship with obviously intelligent men and women. He departed the next morning. I promised

Admiring a Copán stela during a visit to the early diggings at the site (photo by Hugo Bianchi).

to visit Chile as soon as possible, but I didn't get there soon enough to see him again.

There were two other great friends with whom I still correspond: Edith Peters and Martha Peaslee, both evangelical missionaries. Edith followed me in all of my archeological adventures. We went to Copán together along with Hugo in the role of official photographer. We also made intriguing findings in an area of Honduras close to the Nicaraguan frontier. We consulted a Honduran archeologist and asked him to visit the site with us. He was awed and said I must announce the finding. Clifford Evans and Betty Meggers, who were visiting Honduras with other Smithsonian archeologists, agreed that what Edith and I had discovered was important. But soon after our last excursion, problems in Nicaragua were developing. The area was flooded with refugees, first the Sandinistas, later the Contras. Archeological diggings were out of the question.

My other friend was the Guatemalan consul Conchita Arguedas. Her frail appearance belied her stamina and iron will. There was nothing she couldn't do if she set her mind to it. John Griffiths was about to leave for another assignment and I wondered if it would be possible to get a Hon-

Upon my return to Washington, D.C., I am decorated with the Order of Morazán by Ambassador Roberto Lazarus, in the Hall of the Americas, Pan American Union.

duran decoration for him. She mobilized her contacts at the Ministry of Foreign Affairs, and John duly received the Morazán decoration.

Among the scholarships I granted during my stay in Honduras, there was one for Julio Escoto to attend the University of Iowa's international writing program. Since then he has published fourteen books, and at present I'm translating into English one of his later works. Titled *Dawn*, it's a historical novel set in the framework of what happened in Honduras during the Nicaraguan civil war. Other books of his have been translated into Polish, German, and Portuguese. Julio is not easy. He is often lyrical, bordering on surrealism in his imagery. He is philosophical, controversial in his political judgments, honest, and direct.

My time had come to return to Washington. I was to head the Field Services branch. The experience acquired in Central America would serve me well when I set about bringing a rebirth to a department that had been sadly neglected.

Back in Washington, D.C., with my husband Máximo Mewe at our home in Virginia (photo by Rosalind Solomon).

CHAPTER 20

The Field Services branch was an entirely new area for me. Formerly, as chief of the evening operation of the Spanish branch, I had been responsible for shortwave broadcasts to all Spanish-speaking countries in the hemisphere. Field Services was quite a different operation, and the retiring chief briefed me on what it dealt with. Prerecorded weekend programs were offered to the USIS (United States Information Service) posts for a minimal price that covered the cost of the tapes. The posts then offered this free material to local radio stations. The programs were mostly educational, on health, sciences, and agriculture. When I told Máximo, my husband, what my new assignment entailed, he seemed quite excited. As the former owner of a radio station in Valparaíso, he said that, due to the poor quality of the shortwave broadcasts, they could hardly ever use these newscasts and features, yet the packaged programs distributed by USIS Santiago were invaluable.

During my stay in Honduras, I had become aware of this. So I was happy that I would be taking care of a very useful public relations instrument of USIA. My joy was short-lived. As soon as I started to work, I realized that the branch had been not just neglected but practically destroyed. The posts complained that shipments failed to arrive on time, so they lost placement on local radio stations because deliveries were unreliable. I had to find out what system was used for our shipments. Visiting our own mail room, I found out that the tapes were sent to the State Department's mail room, which in turn placed the packages in the corresponding bins for shipment. Everything looked fine until I asked this question. "Shipments are mailed regularly every week?"

"Not weekly, but as soon as the bins are full."

This reminded me of a story Father would tell about a trip to Spain at the turn of the century. He left Madrid for Barcelona, but about one hour after departure, the train stopped at a small town. Inspector and engineer stepped down to smoke and snack. Father approached with a question: "May I ask what we are waiting for?"

"We are waiting for passengers."

I realized that my packages were waiting for bulk. I took the necessary provisions to step up the shipments of our tapes, which hardly endeared me to mail room people, either at State or USIA, but the posts were delighted.

Shortly before retiring, my predecessor had advised me to include in my operation the recently independent Caribbean countries. I suggested to division chief Mel Niswander that he send me on a tour of the islands. A whole new world opened up to me. Trinidad, Tobago, Barbados, and St. Lucia were my first visits. I was surprised to find in Trinidad a population predominantly Hindu. I had a brief interview with the public affairs officer to explain the purpose of my trip. He requested samples of the programs in English, and due to my inexperience I missed a chance to offer them in Hindi.

He entrusted the rest of my stay to his driver, who would take me to see the sights. Would I be interested in seeing the buildings left by the American troops after their World War II occupation? I felt embarrassed at the sight of decaying barracks and a crumbling auditorium; there was no possible comparison to the Roman ruins left in Western Europe. They were pitiful, tacky remains, and I wished that the American military authorities had rather razed these miserable buildings before they left.

The next day the driver picked me up at the hotel, apologizing for his tardiness. He asked if I would mind stopping by his house on the way to the airport. We still had enough time, so I agreed. His house was extremely modest, with the Hindu pennant blowing in the wind. His wife stepped out and invited me to a cup of jasmine tea. When we were ready to leave, the driver smiled ingratiatingly and said: "My wife would like to drive to the airport with us, if you don't mind."

I smiled back, acquiescing. But following the wife came six children. During the thirty minutes to the airport, the USIS car became an aviary and a monkey's cage. I wished somebody had warned me about the smiling courtesy of Hindus.

The next stop was Barbados. The PAO listened to my project and assured me that he would consider ordering programs. He requested samples and gave me a letter of introduction to the owner of the main radio station in St. Lucia. Both Barbados and St. Lucia dazzled me with the exquisite beauty of beaches and gardens. In time, I did succeed in placing our programs in both islands.

I was also interested in Jamaica and Haiti. Kingston, Jamaica, was a revelation. I hadn't expected to find there such a fine museum, showing the best of local artists. I also enjoyed visiting a market that offered art treasures and wood-carvings. The PAO escorted me around, and my discovering a common interest in art made it easier for me to push my project for the benefit of local radio stations and public relations for *VOA*.

In Haiti I hit gold. The PAO was a woman who was immediately excited about the possibilities of my work. Her questions reflected her interest: "What is the content of the programs?"

"Mostly educational, health, agriculture, sciences, and medicine."

"Tropical agriculture and medicine?"

"Within a general view on these subjects, we also approach tropical aspects in both fields."

"Why give away the programs?"

"It's good public relations."

"But your programs are in Spanish, and Haitians speak French and Creole. Can you send me programs in Creole?"

"I'm quite sure I can."

I had set my heart on visiting Toussaint L'Ouverture's Citadelle, the fortress of the liberated slave who became emperor. His tragic life story was made famous by Paul Robeson in *Emperor Jones*.

So the day before I returned to Washington, I flew to Cap Haitien and hired a cab to take me to the foot of the mountain, where horses waited to take the tourists up the hill to the fort. I was amazed at the magnitude of the structure and wondered at the effort it must have taken to place on its ramparts heavy artillery and cannons obviously of European origin, displaying fine artwork on their iron bodies.

An hour later, I rejoined the cab driver and we returned to Cap Haitien. On the way he asked me what I was doing in Haiti. I told him that I was on an assignment for *VOA*. I asked for a place to lunch. He took me to a small hotel with an excellent restaurant. He would return for me in one hour.

I never suspected what he did in that hour until we drove along Cap

Haïtien's main street. It was now crowded with excited people handing me letters for their favorite *VOA* broadcasters in English, French, and Spanish. I had earlier proof that Haitians are polyglots at an early age. I realized that I had stumbled upon a secret audience of hundreds that nobody knew anything about.

In Washington, I set about finding a Creole broadcaster. Henry Krieger, chief of French language broadcasts to Africa, put me onto Henri Francisque, from Haiti, who was fluent in Creole. His daily correspondent reports were added immediately to our ninety-minute correspondent feed. Word got around fast and soon a second Creole speaker, Sandra Lemaire, joined us.

Now clients were coming to us, including Prime Minister Charles of Dominica, who said that her island had a considerable Creole-speaking population. At the time *VOA* was broadcasting in forty-two languages. Creole became the forty-third, and eventually grew into a specialized branch with Sandra as the star. She called me early this year to ask for an interview to be broadcast on the tenth anniversary of the Creole branch.

By the mid eighties, Field Services had gone through several division chiefs. It had moved to larger offices and hired more personnel. Changes in division chiefs scarcely made a ripple. All of them were Foreign Service officers on their two year stay in Washington. They knew little about our operation and gave us plenty of space to function autonomously.

Division chiefs came in all shapes. Some aloof, others aggressive, a few interested in what we could do together. The aloof category has slipped my mind, as it should. Among the aggressive, I remember one whose name is best forgotten. Field Services had a late evening broadcast, with ninety minutes to feed correspondent's reports in four languages: Spanish, Portuguese, English, and Creole. I had to stay until the end. Breaking news items had first to be translated into Spanish, then recorded and added to the feed. Sometimes we had to do it live.

The new chief called me in to say that I must change my schedule and finish by five o'clock. I protested that I had to stay until the end of the feed, usually about 7:30 P.M. He said in the rudest tone, "I don't care about the feed. You are here to serve me, and that is all you must keep in mind."

"Then you must change my job description." He didn't do it.

Bernice Fleming, our administrative officer, had heard him yell. She stepped into his office and told him he must never again call me in alone. She must always witness our meetings. To my surprise he complied.

Among the chiefs interested in a smooth and creative operation was Eli Flam. He interviewed every staff member about past achievements and new projects. He would start conversations by saying: "Come on, beat your own drum."

I did, with gusto. Having worked earlier in the Spanish branch I knew that between the morning and evening broadcasts there was a ten-hour gap of total silence. My idea was that we should have an answering service, which would use one-minute reports that any Latin American radio station could copy and beam into its area. I submitted the idea to Eli Flam, who enthusiastically approved it. We purchased five machines with counters to follow the frequency of calls and then announced the service. We scheduled machines by time zones in Latin America and the Caribbean.

Our biggest success with this service occurred during the Falkland Islands war. Each of our machine counters recorded over a hundred calls every day. The BBC and Deutschewelle sent observers to find out what we were doing. Radio France introduced a similar service, although only nationally. As a result of this system's success I was rewarded with a Meritorious Honor award.

I missed writing. I talked about it with Eli Flam. He approved the idea of a series on drug abuse. I would write five twenty-minute programs on the effects of drugs on health and on the economy, as well as the reduced intellectual capacity of addicts and the ravages in family relations and foreign affairs due to trafficking. I stressed the notion that producing countries become consumer countries. Time has proved me right.

Bolivia and Peru are the main producers and traffickers of cocaine. We needed programs in the Indian Quechua language. I found Professor Bernardo Vallejos, fluent in this language, at the Community College in Houston. I wrote a number of plays dramatizing the situation of coca growers in the Altiplano and American efforts to provide alternative crops which would create new sources of income. Dr. Vallejos translated and produced the program in Quechua.

My next subject was terrorism. I researched and wrote a set of five programs under the title "The Cost of Terrorism." The Tupa Marus in Uruguay had been active, and the Shining Path in Peru was beginning to make headlines worldwide.

I was so engrossed in my work that I had paid little attention to developments in my marriage. Máximo had often said that he wanted to move to Europe. He had relatives in Italy and friends in Spain who painted a rosy picture of their life on the Costa del Sol. We had talked about it, but I said that I was close to retirement and thought it unwise to depart without a full pension. Besides, I would be too far away from Ximena and Rosa. The idea of setting such a distance between us made me extremely uncomfortable. We divorced, and Máximo settled down in Fuengirola. He insisted that I visit.

I spent a week in the Costa del Sol. We drove through the country stopping at picturesque old villages, dining at roadside restaurants on the food Máximo likes best: fried squid, squid salads, squid in its own ink, paellas bristling with unshelled shrimp. Food has never been important to me. A friend once told me, "If you don't crave for food, it means that you are frigid." I can prove it's not true. Rather, I'm like my grandfather, who used to comment on his wife's gluttony: "She lives to eat, I eat to live."

Máximo had reserved a room for me at a beautiful hotel. The view from the tenth floor on the Mediterranean was breathtaking. But when the water didn't reach the bathroom, I had to look for other lodgings. I asked for a porter to pick up my suitcases only to be informed that there was a strike, and I must carry my own luggage down all those stairs, because the elevators were out of order. During my week there I tried daily to telephone Ximena or Rosa, but never got through. Máximo said America had spoiled me with unnecessary comforts. We realized that differences scarcely noticed during ten years of marriage had deepened. Yet this didn't spoil our friendship.

Returning to Washington, I found that Eli Flam was leaving for another assignment. His replacement was a disappointment. Starting proceedings for my retirement, I reviewed my life at the *Voice*. It was satisfying that my career had been far from mediocre.

I had created a news program whose writing I carried single-handed for six years. It made famous the broadcasters who voiced it.

I had assisted in the coverage of the space program until the landing on the moon.

For three years I had served in Honduras. That country's government awarded me its highest decoration, the Morazán, for my efforts in raising funds for the survivors of a hurricane that killed more than 20,000 people. My sponsoring of U.S. grants assisted university professors, artists, writers, and businessmen. This was mentioned in the ceremony held at the Hall of the Americas at the Organization of American States when the Honduran ambassador, Roberto Lazarus, pinned the decoration on my chest.

As the chief of Field Services, I opened up the Caribbean to our programs, adding Creole to the languages already broadcast by *VOA*.

I devised the Codaphone to provide news services to local radio stations throughout the hemisphere, for which I was given a Meritorious Honor award.

I wrote documentaries on drug abuse and terrorism, which led to the addition of Quechua to *VOA*'s languages.

Having noticed during my trips through Latin America and the Caribbean that the shortwave sound was unsatisfactory, I consulted Michael Kristula, director of policy and programming for USIA TV, about the possibility of using their satellite to beam broadcasts to our area. He offered his expertise and counsel to achieve this goal. Shortly before I retired I had the satisfaction of sending our first programs by satellite to all USIS posts. Gradually, most broadcasts have followed our lead.

I could leave without regrets, having done a good job.

But I did have one regret. Except occasionally on an individual basis, I had been unable to assuage the deep disappointment that our staff members felt at work. The *Voice* had chosen them among the best journalists in Latin America. Yet they had to use secondhand news in translation for their broadcasts. This smothered their natural impulses as active journalists. When they got their two-year contracts from *VOA*, they thought they'd reached the pinnacle of their careers. Instead the system seemed to emasculate them. If they returned to their countries, it would be seen as a humiliation. Nobody would believe they were back because they were dissatisfied, but rather would think they had failed. In their own countries they had enjoyed the status of minor celebrities. The anonymity of their work at the *Voice* devastated them.

I remember only two who left successfully. One accepted a position as a public relations officer for the UN Food and Agriculture Organization (FAO), with residence in Santiago, Chile. The other opened restaurants in Washington and was extremely successful. Today he is a millionaire. That was in the eighties. I understand that things have changed for the best and many colleagues at the time have found the courage to exit and develop careers elsewhere.

As for myself, after twenty-five years at USIA-*VOA*, I was ready to go. I looked forward with growing impatience to being close to Ximena, Rosa and my grandchildren in Texas.

CHAPTER 21

After selling my house in McLean and giving friends objects to remember me by, I watched the movers load my belongings. As my plane winged away into the sky, I glanced down at the city where I had lived so excitingly for twenty-five years. It was a bittersweet feeling, for I simultaneously regretted leaving Washington yet looked forward to being with my daughters again. And Texas was to be a new scene for me.

On earlier trips there, I had been introduced to Austin and to Lakeway, the lovely development on Lake Travis. A beautiful house awaited me, bought in partnership with Ximena and Walter, her husband. The house had everything I had ever dreamed of: big windows opening onto a wide view of the lake, which was dotted with sailboats on weekends; a pool to entertain the family; a big yard to grow a splendid garden with hibiscus, jonquils, roses, morning glories, gardenias. The planning had been perfect. I spent a few days in Houston before the date scheduled for the movers' arrival with all my possessions. Ximena drove me to Lakeway and helped to decide where things should go.

By the time the truck was empty, it was too late for her to return to Houston. We spent the evening making great plans for the future. A brand-new intimacy had started. She left at dawn, and immediately I got down to the task of finding the right place for every piece of furniture, painting, and bibelot. Suddenly I felt a tickling on my cheek. A drop of sweat was running down my face. I washed it away then decided to get in the pool. I slipped into my bathing suit and stepped outside. To my

horror the water was dark green! What had happened? What was I supposed to do? I didn't know anybody in Lakeway. I described the situation to Walter on the telephone. My voice must have sounded panicked.
He said: "Don't you have your chemicals? You must use the proper
chemicals in the right amounts to restore the balance in the water."

"I don't know what you are talking about. What kind of chemicals?
What amounts? Wouldn't it be easier if I empty the pool and fill it up
with clean water?"

"NO!" he said, excited. "That would cost a fortune. Look for pool
services in the Yellow Pages. But *don't* empty the pool!"

All pool service companies were closed at that hour. I had to wait till
next day. I took a shower. Lit a cigarette. Skipped dinner. Watched TV,
the opium of the century. I was lucky that I didn't have a crystal ball
handy, for it would have told me that the green water would be a recur-
ring problem. Or that within a few months a tornado would cause half
of the pool to overflow onto the first floor, ruining carpeting and furniture. Any gust of wind covered the water with leaves and broken twigs.
In short, it was a full-time operation, and the pleasure I expected from it
wasn't worth the attention it required, or the money for the pool man.

A flock of deer visited every day. I got some deer corn to feed the
lovely creatures. A neighbor came running out of her house. "Don't feed
the deer!" she cried. "They are so voracious you will never have a decent
yard. I even have electric wires around my garden. They jump over to eat
the bulbs I have just planted. *Don't* feed them!"

Listening to her, I felt something crawling on my left leg. I looked
but was unable to detect a bug. Minutes later I was desperately scratch-
ing. I hardly slept that night. When I looked at my leg in the morning,
it was purple from ankle to knee. I rushed to a doctor: "If you have to
amputate, please do it quickly," I said.

"What are you talking about? You have a severe allergic reaction to
fire ants."

He gave me a shot of cortisone and prescribed lotions and ointments
to stop the itching. I feared that my honeymoon with Texas was over.
The house that was meant to be a pleasant watering hole for the Houston family turned out to be too far away for weekends. The two-and-a-
half-hour drive was really a drag. Regular visits from Rosa, Ximena, husbands, and their children, frequent at the beginning of my stay, gradually
became less regular.

I started teaching conversational Spanish to a group of men who had learned the language during trips overseas and wanted to keep up this skill. Most of them were oil company CEOs. Through their stories and experiences I realized that their assignments worldwide were like diplomatic missions.

The main occupations for these retired men and their wives were sports, primarily tennis and golf. I had played both in years past, and they tried to encourage me into playing again. I declined. I'd rather concentrate on our classes, which gave me more knowledge of their backgrounds and experiences, becoming occasions for reminiscences, with Spanish taking a back seat. I wasn't a very strict teacher.

I also filled the days translating into English some short stories of a Costa Rican author, Rima de Vallbona. They were highly imaginative, and she handled suspense well and, at times, displayed a bitter humor. "Flowering Inferno" was published by the Latin American Literary Review Press under director Yvette Miller, who commissioned from me later the translation of a Chilean author, Jaime Collyer. His book *People on the Prowl* was also a series of short stories. My granddaughter Teresa — Rosa's daughter — and her two-year-old child, Abigail, were my favorite company. Teresa had spent a couple of months with me in Washington, but her emotional problems at the time, and my own due to my recent divorce from Máximo, weren't conducive to good communication.

In Austin I found that Teresa was developing a personality that fascinated me because of the different directions it took from day to day. We spent hours discussing current events, the American system, the American way of life, her own ambitions, and her frustrations. Together we laughed and made wild plans. Shortly before I left Austin she had her second child, Nika. Eventually she divorced and is now on her way to do with her life what she always dreamed of doing — making a mark. How? She will know. She is intelligent and has the right instincts. She is a rebel and a fighter.

Tina, my second granddaughter by Rosa, also spent some time with me in Washington. She took good advantage of it by attending Virginia's Community College in Alexandria, where she learned computer sciences. Later she moved to Chicago, married, had her first son, Gabriel Borja, and decided to return to Houston where she had grown up. There she had her second son, Jackson Arturo, named for my father. She is beautiful and practical, and doesn't go in for flights of fantasy like Teresa and myself. She concentrates on her family circle and projects a feeling of serenity. Could there be an undertow of dormant restlessness in her?

It's hard to know. She likes to read, and García Marquez is one of her favorite authors. That should mean something.

After living away from my daughters for so long, I found that we had to get to know each other again. Ximena's two boys didn't have a chance to know me in their early years. We didn't have a chance at bonding, as was the case with Rosa's girls, who were born in Washington and lived near my home. Although a good relationship with the boys still eludes me, I'm sure that the day will come when we reach the closeness I long for. The potential is there, but both my grandsons have thick shells of pride difficult to crack. Alex is a successful businessman who had his early knocks but came through all right. He is the proud father of Blake, Ximena's first grandson. It was probably the couple of years spent in a military academy that gave Alex the "stiff upper lip" he often displays. Ben followed his older brother to the military academy, where he may have acquired the beginnings of his reserved character. He hides well a sensitivity that he occasionally pours into short stories and essays. He graduated in computer science and is finding his way with creative projects in a fairly crowded, ever-changing field.

With my daughters, it has been a Pandora's box. I found conflicts I had never suspected. I also found successes I felt proud of. Like Rosa, who, after two painful divorces, organized her life to become financially independent and surrounded by a strong group of supportive friends. Ximena graduated in psychology and took a job, while her husband, Walter, who was a successful architect until the oil crisis of the seventies, did likewise. Both disliked their work.

When Walter decided to move to Colorado, where his daughter Anne lives, it meant that our house in Austin had to be sold. I didn't mind, although I had already adjusted to heat, pool, voracious deer, and poisonous fire ants, which needed a daily dose of Diazinon. But I'd made friends that I still miss. The house went on the market and as it wasn't selling fast enough, a friend sent me a St. Anthony with instructions to bury it behind the house, head down. It worked. Real estate people in Lakeway now keep a supply of the statuettes in their offices.

All my belongings went into storage. Then I flew to Miami, where Ximena waited for me to take the midnight flight to Chile. At the Santiago airport the whole family was expecting us. It was like a replay of my childhood scenes in Valparaíso. Luz held a baby for me to cradle.

"Lillian, this is Arturito's fifth grandchild."

"You mean child."

"No, several of his daughters are married and this is his fifth grandchild."

"My God, that makes me feel so old. I still think of Arturito as my favorite nephew playing soccer with Enrique, who called him Champion." Eugene looked fine. He just walked with some hesitation. Otherwise he seemed strong as ever. He had insisted for months that I come to Chile. A few days after my arrival I found out what he had on his mind. We had finished dinner and were sitting all three, Luz, Eugene, and myself by the table having a liqueur, when Eugene said, "Mother was unfair and cruel to you."

For a moment I was speechless. Then I understood why he had pressed me so strenuously to come to Chile. The thought that he might have done more to protect me from Mother had haunted him for decades. What could I say? Mother had her convictions that I didn't share. We were so different. Such conflicts happen in every family.

Eugene's words took on a different meaning when, ten days later, he had a stroke from which he never recovered. He died soon afterward. I realized that his feeling of guilt had kept him alive until he could unburden his torment and be absolved by me.

Returning to Austin, I spent three months in a friend's home trying to make up my mind about buying a house there or moving to Colorado, where Ximena and Walter had already settled. I took a short trip to Colorado and in one eventful morning found a place that I loved at first sight and still enjoy today.

Daybreak wakes me up with the sun shining on my face through a lace of foliage. Sundown throws magnificent colors into my living room. The surrounding mountains display the deep green of pines with ample patches of lighter aspens. In the fall these delicate trees turn into pure gold, before being covered by snow. All year round nature luxuriates in different pageants of splendor: wildflowers as delicate as orchids in spring and summer, and in winter the majestic bulk of mountains under snow with frozen waterfalls arrested into bluish stalactites of ice. All this presents a spectacle of never-ending beauty. It conspires to encourage contemplation and idleness.

However, in a few months I had exhausted this mood, and I longed for action. I went to Texas to attend Rosa's wedding to her longtime friend, Tom Reilly. Rosa has always been fairly indifferent to fashion, becoming hairdos, makeup. I tactfully suggested that I would like to help in choosing her wedding dress, but I was just as tactfully discouraged. I didn't have time to mull over the rejection. The wedding day was imminent. Ximena and I drove to the church. We were escorted to a pew.

At a signal, everyone stood up. At the top of the aisle, Rosa stood smiling, tall, elegant, gorgeous, her hair in a French chignon interspersed with flowers. My eyes filled with tears of pride at her beauty. "Unforgettable," Rosa and Tom's song, started to play, and then the tape broke. Tom stepped forward and sang it a cappella. My tears dried up and I joined the laughter that Rosa began, walking down the aisle toward him.

Ximena worried me. She had grudgingly moved to Colorado, leaving behind her sons and twenty years of friendships in Houston. For the first time in her life she started a small business, a gift shop that she promptly turned into an art gallery. She probably hoped that her good taste and knowledge of art would carry her through. She had much to learn. But then so did I. At one point she decided to take consignments. Sometimes these were absolutely ghastly, and yet they sold faster than what we considered more attractive and appealing. We realized to our dismay that Western taste is peculiarly odd and unpredictable.

Sometimes I would advise Ximena to hide some hideous object that a consignment client had brought in. For sure, that would be the sale of the day. Both Ximena and I started to doubt our taste. Ximena had discovered outstanding artists and tried to promote their work. One, a wood carver, made miracles of sheer beauty with simple pieces of wood. Another one worked with alabaster, scraping the stone so thin that the veins showed through. No other gallery in town had them. Yet sales were exceptionally poor, and the less important pieces of minor artists had a sure clientele.

Much to my distress, after having exhausted every trick of the imagination to call attention to her gallery, she started to dress only in black. She was obviously mourning her captivity in a situation that she didn't know how to disengage herself from.

Then she heard about Pacifica University with its accelerated programs for graduates, and decided to enroll for her master's degree in psychology. She revived. Being bilingual, her chances of a successful career as a professional counselor should be excellent. Having now her masters she is bracing herself for the Ph.D.

During my years at the *Voice of America* I heard about a General Motors project to build a city around the manufacturing plant of its new car, Saturn. To witness the birth of a city seemed to me fascinating, so I submitted a request to follow this event as something that only happens in America. Unfortunately I was unable to make our chiefs see my point of view and the series never started.

Yet today I find myself in a valley where a string of towns is being built fast, from Denver to Glenwood Springs. One day this will be a megalopolis. I am witnessing the birth of a city. There is also adventure here. Whether I can manage to become a participant is something that I'm looking into. There are many things that I could do. It's a matter of watching for the opportunity to step forward and say, "I can do that." Time will tell — but do I have enough?

EPILOGUE

Once you're an exile, you're always an exile because during your time away you start up a life . . . and those ties are severed when one returns.
— *Mario Benedetti,* Americas *magazine, August 1998*

A year after I left Chile my brother, Eugene, wrote me a long letter telling me that Mother's doctor had advised the family that she was showing symptoms of Parkinson's disease. He had suspected this for a while but delayed saying anything about it because he knew that nothing could be done. Eugene asked me to inquire if the disease was really so hopeless. I had already noticed that her handwritten letters showed a definite change. The tremor was affecting the typical Sacred Heart penmanship of which she was so proud. I called her and her voice came over the phone with a cracked sound as though she was speaking through a wooden box. I didn't mention that I knew what ailed her. I told her instead that perhaps she might want to visit us in Washington. She laughed briefly and said: "Impossible. You don't know how much I've aged this year."

I set out to find if it was true that there was no cure or relief for Parkinson's patients. I read in a magazine that the photographer Margaret Bourke-White had interrupted her career because the tremor in her hands didn't allow her to hold her camera steadily. But she found a physician in New York who had been successfully operating on Parkinson's patients. She submitted to surgery with dramatic results and was able to resume her work. I found the name of the physician and made an appointment with him to consult on Mother's case. He listened attentively then asked: "How old is your mother?"

"I'm not sure, but she must be close to seventy-five."

"I'm sorry. I can't take the risk. If I fail I would ruin my record."

I insisted, but to no avail. I asked if there was any medication that he could recommend but he couldn't think of anything that would help. Levodopa, the drug that increases natural production of dopamine and has successfully helped so many Parkinson's patients in the last few years, was not available until long after Mother passed away in 1963.

I couldn't help but think that if her disease had been slowly incubating in her brain through the years, could it have determined some of her drastic, often unreasonable conduct? If the disease forged her character, how responsible was she for her actions? I felt deeply disturbed upon realizing that Mother was probably helpless. Having first been influenced and molded by a turn-of-the-century Latin American society, and belonging to a proud ruling class, in the dusk of her life she found herself victimized by the ravages of a disease that had neither cure nor relief. When did it start? Was it long before or close to the time when she banned me? I will never know.

And as a cast out, what did I do with my life? I focused on my children and myself. I knew, yet I refused to dwell on the fact, that banishment had a traumatic effect on both my daughters. Their solutions of choice were quite opposite. While Ximena never has overcome her nostalgia for Chile, Rosa cut the ties and created her own American self. And I hover between the two, knowing what I left behind with small regrets and loving what I have found in my American life.

Sometimes I remember melancholic walks with Father, silently regretting lost opportunities. Perhaps he thought then that in yielding to Mother he had deprived his children of them. But as things whimsically work out in life, when she banned me, I opened a whole new world to my own and to others in the family.

On that fateful evening of my banishment by Mother in 1952, I vowed not to return. And I did not — at least not in her lifetime. In the eleven years up to her passing in 1963, our only communication was by telephone and letters. My exile had lasted eighteen years when I finally returned to Chile at *VOA*'s request, but things did not go as planned.

My first return to Chile after eighteen years was frustrating. *VOA*'s call to attend and report on Mrs. Nixon's visit to Peru after the earthquake in 1970 completely upset family and relatives' plans to see me. One small incident at the only party I was able to attend stressed the feeling of alienation I already strongly felt, as though I were intruding in a world totally foreign to me.

An old aunt with a particularly strong personality arrived late and proceeded to excuse herself in a loud voice. She had been founder and president of the Chilean Red Cross. I had remembered some of her ground-breaking deeds and requested from USIS Santiago an interview for a program that I had started offering profiles of Latin American women. It was the broadcast of this interview that had led to her nomination and award of the title "Woman of the Year." She sat next to me and went into an ear-splitting tirade on her new status and all ensuing celebrations. Then she turned to me and ordered: "I understand that Lillian is here. Go fetch her for me. I want to be sure that she hears about the award." I got up and went in search of the young woman in her mind that I knew didn't exist anymore.

Another trip to Chile had a wrenching effect on me. Betty had a terminal cancer and I had to see her. When I walked into her hospital room I saw she had pulled out all the tubes that were supposed to feed her and was busy arranging a flower bouquet in a vase. She turned and smiled wanly. I knew better than to tell her to lie down or call the nurse. She finished the flower arrangement and signaled me to follow her to a couch, where we sat. She couldn't speak. She used a tablet to write messages. She quickly wrote on it and handed it to me. It was a plea to tell the family to stop all interventions and let her die. I hugged her and promised to do it. I fully agreed that she had a right to die. The cancer had been slowly progressing for eight years. She had had several disfiguring operations but refused chemotherapy. I talked with the family that evening but was unable to make them see my point of view or to respect Betty's wish. It was a painful six months later that she passed away in her sleep. On her night table they found her obituary written by herself.

Only in 1990 was I able to spend a whole month in Chile. I almost overlapped with Ximena, who had traveled to Santiago with her two sons, Alex and Ben, and her husband, Walter. When I arrived, my niece Luz Lorca invited me to go to Eugene's cabin on Lake Lican Ray. We decided to head farther south to Valdivia, where I found vestiges of the Lorcas at the Governor's Museum. On the way back I asked if we could make a detour toward Mulchén, the small town that decades earlier had been the hub of our activities to and from San Martín, the magical hacienda where vacations were spent with our Bunster cousins. One of Luz' daughters asked in the brash manner of today's young: "Why do we have to stop at this shit of a town?"

Her words made me snap out of the foggy dream recalled in Mother's stories about our grandmother Rosario on a last farewell visit to relatives in Mulchén before entering a convent, and the tall, slender Martín

Bunster falling in love with her at first sight and changing her destiny. In more recent memory the images of a 1920's model car carrying the grown-ups to San Martín, and a number of huasos (cowboys) in their colorful striped ponchos and wide-brimmed hats leading the horses for the young vacationers. The creaking oxcarts, loaded with our suitcases, starting on the long trek to the fundo (ranch). The dream evaporated, and I saw the reality of dusty streets strewn with the trash from cans overturned by hungry dogs, the peeling paint and broken window panes of modest one-story houses. Another dead end in time. We left for civilization, leaving memories to rest in the silence of years gone by.

In Santiago it was suggested that I visit the Lorca and Bunster crypts. I declined. To this day I have not seen Mother's final resting place. My choice was to better know the upcoming generation of relatives.

Were they talented? Were they ambitious? Had they been crippled by the terror of seventeen years of harsh dictatorship? The silence that answered this last question revealed that, yes, they had been touched. How deep was hard to tell. As for my contemporaries, they seemed frozen in time, most of them living in a sort of cryogenic suspended animation that smothered desires, enthusiasms, and expectations, although there were a few noble exceptions still breathing deep, eyes sparkling, laughter ready.

I had been raised mostly in Europe and within a South American society that looked up exclusively to the Old World's culture, which considered America a rough land of cowboys, gangsters, and money-grabbing, unscrupulous industrialists and entrepreneurs. Once banned I had an extraordinary opportunity to look at the reverse of the coin, and I joyously found that America didn't always fit the cliché.

When I married and moved to Tennessee, my Washington friends would laugh, telling me, "Don't bother to buy shoes. You won't need them there."

Contrary to their opinions, I was soon to appreciate the refinement and sophistication of the South's elite. I was able to participate in worthwhile projects that sparked a high level of healthy curiosity in the community, which itself was a concept fairly unknown in Chile at the time I lived there. This was a lesson I rapidly assimilated, devoting time and energy to the Experiment in International Living and a weekly half-hour television show on the goals of the League of Women Voters.

Several of our new friends traveled yearly to Europe. Then came the time when they and others said, "We want to know our own country better." Their reports were crowded with intelligent observations and exciting discoveries. I was able to follow in their footsteps when, as a State Department escort-interpreter, I traveled all over the United States getting acquainted with institutions, personalities, and artists, and speaking with ordinary people with amazing experiences.

My years at the *Voice of America* were equally valuable in dressing up this cultural picture that had eluded me for so long. Even Americans refused to believe in it, as if they were sustained by a sort of snobbery in reverse, or false modesty, choosing to accept the cliché of the frontier American, rough, uncouth, and practically illiterate.

But a country doesn't lack culture when it has the largest number of important museums of any other nation on the planet, stretching from coast to coast. Where every medium-size city sustains a symphony orchestra and where more than forty thousand books are published every year. And in this mass of literature one can find, beside the most well known bestsellers, authors such as Sam Keen with *Fire in the Belly* and Michael Dorris with *A Yellow Raft In Blue Water,* to name only two of my latest discoveries among a prolific generation of insightful chroniclers of our times.

In the last thirty years writers from faraway lands have become part of the American culture: Gabriel García Marquez, Pablo Neruda, Salman Rushdie, and Isabel Allende among many. And this is what I have found and enjoyed in the second phase of my life in America: the shiny reverse of the coin.

I also know that this American society is far from perfect, but one of its characteristics is its everpresent willingness to face its flaws and find ways to reduce its effects on society at large. The media is usually the watchdog, and its role demands constant vigilance and professional acumen, of which I have been a witness during my years as a journalist.

I once said that I had prostituted myself by using my writer's skill to earn a living, translating and writing scripts for news broadcasts. The truth is that . . .

I wanted to use what I was, to be what I was born to be . . . not to have a career, but to be that straightforward, obvious, unmistakable animal: a writer.

— Cynthia Ozick, *Metaphor and Memory,* 1989